TAKASHI SUZUKI

THE HISTORY OF
SRIVIJAYA, ANGKOR and CHAMPA

mekong

THE HISTORY OF

SRIVIJAYA, ANGKOR
and
CHAMPA

TAKASHI SUZUKI

The History of Srivijaya, Angkor and Champa

All rights reserved. No part of this publication may be reproduced or transmitted in any form or by any means, electronic or mechanical, including photocopy, recording, or any information storage and retrieval system, without permission in writing from the publisher.

Copyright © Takashi Suzuki, 2019

Published in Japan by Mekong Publishing Co., Ltd.
3-7-1 Hongo, Bunkyo-ku Tokyo JAPAN 113-0033

First published 2019

Basic typeset in Times New Roman 16Q and Ryumin L-KL 12Q

ISBN 978-4-8396-0316-8 C3022

*For my parents
Rokuro and Setsu,
And my wife Taeko Suzuki*

CONTENTS

List of Maps   viii

Preface   ix

1. FUNAN   1

1-1   Early History of Funan（扶南）   1

     1-1-1   On-land trade route from the Lower Burma to Oc Eo   3

     1-1-2   Trans-peninsula route after Fan Man's conquest   7

     1-1-3   The Meaning of Indianization   11

1-2   Religion   13

1-3   Funan regime   16

     1-3-1   East-West Trade   17

     1-3-2   Si Thep   19

2. SHI-LI-FO-SHI（SRIVIJAYA）   23

2-1   Shi-li-fo-shi was located in the Malay Peninsula   23

2-2   Marine-route of Jia Dan（賈耽）   24

2-3   Java（闍婆）often meant the Malay Peninsula

       before the Song times   30

2-4   A Short History of Srivijaya   33

2-5   Disappearnce of Funan and

       the establishment of Shi-li-fo-shi   35

2-6   Tributary states to China, around the Malay Peninsula   37

     2-6-1   Langkasuka（狼牙須國）   38

     2-6-2   Dvaravati（墮和羅鉢底）   39

     2-6-3   Kan-da-li（干陀利）, Chi-tu（赤土）and Srivijaya（室利佛逝）   42

     2-6-4   Funan ⇒ Shi-li-fo-shi ⇒ Sailendra ⇒ San-fo-chi（三佛斉）   43

2-7   Disappearance of Shi-li-fo-shi and emergence of Sailendra   48

     2-7-1   Ligor Inscription   50

2-8	Sailendra Dynasty	53
2-9	San-fo-chi（三佛齊）	63
	2-9-1 Function of San-fo-chi（三佛齊）	63
	2-9-2 Chola's invasion（1025-1080?）and its influence	64
Conclusion		69

3. CHENLA AND PRE-ANGKOR KINGDOM 73

3-1	Origin of Chenla and Funan	73
3-2	Si Thep as the original base of Chenla	81
3-3	Pre-Angkor Kingdom	84
	3-3-1 Isanavarman	86
	3-3-2 Adhyapura family	91
	3-3-3 Jayavarman I and decline of Pre-Angkor	92
	3-3-4 Division of Chenla	96
	3-3-5 Tributary missions of Chenla	97
3-4	The end of Pre-Angkor (Chenla)	99
3-5	Theoretical problem of Michael Vickery	102
	3-5-1 Michael Vickery criticizes Cœdès	102
	3-5-2 Michael Vickery's misunderstanding	107
3-6	Summary of the History of Chenla	108
Table1	Chenla Kings	111

4. ANGKOR DYNASTY 113

4-1	Srivijaya group proceeded to Cambodia	113
4-2	Jayavarman II	116
	4-2-1 Jayavarman II conquered Cambodia	121
	4-2-2 Jayavarman II's capital of Roluos	133
4-3	Yasovarman's Inscription of Práḥ Thãt Khtom	133
4-4	From Roluos to Angkor district	140
	4-4-1 Yasovarman transferred capital to Angkor	142
	4-4-2 Jayavarman IV transferred capital to Koh Ker	144

vii

4-5	Rajendravarman II and Jayavarman V	145
4-6	Suryavarman I	152
	4-6-1 Influence of Srivijaya through Thambralinga and Lopburi	155
	4-6-2 After Suryavarman I	161
4-7	The Mahindrapura Dynasty	163
	4-7-1 Hiranyanavarman group, from the north of the Dangrek Range	163
	4-7-2 Suryavarman II	165
4-8	Jayavarman VII	171
4-9	Decline of the Angkor Dynasty	185
	Table2 Angkor Kings	188

5. HISTORY OF CHAMPA

GENERAL ASPECT OF THE HISTORY OF CHAMPA		191
5-1	The Inscriptions of Champa	
	The oldest inscription; Vo Canh inscription	192
	5-1-1 Distribution of Inscriptions by M. Vickery	192
5-2	Three Stages of Champa History Lin-yi, Huan Wang, and Champa	194
	5-2-1 Lin-yi（林邑）	195
	5-2-2 Huan Wang（環王）	196
	5-2-3 Champa-Zhangcheng（占城）	197
5-3	Early relation with China. War and Tributary missions	197
	5-3-1 Tributes of Lin-yi before the Tang Times	204
	5-3-2 Relation with Tang	209
	5-3-3 Srivijaya's invasion	213
5-4	Dong Duong Dynasty	215
	5-4-1 Champa's missions to Song	220
5-5	Vijaya Kingdom	222
	5-5-1 Vijaya's tribute to Song	226
	5-5-2 Confusion of Champa and Jayavarman VII	238

About the Author   242

APPENDIX LIST OF TRIBUTARY COUNTRIES   243

Bibliography   263
Index   265
Chronology   284

LIST OF MAPS

1 Fa-xian's sea route（法顯）   xiv
2 Takua Pa area   8
3 Jia Dan's Sea route from Southeast Asia to Ceylon   28
4 The sea trade route of Srivijaya (6-7centuries)   47
5 Territory of Srivijaya (At the end of the 7th century)   79
6 Territory of Angkor Dynasty   149
7 Angkor Centre   158
8 Royal roads（12-13 centuries）   177
9 Champa   200

PREFACE

The history of the ancient Southeast Asia written in the 20th century was full of mistakes and misunderstandings. Many of western historians have no knowledge of the Chinese script and did not read the Chinese text, for instance "The official history of the Chinese Dynasties". Of course, there are some translations of the Chinese text, but the translators did not fully understand the historical situations. The main sources of these Chinese texts are reports of the foreign envoys. There are some exaggeration and lies, but generally their reports were correct and reliable compared with other sources.

After G.Cœdès established 'Palembang hypothesis', all the historians had gone to the wrong way, and the histories of Southeast Asia were misguided to the unrealistic direction. The existing history of Srivijaya has been totally wrong. Wrong history has been lectured to students for 100 years. Even today, many people believe that the capital of Srivijaya was located at Palembang in the Sumatra Island. However, I have discovered that Palembang theory is completely wrong. The location of Srivijaya (Shi-li-fo-shi) was in the Malay Peninsula and its capital was Chaiya, Surat Thani province of Thailand. In the *Xin Tang Shu* (New History of the Tang Dynasty, 新唐書) clearly states that "the west of Shi-li-fo-shi is the Nicobar Islands". So, Shi-li-fo-shi was in the Malay Peninsula, not Palembang.

室利佛逝, 一曰尸利佛誓。過軍徒弄山二千里, 地東西千里, 南北四千里而遠。有城十四, 以二國分總。西曰郎婆露斯

郎婆露斯 (Lang Po Lu Si)=Lang-Barus is the key word here. In the past, few modern historians could understand this word. I almost gave up reading this word. It sounds like Barus, so I understood this

x   THE HISTORY OF SRIVIJAYA, ANGKOR and CHAMPA

is 'Barus' of the west Sumatra., but someday a Malaysian Facebook friend asked me the meaning of this word. So, I checked again, and found out what was 'Lang-Barus'. In the 9th century, Arab merchants used this word frequently. In this case, Lang Barus is the name of island between Sri Lank and Kedah, 'the Nicobar Islands'. Ibn Khordadbeh says that from Serendib (Sri Lanka) to 'Langabalus', it takes 10-15 days to cover its distance; from 'Langbalus' to Kalah (Kedah), it is 6 days". Chinese monk. Fa Xin (法顕) wrote similar itinerary from Ceylon to Yabadvipa (Malay Peninsula) in the early 5th century. Yabadvipa means the Malay Peninsula, not the Jawa Island. In the 9th-10th century, Persia and Arab sailors (traders) generally called the Nicobar Islands as 'Langabalus'.

I wrote "The History of Srivijaya" (Mekong Publishing Co., Tokyo) in 2012. In my story, I have presented many views which are different from the preceding theories. But I am convinced without the knowledge of 'Lang Barus', I could have proved Chaiya is the capital of Srivijaya, by using other Chinese text, for instance Yi-Jing's "*Nan-hui Chi-kuei Nei-fa Chuan* (南海寄歸内法傳)", "The Standard Histories of China Dynasties (正史)" ,especially the *Xin Tang Shu* (新唐書) and classical Chinese 'Encyclopedia' such as "*Tong Dian* (通典)" and so on. Of course, I can use the translations of the inscriptions. I cannot read Sanskrit, Khmer language, Cham language, but I can read the Chinese characters. Japanese historians had made great works in the past. Dr. Toyohati Fujita, Dr. Rokuro Kuwata, Dr, Naojirou Sugimoto, Dr. Junjiro Takakusu and some others, however they could not break through the theories of G.Cœdès. Japanese historians have tendency to respect the western historians, for instance, the history course of University of Tokyo, had demanded post graduate students to have knowledge of French. That means UOT would use the text of French scholars such as G.Cœdès. However, I think, Japanese students should read the Chinese classical text first. Fortunately, I was a student of the Faculty of Economics, so I could have started my study by reading the Chinese Chronicles. When I read G.Cœdès. I was confused.

G.Cœdès says Palembang was the intermediary port of East-West trade. Considering geology, I thought it was impossible, Indian or Persian merchants should have used the Riau Islands, just in front of Singapore. After, I finished UOT, I worked at a Japanese steel making company. I continued reading many books. But my basic question had never been answered.

G.Cœdès had made two fatal mistakes at the starting point of 'the history of Srivijaya'.The first he thought Funan rulers fled to the Jawa Island after kicked out from the Mekong Delta by Chenla. However, they actually fled to Chaiya (Ban-Ban or Pan-Pan) which used to be a subordinate state of Funan, since the 3rd century. The most European historians had not noticed the importance of the Malay Peninsula. They had no knowledge of geological importance of the Malay Peninsula and influence of the monsoon. In the 4th century, the western merchants began to utilize the monsoon and directly crossed the Bay of Bengal from Ceylon (Sri Lanka) and South India, and they could arrive at the ports of the Malay Peninsula, for instance Kedah and Takua Pa. However, in the summer time they could not go down the Malacca Straits directly to the south, due to the southern head wind. So, they had to wait for the north-eastern wind until the winter time for nearly 5 to 6 months. So, some of them developed the trans-peninsula route to the East coast of the Peninsula. From the east coast ports, they used other ships and went to China in the same year. G. Cœdès did not understand the importance of the Malay Peninsula, and he thought the middle point of East-West trade was at the Sunda Straits. He overestimated the importance of the Jawa Islands in the ancient times.

The second misunderstanding of G. Cœdès is the meaning of the Kedukan Bukit Inscription dated 683. He understood the inscription was the memory of the 'establishment of Srivijaya'. So, he thought Srivijaya was founded in 683 at Palembang. However, Srivijaya force came from the Malay Peninsula with fleet of rowing boats and

THE HISTORY OF SRIVIJAYA, ANGKOR and CHAMPA

occupied the Palembang kingdom in 683, and the inscription was the 'monument of victory' for Srivijaya. Actually, Srivijaya had sent the first mission to the Tang Dynasty between 670-673, according to the *Xin Tang Shu*. Yi-Jing left Canton for India for pilgrim in 671, at that time he already had known about Srivijaya, where he studied the Sanskrit grammar for 6 months as scheduled.

When we study the history of Southeast Asia, local inscriptions and the Chinese Chronicles are major sources. But Chinese text is very difficult for western historians to read directly. Fortunately, we Japanese have knowledge of the Chinese script, and are comparatively easy for reading the Chinese text. But in this case, the word 'Lang Barus' have been very difficult and overlooked occasionally. Perhaps, G.Cœdès decided 'Srivijaya is Palembang', so Japanese historians might have easily followed him, and had not doubted his theory. In the *Sui Shu* (『隋書』=History of Sui), the word Barus (婆羅娑) is used for the Chi-tu (赤土國、Red-Earth) country. In this case, Barus is same as'Lang Barus (郎婆露斯)' in the case of Shi-li-fo-shi (Srivijaya), so Chi-tu was located at the Malay Peninsula. So, I can suppose Chi-tu was merged with Srivijaya in the 7th century. Thereafter, Shi-li-fo-shi had unified the middle of the Malay Peninsula before 670.

After 741, Srivijaya suddenly stopped sending missions to Tang, but no record explained the reason. Srivijaya was located at Chaiya area in the Malay Peninsula, which was probably attacked by Khmer (Water Chenla) around 745. That is the only conceivable reason why Shi-li-fo-shi disappeared from the Tang Chronicle. However, Srivijaya had 14 vassal states and the Sailendra kingdom (central Jawa Island) organized big fleet of navy and counter attacked Chenla and recovered Chaiya and Nakhon Si Thammarat area around 760. After the victory, The Srivijaya group set up the victory monument at Chaiya. That was the 'Ligor inscription' dated 775. After the victory Srivijaya group proceeded Cambodia and Lin-yi (Champa) and occupied major ports of the Mekong River. Srivijaya sent army

Preface   xiii

to Chenla to occupy the inland of Cambodia and the commander
was Jayavarman II, who possibly came from the royal family of
old Funan (Srivijaya). Jayavarman II is the founder of the 'Angkor
Dynasty' and he is said to have declared independence from 'Java',
according to the Sdok Kok Thom inscription dated 1053. In this
case 'Java' means the Malay Peninsula, namely Srivijaya. Quaritch
Wales has the similar opinion, but Michael Vickery and Claude
Jacques strongly oppose the influence of Srivijaya over Angkor.

The Angkor Dynasty had been under control of Srivijaya until
Jayavarman II told a lie to the local chiefs of Khmer. He had
no intention to oppose, but to obey the instruction of Srivijaya.
Because, Angkor had not sent the tributary mission for 300 years
(814-1116) to China, which was probably prohibited by Srivijaya.
Furthermore, Jayavarman II, propagated Mahayana Buddhism
in Cambodia. Former Chenla kings had prohibited to worship
Buddhism, according to Yi-Jing's description.

The Angkor Dynasty had been under control of Srivijaya until
Suryavarman I' reign (1002-1050). He was a prince of Nakhon Si
Thammarat. However, after Jayavarman VI (1080~), the throne of
Angkor was taken over by the Phimai group, which had no direct
relation with San-fo-chi (Srivijaya group). Srivijaya group had lost
strong military power after the invasion of Chola (1025).

About Lin-yi, a strong rival of Funan and Srivijaya, suddenly
stopped sending mission to Tang after 749. No record was left about
this matter, and no historian discussed the reason. But I suppose, Lin-
yi had been also attacked by Srivijaya navy, around 760. Probably
Srivijaya might have destroyed shipping facility (merchant ships) of
Lin-yi. Lin-yi could not have recovered from the damage. But few
historians believe Srivijaya had destroyed the trade facilities of Lin-
yi. On the contrary they believe Srivijaya (Sailendra) was expelled
by King Satyavarman, who left inscription dated 774. Srivijaya's
attack was much earlier than that. Sailendra (new Kha-ling) sent the
first mission in 768, so before that they might have destroyed trade
facility and navy of Lin-yi.

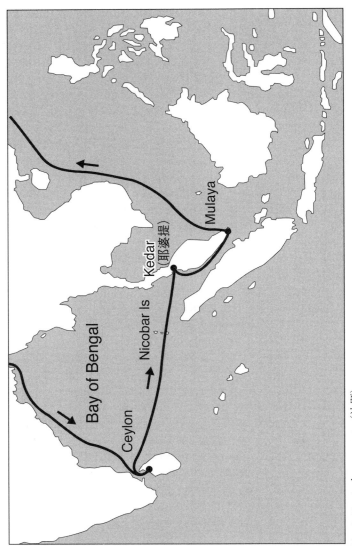

Map1: Fa-xian's sea route (法顯)

Preface   xv

Very few historians had criticized G.Cœdès' theory. However, M.
Vickery has correctly criticized G.Cœdès about his historical theory
on Khmer, but M. Vickery has probably embraced Palembang
theory. There have been so many followers of G.Cœdès. Q. Wales
had opposed G.Cœdès in many points but admitted that Yi Jing
had been to Palembang. Yi Jing had never been to Sumatra, he just
stopped over the Mulayu (末羅瑜) kingdom in his itinerary. Mulayu
was located at the Riau Islands, just in front of Singapore in the 7th
century, and which was an intermediary state of 'East-West' trade.

Dr. Junjiro Takakusu put a sheet of map, in his translation of
Yi-Jing's (義淨) *Nan-hui Chi-kuei Nei-fa Chuan* (南海寄歸内法傳).
His map contains serious mistakes. Yi-Jing had never been to
Palembang and he stopped over Kedah not Aceh. Yi-Jing's real
itinerary course was Chaiya (室利佛逝)⇒Mulayu (末羅瑜=in front of
Singapore)⇒Kedah (羯荼)⇒Nicobar Islands (裸人國=Naked people
islands)⇒Tamralipti (Bengal port)⇒on-land route to Nalanda
(India). However, Dr. Takakusu had been misguided by Chinese
historian, Ma Huan (馬歡). He believed what Ma-Huan (馬歡) wrote,
the"*Ying-Yai Sheng-Lan* (瀛涯勝覽)", in 1416, in which Ma dictated
that Ku-kang (旧港=Old Port) is the same country as was formerly
called San-fo-chi (三佛齊), and Ku-kang was also called Palembang
(渂淋邦), under suzerainty of 'Jawa (Indonesia)'.

旧港、卽古名三佛齊是也。番名曰渂淋邦、屬爪哇國所轄。

It goes without saying that the ancient Southeast Asian history
has many 'missing links'. It is historians' duty to compensate for
'missing links', but as far as I know very few of them have been
successful. On the contrary, many mistakes have been propageted
around the world. That is because historians are lack of imagination
and ability to make the scenario of the ancient history of Southeast
Asia. So, there is no integrated theory to explain starting Funan
to establishing the Angkor Dynasty. G. Cœdès tried to make such

xvi THE HISTORY OF SRIVIJAYA, ANGKOR and CHAMPA

story, but miserably he failed at the starting point.

I want to point out here is that 'economic geographical' perspective must be incorporated more in the Southeast Asian ancient history research. Of course, past historians also introduced geographical elements, but so many historians have been dragged to the wrong directions. It is because they have accepted uncritically the theory of G. Cœdès.

So, we should not forget nor neglect to study the approximate economic development and evolution. However, they made too many misunderstandings and mistakes. The western historians contributed very much to read inscriptions, but their theories are often incomplete and derailed. They have been regarded as authorities, so few of them would change their historical view. Now is the time when the ancient history of Southeast Asia should be revised and rewritten.

I have no intention to accuse the mistakes of preceding historians. I have lot of things to study from them. I have no teacher nor friend who taught me history, I only attended the class of Prof. Koji Iizuka at UOT more than 55 years ago. He taught me the splendors of the oriental culture. I have continued my study for more than a half of century, I have still many problems to solve by myself. Our history is deep and heavy.

I must thank for the effort and sacrifice of Mr. Shin Kuwahara, president of Mekong Publishing Co., Ltd. and prominent editor Ms. Yuka Omokawa. Without their dedicated support, my theories could not be published and perished in the dark.

Takashi Suzuki

CHAPTER
1

FUNAN

1-1 EARLY HISTORY OF FUNAN（扶南）

The kingdom of Funan was first recorded as a tributary state from the Mekong Delta to the Wu Dynasty（呉）in 225 AD. The origin of Funan was supposed to be founded in the first century and was kicked out around 550 from the Mekong Delta by Chenla（眞臘）which had been a former subordinate state of Funan. The word of Funan is supposed transcribed by the Chinese officials, from the Khmer language 'Bhnam or Vnam' meaning modern language 'Phnom=mountain'.

In Chinese characters, '扶（Fu）' means 'support' and '南（nan）' means 'south', so '扶南' means probably 'Support South（of the Wu Dynasty）'. From the beginning, the Wu Court treated Funan as a friendly state and sent two high ranking officials to Funan, Zhu-Ying（朱應）and Kang-Tai（康泰）. Both left very important information about Funan and neighboring countries.

In the formal dynastic histories of China（正史）, Funan had been described as the major state of the Mekong Delta area. Funan had sent missions to China many times. Probably the Chinese chronicles were mainly written according to the information brought by the tribute missions. So, there might be some exaggerations and biased reports.

Kang-Tai had written a legend of the origin of Funan in his report, which is quoted in the *Tai Ping Yu Lan*, vol.347（太平御覽、巻347）as

2   THE HISTORY OF SRIVIJAYA, ANGKOR and CHAMPA

follows:

According to the legend, a young Brahman (or Kshatria) named 'Khon-Tien (混塡=Kaundinya)' came over to a certain seashore of the Mekong Delta area from Tamralipti (Bengal port) on a large Indian merchant ship. A local princess named Liu-ye (柳葉) tried to take over the ship, then Khon-Tien used the sacred bow given by God and the first arrow had penetrated the queen's boat. She was strongly panicked and surrendered to Khon-Tien and they married. Then they established a new country 'Funan'. They got seven children, and distributed them seven small states.

The similar story is recorded in the My-Son (in Champa) inscription dated 658, that Kaundinya, the foremost among Brahmans, planted the spear which he had obtained from Drona's son Asvatham, the best Brahman. There was a daughter of a king of serpents, called 'Soma'. She was taken as wife by Kaundinya. Funan people believed their origin was established by Kaundinya and Soma.

A Japanese historian, Dr. Naojiro Sugimoto (杉本直治郎) estimates Funan was founded between the end of the first century or the beginning of the second century.

More details were quoted in the *Liang Shu* (梁書).

"Hundred years later, King Ban Kuang (婆況) integrated these small states. He died at the age of 90. His son 'Ban Ban (婆婆)' inherited the throne, and he left administration to 'Great general Fan Shi Man (范師蔓)'. King Ban Ban died three years later. Then the Funan people all together recommended Fan (Shi) man to succeed the throne. Fan Man was a strong and tactical general. He had conquered the neighboring states, and called himself 'Great king of Funan'. He made fleet of rowing large boats and invaded major international ports of the region. For instance Qu-du-kun (屈都昆)、Takua Pa (九稚)、Tenasserim (頓遜) and other states, totally more than 10. He expanded territory 5-6 thousand li (2000-2400 km) along the sea shore. Next he intended to conquer the Jin-lin state (金隣國), probably Kanchanaburi (or U Tong), but unfortunately he had a serious illness. He dispatched his son 'Jin Sheng (金生)' as a commander. However, a son of Fan Man's elder sister, 'Fan Zhan (范旃)', at that time a general with 2,000 soldiers killed Jin Sheng and usurped kingship. Fan Man's youngest son named 'Chang (長)', who had lived among ordinary people until age 20, organized brave friends and killed Fan Zhan. However general Fan Shou (范壽), a subordinate of Fan Zhan killed Chang and became the King of Funan. In 243, Fan Zhan (范旃) sent his envoy to the Wu Dynasty."

Funan had been a giant maritime state which financially depended on the trade. The nature of the maritime state had not changed after they established Srivijaya based on the ocean trade in the middle of the 7th century. The name of polity had changed after 'Srivijaya' to 'Sailendra' and finally 'San-fo-chi' (meaning three Vijayas).

Of course, in the hinterland of Funan, there was rice-growing area but Funan did not depend upon the tax from their people for the fiscal revenue. Funan government had sufficient income by foreign trade. But some residents had to be navy soldiers in case of war.

1-1-1 On-land trade route from the Lower Burma to Oc Eo

In the ancient time, at first Funan transported imports from West (mainly India), from the ports of the lower Burma to Oc Eo in the Mekong Delta by three on-land routes.

The first; commodities unloaded at Thaton, Martaban and Moulmein (Mawlamyine), shipped from the Bengal were carried to Tak via the Mae Sot mountain pass and further transported to Sukhothai or Nakhon Sawan. Si Thep was the main intermediary city and transported them to Oc Eo port of the Mekong Delta. This route was historically main route from the Lower Burma to Thailand.

THE HISTORY OF SRIVIJAYA, ANGKOR and CHAMPA

Trade route of Funan
(Route1)

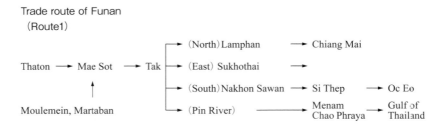

From Tak, cargos were transported by using the Pin River and via Ayutthaya, entered the Menam Chaophraya River, and finally were carried to the Gulf of Thailand.

From Tak to Nakhon Sawan, then commodities were carried to Si Thep. From Si Thep, the cargoes were carried to Oc Eo via the Pa Sak, Chi, Mun and Mekong River.

The Menam Chaophraya River was available from Nakhon Sawan to Suphanburi (near U Thong) and the Gulf of Thailand.

A classic type of Buddha Footprint is left at Wat Doi Khoi Khao Keao, Tak city, where was an intermediary exchange point between Burma and Thailand. This Footprint suggests Buddhism came to this area through Burma. Probably the Mon people were populous there and accepted and worshiped Buddhism. From Tak to Sukhothai is very near. Theravada Buddhism probably penetrated Sukhothai by this route from Thaton area after the 10th century.

Buddha Footprint of old temple Wat Doi Khoi Kaeo, Tak city, which may be the work of the Mon Buddhist before the 10th century.

1. Funan

Photo 1 : Buddha Footprint of old temple Wat Doi Khoi Kaeo, Tak city

Photo 2 : Buddha Footprint of Wat Phra Chai Mongkol, Mae Sot, Burma origin

(Route2)

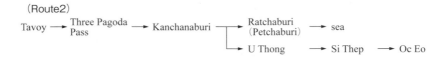

Second route; From Tavoy, which is situated in the south than the first route, western commodities were carried to Kanchanaburi, via the Three Pagodas Pass and were easily transported by using river facility to Kanchanaburi. From Kanchanaburi commodities were transported to U Thong, Si Thep then finally to Oc Eo. It was very long way, but in the 2nd to the 4th century it was usual route. Of course, from Kanchanaburi to Ratchaburi route existed. Ratchaburi faces the Gulf of Thailand, and they could use the sea route.

This 'Three Pagoda Pass' was used broadly by the Mon, because the access to Ratchaburi was convenient by using nearby rivers (the Kwai, Maeklong River). Ratchaburi was the trade centre of Dvaravati.

I suppose from 'Kanchanaburi ⇒ U Thong ⇒ Si Thep ⇒ The Mekong River' route was used frequently until the end of 4th century. However, after Funan had developed the trans-peninsula route from Takua Pa to Chaiya, this new route became main, since the 4th century.

(Route3)

Tenasserim → Sing Khon Pass → Prachuap Khiri Khan → Gulf of Thailand

Dun-Sun (頓遜 or 典孫) = Tenasserim (Mergui) appears on the Chinese text frequently. Mergui - Tenasserim was very important port, where Great General Fan Man (范蔓) occupied in the 3rd century. The Mon people had used the shortest route to Prachuap Khiri Khan, Hua Hin and Ratchaburi by crossing mountains (Sing Khon Pass) then they used the Gulf of Thailand.

1. Funan   7

Traditionally Funan had a major port Oc Eo at the Mekong
delta. Funan had stocked there the imported commodities from the
western countries, such as India, Persia and Arab and shipped them
to foreign countries especially to China.

1-1-2　Trans-peninsula route after Fan Man's conquest

On the other hand, new method of transporting of imported west
goods had been developed since the middle of the 3rd century.
Funan's new trans-peninsula route was from Takua Pa to Chaiya, at
the Bay of Bandon.

There was the development of the passage to directly crossing the
Bay of Bengal from South India and Ceylon by using the westerly
monsoon in the summer time and to arrive at the west coast of the
Malay Peninsula. However, even after the ship arrived at the Malay
Peninsula, due to the seasonal head-wind from South, they could not
immediately, go down the Straits of Malacca. The merchant ships
had to wait for the northeast wind to go down the Malacca Straits for
nearly 5-6 months at the harbor on the Malay Peninsula. In this case
Kedah was the most convenient port, considering sufficient supply
of rice and clean water.

Therefore, the officials of Funan and the Indian merchants of the
Malay Peninsula developed the land transport method to carry the
commodities to the east side ports of Peninsula. At that time, Takua
Pa to Chaiya was the shortest and within a territory of the 'Ban-Ban'
state. Ban-Ban was governed by the Mon king, but substantially a
subordinate state of Funan.

Funan people used Takua Pa to Chaiya route, then by ship to Oc
Eo or sometimes directly to China. In front of Takua Pa, there is the
'Ko Koh Khao' Island, in which 'Thung Tuk' was the international
market place, probably called Ko-ku-lo (哥谷羅) by Chinese. On the
other hand, the rulers of Kedah independently sent their commodities
by using the eastern side ports (for instance Kelantan, Songkhla) to
China and other countries. At that time Kedah was prosperous by

THE HISTORY OF SRIVIJAYA, ANGKOR and CHAMPA

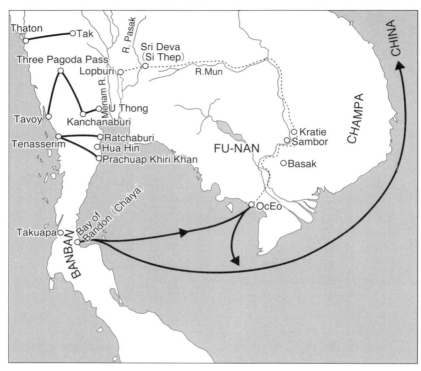

Map2: Takua Pa area

making iron at Sungai Batu.

In case of Ban-Ban, they can use the more convenient route which carries commodities mainly using small rivers from the west coast (Takua Pa) to the east coast, since the middle of the 4th century. There was a route, starting Khao Phra Narai, then use the Khlong Sok River to 'Ban Ta Khun' (near Wat Kraison), and then connected the Phum Dung River to arrive Phun Pin. Khao Si Wichai (Srivijaya hill) is near Phun Pin, Surat Thani, where are remains of several Hindu and Buddhism temples.

At Khao Phra Narai, Indian merchants set up their colonial village, where they built a Vishnu temple. At Khao Si Wichai, Surat Thani, Thai excavation team discovered a beautiful Vishnu statue. (Photo 3)

Funan further developed the new tributary route from Chaiya to China directly. In this case, Ban-Ban became a tributary state since the first 'South Song (Liu＝劉)'. It is recorded that Ban-Ban sent its first mission during 424-453.

Funan could not have controlled Kedah due to the distance, so Kedah enjoyed significant profit by sending tributary missions to China. There were on-land routes from Kedah to Kelantan, Songkhla. Later, Kedah can use 'Satun', a little north port, to unload the goods and carry them to Songkhla. In 441, Kedah sent the first envoy to South Song, under the name of Kan-da-ri (干陀利). Kandari later changed its name in the 6th to 7th century as 'Chi-To (赤土＝ Red Earth)' after merger with Langkasuka.

At first Kedah was recorded as Kola (個羅), Kedah (羯茶), Kadaram, Kidaram (Tamil), Kataha (Sanskrit) etc, but it was recorded as Kin-da-ri (斤陀利) or Kan-da-ri (干陀利) in the First South Song (劉氏宋: 420-479). So, Kan-da-ri (干陀利) means Kedah. However, G.Cœdès says Kan-da-ri was located in Sumatra, because the majority of historians say so.

The *Ming Shi* (明史, History of Ming Dynasty) says that Kandari

THE HISTORY OF SRIVIJAYA, ANGKOR and CHAMPA

Photo 3: Vishnu image of the Sri Vijaya Hill (Khao Si Wichai) now displayed at the Bangkok National Museum. (by T.Suzuki)

was 'San-fo-chi'. So, G.Cœdès might have thought Kandari was 'San-fo-chi (=Srivijaya)', and located at Palembang (Sumatra). As the result, many historians also considered 'Kandari was located in Sumatra'. This seems funny story, but many historians believed so and prevailed in the whole world for nearly one century.

In 441, Kin-da-ri sent the first envoy to the South Song Court. Before then, Khalatan (呵羅單) had sent missions in 430, 433, 434, 436, 437. Khalatan looked like the substitute of the Kedah kingdom. Kedah and Khalatan might have had strong connection on the trade.

But, later the kingdom of Khalatan might have some independence which also sent the last envoy in 452, and since 531, and possibly changed its name as 'Tan-tan (丹丹 or 單單)' which continued until 670. Kelantan had accepted Buddhism very early, probably in the

1. Funan   11

5th century. In 430 King of Khalatan sent the first mission to the South Song with an official letter, in which stated that in Khalatan Buddhism was prevailing.

At that time in the Malay Peninsula, the Mon people were active in the commerce especially around the Bay of Bandon area, and the west coast. Later the Indian merchants joined them. Funan used the Mons people for their business. In the *Old Tang Shu* describes that all the people study the Sanskrit and worship Buddhism at Ban-Ban. Chaiya area had been very civilized at that time. In the 7th century, normally reading and writing were privilege for a small group of officials and priests.

1-1-3   The Meaning of Indianization

The trade between India (including Bengal) and Thailand (mainland and the peninsula) is estimated to have begun from the time of the Maurya Dynasty of 3-4 BC century. Merchants from India had visited the Lower Burma ports, the Malay and Indochina peninsula. Necklace of beads appeared from the 3rd BC century. Furthermore, not only trade purpose, Indian migrants came to the Malay Peninsula and the Sumatra Island to look for gold and tin mine. The Indian merchants have brought trade goods such as cotton clothes and beads of necklace and pottery, to exchange with food, fragrant wood, gold etc. At the same time, they accompanied Brahman and Buddhist monks, so Hinduism and Buddhism penetrated into these regions. Some Indian people settled in Thailand and merged with local people gradually. Indian people taught the technology of agriculture and metal working to the local people.

The Indian merchants bought silk, craftworks from China and spice and incense in the Southeast Asia and got a big profit by re-exporting them to the Roman Empire, Egypt, Mediterranean area.

India got huge gold coins from Rome and the currency changed from 'the silver standard to the gold standard' system, thus the demand for gold increased rapidly in India.

12   THE HISTORY OF SRIVIJAYA, ANGKOR and CHAMPA

Therefore, Indian's gold search fever occured and many Indian adventurers went to Suwarnadvipa (Sumatra and the Malay Peninsula). 'Suwarnadvipa' means the golden country, with both sides water. About Suwarnadvipa, there are many scholars and students of history who understand simply as only 'island or Sumatra'.

'The silk load by the seaway' was much more efficient than so-called 'the silk load on- land' which depends on the long land route to trade with China. The Indian, Arab and Persian merchants found the sea-route was much easier and more efficient and profitable than transportation with a long caravan of camels.

Also, the Indian merchants came to the Southeast Asia in group and were strong in the fellowship sentiment and they decided many important matters by their group meeting. Therefore, a decision making was done after well discussion among the top leaders about the policy and operation. This is the same in case of Funan.

Funan's Great General 'Fan Man' was recommended by the people to take the throne of Funan after the previous king's death. Another example was Chiao Chen-Ju (the 2nd Kaundinya, 僑陳如), who was a Brahman staying at Ban-Ban. Amid the political confusion in Funan, he was welcomed by the Funan people and was recommended to be the king of them. He introduced many advanced Indian system to Funan and established the base of development.

There remain scarce examples of the inscriptions of Funan. It may be the reason that there was not habitude to emphasize the achievements of specific individual.

In the *Nan-Ji Shu* (南齊書), King Kaundinya Jayavarman (478-514) sent his envoy to the South Ji (南齊) Dynasty in 484, the ambassador, an Indian Brahman named Nagasena (那伽仙) explained about the religious situation of Funan.

He explained to the emperor that in Funan the people worship 'Mahesvara (Siva)', and believe that God would come down on the top of the 'sacred mountain Meru' and people believe under this God, the climate is always good, and the peaceful life is guaranteed.

Therefore, the king found a suitable sacred mountain every time he transferred his capital. In the Angkor times, the king constructed a high tower on the pyramid, he chose there as Meru mountain and the people worshipped it as 'the centre axis' of the universe.

Dr. Naojirou Sugimoto says that the Funan seems to have selected a mountain at 'Ba Phnom' (Sugimoto, p376). However, it doesn't seem to have been originally a capital city of Funan. It seems that Angkor Borei (Phnom Da) was the original metropolis, judging from the numerous ruins and the geographical conditions. At Angkor Borei and Phnom Da, there are many Hindu images and remains. Vishnu images were spread from Angkor Borei to the Bay of Bandon and other regions.

1-2 RELIGION

Worship of the ancestral spirit and animism was pre-Hindu practice of South East Asia. Later Indian migrants brought worship of Hinduism and deified kings. Kings willingly accepted Hinduism. From migrated Indian Brahman and Kshatria class, who came into this area as the leaders of Indian merchants, and introduced Hinduism first and often married daughters of local rulers. Buddhism came later and penetrated mainly among the Mon people.

It will be permitted to say that the 'Meru mountain' worship was brought into Funan as Siva belief from the beginning, and the ancestor-worship and the Hinduism seem to be connected among the common people.

On the other hand, for Funan, Mahayana Buddhism was introduced among the leaders and the popularization of Buddhism was beginning in the 4th century. Probably Mahayana Buddhism was introduced from Ban-Ban to Funan. Ban-Ban was the subordinate

14　THE HISTORY OF SRIVIJAYA, ANGKOR and CHAMPA

Photo4: Buddha Footprints at Wat Kraison　(in the middle of Takua Pa and Chaiya)

state of Funan since the 3rd century after the conquest of General Fan Man. The communication between the both states were quite usual and frequent, so Buddhism was introduced in Funan gradually.

The penetration of Buddhism to the Malay Peninsula was very early. There are many primitive 'Buddha Footprints' in the Peninsula. From Chumpon, Takua Pa, Krabi, Trang, Chaiya, Nakon si Thammarat etc. The ancient and primitive type Buddha Footprints were just directly chiseled on natural rocks.

'Ban-Ban' was the most advanced Buddhist state in the Malay Peninsula where many Indian merchants were coming in and some Hindu Brahmans and Buddhist monks also visited there with them. The kings accepted them and supported Buddhism. At first Buddhism seems to spread among the local Mon people.

In this area, Buddha Footprints which only engraved a footmark of Buddha on natural rock, were introduced by Indian monks. Before

1. Funan

the 2nd century, the Buddha images were not popular even in India, or prohibited to make the image, so Buddhist monks in the Malay Peninsula made Buddha Footprint for worship.

Trade relation between Ban-Ban (under Funan) and Indian traders was strengthened since the 3rd century, especially after the conquest of Fan Man , Funan and India established 'direct' business relation. At Takua Pa, Ban-Ban was the sole buyer of the western goods, and the people of Ban-Ban (mostly the Mon) became intimate with Indian merchants and monks.

Owing to the international trade, Ban-Ban had been opened earlier and many Indians came in. So, Ban-Ban was much advanced as for the acceptance of Buddhism. On the other hand, Buddhism in Funan was stimulated by the Buddhism heat in China. So, leaders of Funan were affected from both sides, Ban-Ban and China. Buddhism surged in Ban-Ban, where were more than ten Buddhism temples and more than 1,000 monks were studying Buddhism in the territory. Once the leaders of Funan knew Buddhism, many of them were attracted by the depth of the philosophy of Buddhism and became devotees of Buddhism. Later Mahayana Buddhism became the 'state religion' of Srivijaya group.

Mahayana Buddhism became the common philosophical basics of the leaders of Funan and Srivijaya. The last king of Funan, Rudravarman was known as a Buddhist. However, Chenla kings believed in Sivaism and hated Buddhism as Yi Jing wrote.

Later, in Srivijaya regime, Mahayana Buddhism became popular in the states Srivijaya dominated. The typical example was the Sailendra kingdom in the central Jawa where the Borobudur temple was built which is the biggest Mahayana temple in the world. Jambi also constructed huge Mahayana Buddhism complex, even now 'Muaro Jambi' remains outside of Jambi city.

1-3 FUNAN REGIME

In the 3rd century, Great General Fan Man was a superior strategist of genius and made the plan to monopolize procurement of western goods, then he organized the navy which consists of large-sized rowing boats to secure a trade route (purchasing and transporting the western goods) in Funan, and captured several main trade ports one after another and put them under Funan's control.

King Fan Shou (范尋) sent mission to the Western Jin's, Emperor Wu-di's first year (265).

After that, King Fan Shou had continued sending 4 envoys to the Western Jin until 287.

There is a record that in 357 King Chu Chan-tan (竺旃檀) sent tribute of elephants to Emperor Bok (穆帝) to the Eastern Jin Dynasty.

The Emperor, at that time was 15 years old, frightened by elephants and showed straight uncomfortable feeling and ordered the envoy not to bring such an animal again because it is astonishing people and need so much attention to breed. (梁書、The *Liang Shu*)

King Chu (竺) means an Indian origin, Chan-tan (旃檀) means 'Chandana'. After this trouble, Funan could not have sent the mission for a long time. The next chance was in 389. After this, Funan sent next envoy in 434 to the South Song Dynasty.

On the other hand, Lin-yi had sent 7 envoys in the 4th century. As the importer of the western commodities Funan's position was superior to Lin-yi's, but Funan could not send mission to China. During that time, it is said there was severe political confusion in Funan. So, Funan rulers had arranged to send mission from Ban-Ban at the same time, they invited Chiao Chen-Ju (the 2nd Kaundinya, 僑陳如) as their king.

According to Chinese records the *Sānguó zhì* 三國志 (Records of the Three Kingdoms) completed in 289 by Chen Shou 陳壽 (233–297), two envoys from Funan arrived at the office of Lu Dai (呂

岱）, governor in the southern Chinese kingdom of Wu （吳）: the first
embassy arrived between 225 and 230, the second in the year 243.

Later sources such as the *Liang Shu* 梁書 （Liang History） compiled
by Yao Cha 姚察 （533–606） and Yao Silian 姚思廉 （~ 637）, completed
in 636, says that in the 3rd century, the mission of Chinese envoys
Kang Tai （康泰） and Zhu Ying （朱應） from the Wu Dynasty were
sent to Funan. The report of these envoys, though no longer extant
in their original condition, were quoted and partly preserved in
the later dynastic histories. Fortunately, we can know much about
Funan from them.

After returning, Kang Tai wrote two reports, the *'Foreign Aspect*
（外國傳）' and the *'Funan Local Custom* （扶南土俗）' after returning
home and the original texts were lost, but, some have been quoted in
the *'Tai Ping Yu Lan* （太平御覽）' （compiled by Lee Feng 李昉, of the
Northern Song Dynasty, compiled around 980）. In Volume 787, he
reported about Zhu Bo （諸薄＝Jawa） and we can know the various
situations of its neighboring states.

1-3-1 East-West Trade

The Indian merchants traded by using the west ports such as
Thaton, Thavoy, Tenasserim, Takua Pa, Krabi and Kedah. Kedah
had been also a big city of its iron products since BC 500. Recently
at 'Sungai Batu', near Bujan Valley, Kedah city, large remains of
iron-making have been found and excavation work is now going.

The main Indian side port was Tamralipiti of Bengal. In the
winter time, they came down from the Bengal area and their main
commodities were cotton cloth and beads. The Persian merchants,
too, came to the ports of Burma. They traded mainly with the Mon
speaking people and local Indian merchants. The Persian merchants
directly visited China with tribute.

In the mainland of Thailand, the Mon people had lived and
were engaged in commerce, rice farming, making bronze, iron
and salt. Their activities were spread into the Isaan area （North-

18   THE HISTORY OF SRIVIJAYA, ANGKOR and CHAMPA

eastern Thailand) and Laos. They, at first accepted Hinduism then Buddhism. All over the inner land, there remains many old Buddha Footprints as the symbol of Buddhism worship.

After Funan was formed, at first, commodities from the west ports were carried overland to the intermediary bases, such as U Thong and Si Thep in the mainland Thailand, before transported to the Mekong delta.

Some commercial cities had existed since the Bronze Age. Along the trade routes and the network of salt, iron, Dongson bronze drums existed. The major residents were the Mon speaking people and some were Khmer.

The group of Indian merchants settled in the cities and villages. With advanced technology and knowledge, those Indian people taught the residents how to cultivate rice and make metal tools, iron making method and so on. With passing through the time, Indian became rulers in the cities. The examples were U Thong and Si Thep (Sri Deva), where they first introduced Hinduism and later Buddhism.

As above mentioned, the cargos which were unloaded on the Lower Burma ports were carried to Tak and Kanchanaburi through the Three Pagodas Pass as above mentioned. These commerce route had existed since the Neolithic era.

At Kanchanaburi, which was the key point of the route. there are ruins from the ancient times, 'Prasat Muang Sing', which was used as stock place, Buddhist temple and fortress. At the age of the Angkor Dynasty it was expanded and fortified. Kanchanaburi faces the Maeklong River which passes Ratchaburi Province and empties into the Gulf of Thailand in Samut Songkhram. From Kanchanaburi to U Tong is short distance on road.

1. Funan

Photo 5: Si Thep (from panel of the museum)

1-3-2 Si Thep

Si Thep used to be called 'Sri Deva' or 'Srideb' meaning of the 'Shrine city', where was full of Hindu shrines and the images of Hindu Gods, such as Surya, Krishna, Vishnu and Siva. The Pasak River flows nearby Si Thep and flows Lopburi and empties into the Gulf of Thailand via Ayutthaya.

Also, from Si Thep they can connect with the Mekong River via the 'Chi' and 'Mun River'. The city was located at the most important point of the traffic, where Funan group had governed since the 2nd century. The early rulers of Si Thep believed in Hinduism. On the other hand, the local residents mostly the Mon people, at first accepted Hinduism, but later, probably since the 9th century changed to Buddhism.

Judging from the scale of the ruins, Si Thep was a very big city enclosed in moat. Historically Si Thep had been prosperous as the commercial city of the Mon people, who generally worshipped

Photo 6: Dharma Cakra of Si Thep & Base of pagoda

Photo 7: Base of pagoda (Si Thep)

Buddhism and built giant pagodas in the city. There are Buddhist temple ruins of the Dvaravati style too, and a huge 'Dharma-cakra' is placed in the centre of the historical park.

In the northeast Thailand iron manufacturing and salt making were popular industries. Generally speaking the northeast area in Thailand (now called Isaan) had been very prosperous compared with south of the Dangrek Mountains, today's Cambodia.

Dr. Q. Wales supposed that cargos unloaded at Tavoy in the lower Burma were carried to Kanchanaburi and further to U Thong and Si Thep. Nakhon Sawan was convenient intermediary city. There was still a long journey via the Chi River, the Mun River and the Mekong River and the final destination was Oc Eo port. It is sure that it depended on the rivers for the main transportation in those days, but many roads which connected river to river existed. From Si Thep to Nakhon Ratchasima, there was road connection. These commercial and transportation network had been developed among the Isaan area since ancient time.

CHAPTER
2
SHI-LI-FO-SHI (SRIVIJAYA)

2-1 SHI-LI-FO-SHI WAS LOCATED IN THE MALAY PENINSULA

As above mentioned, Shi-li-fo-shi was located in the Malay Peninsula. G.Cœdès made wrong interpretation of the Kedukan Bukit Inscription. Srivijaya conquered the kingdom of Palembang in 683, but 'Shi-li-fo-shi' had been founded before in the Malay Peninsula. The location of 'Shi-li-fo-shi' had been clearly identified as above mentioned, by the *Xin (New) Tang Shu* (新唐書) that the west of Shi-li-fo-Shi was the Nicobar Islands, meaning Shi-li-fo-shi was located in the Malay Peninsula. No historians have understood this sentence, except Dr. Rokuro Kuwata and few other historians. In the Malay Peninsula, Chaiya, Surat Thami is the only one candidate as the capital of Shi-li-fo-shi. That is Chaiya. Nakhon Si Thammarat was not so developed in the 7th century.

Furthermore few historians identified the exact location of 'Luo-Yue (羅越)' and 'Ko-ku-lo (哥谷羅)'. They say Luo-Yue was Johore, near Singapore, however Luo-Yue is located at the northern part of the Malay Peninsula. Ko-ku-lo is a major port of the west coast of Peninsula and as Jia Dan (賈耽) says "located at north of Kedah". Ko-ku-lo is without doubt Kho Khao Island, outer port of Takua Pa.

In case of Luo-Yue, most historians had misunderstood the marine-route of Jia Dan, quoted in the *Xin Tang Shu*, so they had

24 THE HISTORY OF SRIVIJAYA, ANGKOR and CHAMPA

no other choice than Johore. However, in the Tang times Johore was not so popular port. The *Xin Tang Shu* writes correctly about this matter. I will explain as follows:

2-2 MARINE-ROUTE OF JIA DAN (賈耽)

The *Xin Tang Shu* has the geographical articles in which Jia Dan's sea route map is quoted. Jia Dan was prime minister of the Tang Court around 800.

"After five days journey from 'the Con Dao Island', one reaches a strait which the barbarians call 'Zhi (質)', and which is 100 li from south to north. On its northern shore is the kingdom of Luo-Yue, on its southern shore the kingdom of Fo-shi (Srivijaya). Some four or five days' journey over the water to the eastward of Fo-shi is the kingdom of 'Kha-ling (訶陵)', the largest island in the south. Then, emerging from the strait, in three days one reaches the kingdom of 'Ko-ko-seng-chih (葛葛僧祇)', which is situated on another island off the north-west corner of Fo-shi. The inhabitants are mostly pirates. Sailors on junks go in dread of them. On the northern shore of the island is the kingdom of Ko-lo. To the west of 'Ko-lo (箇羅)' is the state of 'Ko-ku-lo (哥谷羅)'. Along 'Ko-ko-seng-chih' after 4-5 days journey, the ship arrive at 'Sheng Deng Zhou (勝鄧洲).

From Sheng Deng Zhou to the Nicobar Islands (婆露國), it takes 5 days. From Nicobar to Sri Lanka (師子國) it takes 10 days.

「(到軍突弄山。)又五日行至海硤、蕃人謂之「質」、南北百里、北岸則羅越國、南岸則佛逝國、佛逝國東水行四五日、至訶陵國、南中洲之最大者。又西出硤、三日至葛葛僧祇國、在佛逝西北隅之別島、國人多鈔暴、乘舶者畏憚之。其北岸箇羅國。箇羅西則哥谷羅國。又從葛葛僧祇四五日行、至勝鄧洲。又西五日行,至婆露國。又六日行,至婆國伽藍洲。又北四日行,至師子國.

2. Shi-li-fo-shi (Srivijaya)

In this case, 'Zhi (質)' is generally interpreted 'selat' ('strait' in Malay language), and supposed to be the Singapore Strait. However, the Singapore Strait is too narrow, less than 10 km width. 100li means about 40 kilometers. Furthermore 'selat' has three meanings, 'strait' 'narrow' and 'sound (bay)'. But in this case, selat is not correct reading, 'Zhi' might be a proper name of a certain place. I understand Zhi means a 'S (r) i Surat'=Surat Thani, the Bay of Bandon, of which mouth is about 40 kilometers from north to south. If Zhi is identified as the Singapore Strait (硖), the location of Luo-Yue (羅越) must be Johore at the south end of the Malay Peninsula. And the location of 'Shih-li-fo-shi'supposed be the Riau Islands far from Sumatra, but many historians ignored actual distance between Sumatra and the Riau Islands. This hypothesis is a convenient story for the 'Palembang theory'. Luo-Yue cannot be Johore. In the Tang times, Johore was not developed so much as to be an emporium for the neighboring states.

Jia Dan says from Zhi (質), one can go to Kha-ling (訶陵國) after 4-5 days journey. In this case, Kha-ling means the middle of the Malay Peninsula, probably 'Sathing Phra', a major port of Srivijaya. Then one goes down further and crosses the Singapore Strait to the west, within three days, one can arrive at 'Ko-ko-seng-chih (葛葛僧祇國)', which is unidentified.

Normally 'Kha-ling' was located in the Java island. But, since the middle of the 8th century to the 9th century, Kha-ling had represented the 'whole Srivijaya' as the Sailendra kingdom. Apparently, officials of the Tang Court acknowledged that a part of the Malay Peninsula belonged to Kha-ling, which was used as the shipping port to Tang. Such view was inherited by the writers of the *Xin Tang-Shu* in the Song times.

The Tang Court probably considered the territory of Shih-li-fo-shi covered from a part of the Malay Peninsula including Kedah to the southern part of Sumatra such as Mulayu, Jambi and Palembang. Ho-lo (Ko-la = 箇羅) is Kedah. Ko-la, Kalah and Kadaram all mean

Kedah.

Ko-ku-lo（哥谷羅）is not formally identified yet, but I suppose it means the Kho Khao Island. The Kho Khao Island is located just in front of Takua Pa and its 'Thung Tuk' was the market place for international merchants. Q. Wales found the remains of old entrepôt. 'Ko-ku-lo' is located in the Malay Peninsula, the position of Luo-Yue（羅越）should be northern part of the Peninsula. Furthermore the residents in Luo-Yue were similar to Dvaravati people ('Mon tribe'), so Luo-Yue cannot be Johore. Lou-Yue probably had the territory across the root of the Malay Peninsula facing the Bengal Bay, and the northward was 'sea water' to Bengal.

There is another description in the *Xin Tang-Shu*, "The northward from Luo-Yue is 5,000 li sea water, and the south-west is Ko-ku-lo（哥谷羅）". According to 'the Jia Dan's explanation of the map, Lou-Yue（羅越）is located at northern direction of Ko-ku-lo（哥谷羅）= Ko Koh Khao Island. So, Johore is completely the wrong direction.

The *Xin Tang-Shu* says that traders from various directions gather around Lou-Yue. The customs of the resident of Lou-Yue are same as those of Dvaravati (the Mons). Every year, the merchant-ship of Lou-Yue comes to Canton and reports to the local officials. So, I consider that the location of Lou-Yue was near the mainland of Thailand and the upper north of the Malay Peninsula, near Ratchaburi to Tenasserim（Burma）.

「羅越者北距海5,000里西南哥谷羅商賈往來所湊集俗與墮和羅底同歲乘舶至廣州、州必以聞。」

As the conclusion, Jia Dan's itinerary map is not accurate, so flexible interpretation by readers is needed. However many historians easily decide Zhi（質）means 'strait' so that it is the Strait of Singapore. They have been in haste to connect everything to Palembang. I understand 'Zhi's the proper name of location, near the Bay of Bandon. It is probably 'Si Surat = Surat Thani'.

2. Shi-li-fo-shi (Srivijaya)

As the identification of Luo-Yue, 'Ratburi (Ratchaburi)' may be the proper location. Ratburi has huge historical remains, and is considered once big emporium which had port facilities on the both sides on the west coast (Burma side) and on the east coast, facing the Gulf of Thailand. Historically Ratburi had been under indirect control of Funan, because the Bay of Thai (Siam) was dominated by Funan's and later by Srivijaya's navy. As Dr. Toyohachi Fujita suggested, Ko-lo-she-fen (哥羅舍分)'may be Ratchaburi. Fen (Bun＝分) is apparently 'buri (town)' and 'Lo-she' should be pronounced as 'Ra-cha'. Ko (哥) is meaningless 'prefix'. Ko-ku-lo (哥谷羅) is located at Takua Pa, which is also, intermediary market place for the international merchants.

According to the '*Tong-Dian* (通典)', compiled by Du You (杜祐) in 801, Ko-lo-she-fen (or Kha-la sha-bun) is situated in the southern part of the South Seas. It adjoins the kingdom of To-ho-lo (or Da-wa-la 墮和羅). It can put 20,000 soldiers in the field. In the fifth year of the Xian Qing (顯慶) of the Tang (660), King Pu-yue-jia-ma (蒲越伽摩) sent envoys to tribute.

> 「哥羅舍分國在南海之南按墮和羅國勝兵二萬人其王蒲越伽摩唐顯慶五年遣使朝貢」

According to the '*Ce-fu Yuan-Gui* (冊府元亀)', the ambassador of Ko-lo-she-fen left their port in 659 and arrived to the Tang Court in 662. This fact means the ambassador took the course of the Malacca Straits. Around 660s, the Gulf of Thailand had been under control of Ban-Ban (Pan-Pan) and former Funan's navy, so Ko-lo-she-fen could not use the Gulf of Thailand, the shortest course to China.

The Tang Court probably considered the territory of Shi-li-fo-shi covered from a central part of the Malay Peninsula including Kedah to the southern part of Sumatra such as Mulayu, Jambi, Palembang

28 THE HISTORY OF SRIVIJAYA, ANGKOR and CHAMPA

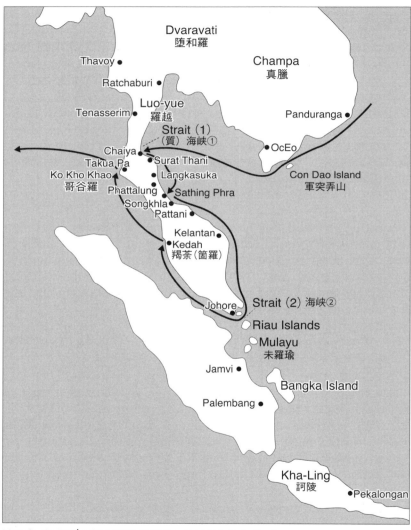

Map 3: Jia Dan's Sea route from Southeast Asia to Ceylon

2. Shi-li-fo-shi (Srivijaya) 29

and the Jawa Island.

G.Cœdès had 'good' intention to discuss the Srivijaya history from the perspective of East-West trade history, but he put the midpoint of East-West trade at the 'Sunda Strait'. This is improper, because the Jawa Island is not adequate to be intermediary to trade with China. The Malay Peninsula was more convenient as intermediary ports, by using the 'trans-peninsula' route.

Academics who have achieved excellent track records in the field such as archeology are numerous, but their conclusion is often wrong, because they stick to the 'Srivijaya hypothesis' of G.Cœdès. For example, they believe that all the Buddhists monks from India had visited Sumatra instead of the Malay Peninsula. Many historians believe that Yi Jing visited Palembang before he went to Kedah and Tamuralipiti. That is incorrect by considering the location of 'Mulayu', furthermore Palembang had provided poor infrastructure for studying Buddhism and Sanskrit. As the result, most historians had ignored the importance of the Malay Peninsula, even Paul Wheatley put the capital of Srivijaya at Palembang.

The ancient history of Southeast Asia had gone to the wrong side owing to the followers of G.Cœdès. Most historians do not aware that they are in the dark and wandering in the labyrinth. I have written in my book "The History of Srivijaya" (Japanese) and how G.Cœdès had repeated serious mistakes. I suppose he had not read the "*Xin Tang Shu*" in the Chinese text or ignored its contents.

2-3 Java (闍婆) often meant the Malay Peninsula before the Song times

In the early 5th century, a prominent Chinese Buddhist monk Fa-xian (法顯) also recorded that after he had shipped from Ceylon to China, the tempest continued day and night. After storms of thirteen days, the ship was carried to an island, where they repaired the leak, the ship started again to the eastern direction.

After nine to ten days they arrived at 'Yaba-dvipa (耶馬提).' Many historians consider 'Yaba-dvipa' is the Jawa Island or Sumatra. However, in this case, ships could not go down the Malacca Straits due to the summer time head wind (monsoon) from south to north. So, the merchant ships must wait for the north-east wind until winter for nearly half of a year. Fa-xian wrote, he waited at Yaba-dvipa for five months. It was unavoidable waste of time. In this case Yaba-dvipa was the Malay Peninsula, probably Kedah or Takua Pa. The word 'Java (闍婆)' written in the Tang text means mostly the Malay Peninsula.

The *Song Shu* (宋書), history of First South Song (420-479) writes "呵羅單國治闍婆洲". This means that Kalatan (呵羅單) governs 'Jawa', but Kalatan was located in the Malay Peninsula, today's Kelantan. So, Khalatan state could not have governed the Jawa Island. It was a simple exaggeration of the king of Kalatan. Actually, Khalatan was located in the Peninsula (Kelantan state, Malaysia) and governed some neighboring area. Possibly some ports were under control of Khalatan state at that time. In Khalatan, Buddhism was flourishing according to the "*Song Shu*". A classic 'Buddha footprint' carved on a natural large stone exists at Buchon, Kota Bharu city and smaller 4 primitive Buddha Footprints exist at Bukit Mara.

There are many primitive Buddha Footprints in Thailand, especially Peninsula area, Takua Pa, Krabi, Chiya etc. However, in Indonesia there is no Buddha Footprints except at the Karimun

2. Shi-li-fo-shi (Srivijaya)

Photo 8: A classic giant 'Buddha footprint' at Kelantan, the 5th century

Island in front of Singapore. In the ancient time, the Karimun Island provided intermediary port facility for foreign ships and some Indian merchants (Buddhists) might have lived there.

'The ancient history of Southeast Asia' cannot be written perfectly if a historian depends upon the hypotheses of G.Cœdès. If you begin with relying on the Palembang hypothesis of Cœdès, you can't write the true history of Southeast Asia. Now it is confirmed, by the above description of the *Xin (New) Tang-Shu* that Srivijaya was located in the Malay Peninsula. It was certainly located at the Bay of Bandon. The rulers of Funan exiled or defected to the Ban-Ban state with their navy, in the middle of the 6th century. Afterward they had integrated the Malay Peninsula and established a polity of 'Srivijaya (Shi-li-fo-shi)'. Srivijaya had sent the first tributary mission to the Tang Court in 670. After that Srivijaya expanded itself to the Straits of Malacca and the Jawa island (kingdom of Kha-ling) to monopolize the tributary mission, or the trade with Tang Dynasty from the Southeast Asia.

At present, Thailand, Cambodia and Vietnam are separated by the border but in the ancient history the concept of the border had been obscure and different.

The activity of Funan had been, so flexible, so many historians cannot follow up the description of the *Xin Tang-Shu* and other texts. The history of Chenla is also very confused, because many historians consider that Chenla's activity had started from within the territory of Today's Cambodia and the Mekong River side (Wat Phu or Vat Phou).

The territory of Funan covered very wide, from the west coast of the Lower Burma to the central part of Thailand, U Thong, Nakhon Sawan, Si Thep and the Chi River, the Mun River and the Mekong River.

The Angkor Dynasty had been established in 802 when King Jayavarman II formally ascended the throne, and until Suryavarman I, the regime had been under the influence of Srivijaya for nearly 250 years. During this period, the Angkor Kingdom had been influenced by Srivijaya. Mahayana Buddhism expanded widely and became popular religion in Cambodia. After Suryavarman I's death in 1050, the new independent family from Phimai region took over the reign.

After I had written "*The History of Srivijaya*" and probably I succeeded to connect some of the key points of the missing links of the history.

However still there are many problems unsolved. For instance, who was Jayavarman II, and why the Angkor Kingdom had not sent mission to China for more than 300 years?

2-4 A Short History of Srivijaya

The history of Funan in Cambodia was once finished after the invasion of Chenla. However, Funan took different course of history. Around 530, the Funan rulers were kicked out from the Mekong Delta area. Where did they go? G.Cœdès thinks they fled to the Jawa Island where they founded the kingdom Srivijaya. However, in the central Jawa, there had existed a strong kingdom called 'Kha-ling (訶陵)' by Chinese character.

Funan and Kha-ling had been competitors as trade states, as 'vassal' states of China.

It was impossible for Funan rulers to conquer Kha-ling kingdom of Jawa with small army. My hypothesis is that the rulers of Funan fled to the 'Ban-Ban (盤盤) state' located at the Bay of Bandon, Surat Thani area. The Ban-Ban state had been a subordinate state of Funan since the 3rd century, after the Great General Fan Man had occupied there. Funan had used Ban-Ban as the trade centre of the western commodities imported at Takua Pa, on the west coast and transported them to the east coast of Chaiya. Funan rulers continued the tribute mission to Tang from Chaiya. Moreover, Funan had used Ban-Ban as its substitute to tribute to Tang since 5th century. So, Funan had two trade routes with China, one is under the name of Funan, and another is under the name of Ban-Ban.

According to the '*Tong Dian* (= 通典), compiled by Du You (杜祐) in 801, Ban-Ban (婆婆 or 盤盤) had weak army and their arrow-head is equipped with 'stone', even though the head of lance is made of iron sword. Ban-Ban had been probably forced by Funan to have weak military. At Ban-Ban, Buddhism was popular and there were more than 1,000 monks with 10 temples for the ordinary monks and one upper class temple for senior monks. Furthermore, the common

34   THE HISTORY OF SRIVIJAYA, ANGKOR and CHAMPA

people were studying the Sanskrit language.

Ban-Ban's economic and strategic value was so great, so Funan had changed the nature of Ban-Ban as its subordinate state for the international trade port.

Even though Funan had lost its base at the Mekong Delta in the middle of the 6th century, the *Xin Tang Shu* says that Funan sent missions two times, in 'Wu-Di (618-26) and Zhen-Guan (627-49) times. Funan presented two white head men, who were captured at the west border of Funan. "武德、貞觀時,再入朝,又獻白頭人二." Furthermore, according to the "*Ce-fu Yuan-Gui* (冊府元亀)" in 643, king of Lin-yi (Champa) asked the Emperor for assistance to stop the attack from Funan.

After appeal of Lin-yi, Funan kept silence. Funan was preparing the next step to form Shi-li-fo shi (Srivijaya). Funan merged Chi-tu (赤土) in the early 7th century. Then Funan changed its name as Shi-li-fo-shi (室利佛逝), and sent its first ambassador to Tang in 670. Actually, Funan was alive and active after they had been expelled by Chenla 100 years before and established a new state Shi-li-fo-shi (室利佛逝). However, many historians have not recognized this fact, but considered the *Xin Tang Shu* is mistaken and unreliable.

Before Tang, after 530, Funan sent tributary missions to the Liang (梁) Dynasty in 535,543 and to the Chen (陳) Dynasty in 559, 572 and 588. Funan had apparently survived after 530.

According to the *Xin Tang Shu*, Funan was located 7,000li (2,800km) south of Ri-nan (日南). People are same as Huan Wang (環王 = Lin-yi) with black color skin and have similar custom (Khmer). When king goes out, he rides on elephant. Paddy can be cropped three times a year. Tax is paid by gold, precious stone and incense. King's palace is rather humble and the royal family had surnamed 'ku-run = 古龍'which sounded 'kunrun = 崑崙'. The word kunrun (崑崙) is unique in the Chinese and Southeast Asian people do not call themselves 'kunrun' . 'Kurun' means 'King' in

2. Shi-li-fo-shi (Srivijaya)   35

Cambodia language, for instance 'Kurun bnam' means 'King of mountain'. The original capital was 'Temu' (特牧城), after sudden attack by Chenla, Funan changed the capital to 'Na-Fu-Na (那弗那)'.

The status of Ban-Ban used to be the subordinate state of Funan, completely under control of Funan. After setting up the headquarters at the Bay of Bandon, Funan rulers had continued international trade not only with China but also their vicinities. Funan had the trade strategy to monopolize the tributary mission to China, and integrated the Malay Peninsula at first.

M.Vickery says Chenla merged Funan peacefully in Cambodia. He says there is the K53 Inscription (667), which tells there were kings minister's families which had worked for Funan and Chenla Dynasty for 4-5 generations (Vickery, Toyo, p 41). Of course, such cases might be, but majority of rulers of Funan escaped to Ban-Ban beforehand.

On the other hand, there is the 'Han-Chey' inscription, at Kompong Cham, which tells us Bhavavarman after chasing the enemy (Funan) princes and cruelly killed them all. After the victory, he dispatched the group of musicians advocating the victory. Without doubt, there existed battle between Chenla and Funan. The two inscriptions on the inner door pillars of the old brick sanctuary at Han-Chey, just above Kompong Cham on the Mekong, were the first discovered. Certainly, some of the royal family members of Funan were killed brutally by Chenla.

2-5 DISAPPEARANCE OF FUNAN AND THE ESTABLISHMENT OF SHI-LI-FO-SHI

Funan of the Mekong area once disappeared in the middle of the 6th century, the neighboring states simultaneously started sending

36   THE HISTORY OF SRIVIJAYA, ANGKOR and CHAMPA

tributary missions to China. Because the controlling power of
Funan suddenly diminished, and the unexpected freedom was given
to Langkasuka, Dvaravathi, Kandari and Chi-tu.

Exiled Funan (Ban-Ban) merged Chi-tu (赤土 = Red Earth)
probably before the middle of the 7th century, and established a new
polity Shi-li-fo-shi (室利佛逝). Chi-tu was former Kan-da-ri (干陀利),
of which major ports were Kedah and Songkhla in both sides of
Malay Peninsula.

Shi-li-fo-shi is explained in the *Xin Tang Shu* that East-West,
width is 1000li, and length from North to South is 4000 li. Number
of their states (subordinate) is 14. The country is divided by 2
(二國分總) to govern it. Shi-li-fo-shi was a long narrow country, so
probably the east side (facing the Gulf of Thailand) was governed
by Chaiya, and the west side was governed by Kedah, which faces
the Straits of Malacca.

Srivijaya wanted to control the whole Malacca Straits and sent
navy to Mulayu, Jambi, Palembang and the Bangka Island. In 683,
Srivijaya occupied Palembang and left there the 'Kedukan Bukit'
inscription. In 686, Srivijaya gathered the fleet at the Bangka Island,
and started invasion to the Kha-ling kingdom in the central Jawa.
The commander was Dapunta Selendra (Sailendra), and they
easily defeated Kha-ling, of which the capital was Pekalongan.
The commander left one simple inscription at Sojometo village.
In this time, the territory of Srivijaya became the largest in its
history. Srivijaya established the 'Sailendra kingdom' in the central
Jawa, however they had not destroyed the 'old Kha-ling (Sanjaya)
kingdom. They co-existed in the central Jawa, Sailendra was
probably in charge of navy and trade, and Sanjaya in charge of
domestic administration. Sailendra sent the tributary mission in 768
to Tang, under the name of 'Kha-ling (訶陵)'. It is another mystery
why Srivijaya took such action? It is because Srivijaya was afraid of
the Tang Court's regulation which prohibited the conflict of among

the vassal states. So, Sailendra had to use the name of 'Kha-ling' to conceal the fact of conquering Sanjaya (old Kha-ling).

2-6 Tributary states to China, around the Malay Peninsula

Paul Wheatley says:

"On the dissolution of the Funanese empire, its successor, Chenla, possibly because of its continental origin, failed to consolidate its supremacy over the Malay Peninsula, whereupon the former dependencies in that region hastened to establish their autonomy by dispatching embassies to the Imperial Court of China". (P. Wheatley, p 289).

Indeed some new states came up to China, after the middle of the 6th century, however every state might have failed to 'establish their autonomy'. Chenla could not dominate the sea-faring, so they could not send envoys by sea for long time.

P. Wheatley picks up some examples:

"At present there are notices of only four kingdoms. Judging by the records still extant it is probable that the Sui (隋) annalist was here referring to P'an-p'an (Ban-Ban), Ch'ih-t'u (Chi-tu), Tan-tan (Khalatan) and Ko-lo (Kedah)" (P. Wheatley, p 289).

Of course, 'Ban-Ban' was substantially, occupied by exiled Funan since the 3rd century.

P. Wheatley forgets two more kingdoms, Langkasuka (狼牙須國) and Dvaravati (墮和羅鉢底). He did not understand the whole situation of the Malay Archipelago.

38   THE HISTORY OF SRIVIJAYA, ANGKOR and CHAMPA

① Dvaravati (墮和羅鉢底): 583 (頭和), 627-49, 638, 640, 643, 649,
② Tan-Tan (丹丹): 535, 571, 581, 585, 616 ,666 (單單), 670.
③ Chi-tu (赤土): 608, 609, 610.
  Kandari (干陀利): 441, 455, 472, 502, 518, 520, 563 ⇒ later became
  Chi-tu..
④ Langkasuka (狼牙須國): 515, 523, 531, 568. ⇒ Later, merged with
  Kandari
⑤ Ban-Ban (盤盤): 423-53, 455, 457-64, 527, 529, 532, 534, 542,
  551, 571, 584, 616, 633, 635, 641, 648, 650-55.
  Shi-li-fo-shi (室利佛逝): 670-673, 701, 716, 724, 727, 741.

  1. Chi-tu is the former Kandari and probably merged Langkasuka.
  2. Shi-li-fo-shi is the former Ban-Ban and merged Chi-tu and
Tan-Tan. After 670, Shi-li-fo-shi became the sole country sending
envoys to Tang from the Malay Peninsula.

2-6-1   Langkasuka (狼牙須國)

Langkasuka country (currently Nakhon-Si-Thammarat) first
made tribute in 515, 523 and 531 and 568. Langkasuka got the
information of Funan's inner conflict over the succession trouble.
They started sending mission in 515, total 4 times. (Rudravarman's
usurpation, in 514). Langkasuka is Ban-Ban's neighbor so they
can get early information. Probably they caught the information of
Funan's trouble and took the quick action to send an envoy to China.
Later Langkasuka might have been merged with Kandari (干陀利) at
the end of the 6th century, and formed 'Chi-tu'.

The contemporary theory that Langkasuka was Pattani, is an
obvious mistake. Without doubt, Langkasuka was today's Nakhon
Si Thammarat. The evidence is the *Sui Shu* which records:
The Sui Emperor, Yang-di (煬帝) sent 'Chan Jun (常駿) as a special
envoy to 'Red Earth (Chi-tu)', and he reported that after he passed
the Condao Island, 2 days later he saw a high mountain toward the

2. Shi-li-fo-shi (Srivijaya)   39

west direction. It is a land-mark of Langkasuka, behind Nakhon Si Thammarat. There is Mt. (Khao) Luang (1820m), which is the highest mountain in the region. Unfortunately, at Pattani there is no mountain at all.

Curiously, many Thailand's modern historians believe that Pattani is Langkasuka. The western historians made up such a story and many Thai people still believe it.

The "*Zhu-fan-zhi* (諸蕃志)" is often referred as the reason of Langkasuka's Pattani theory. But the author Chao Ju Kua (趙如适) did not use the same script as the *Sui Shu*. The *Sui Shu*'s Langkasuka is 狼牙須國、but the *Zhu-fan-zhi*'s Langkasuka is 凌牙斯加. Furthermore, in the *Zhu-fan-zhi*, Pattani is quoted as '拔沓 (Pa-Ta)'.

The *Liang Shu* says that Langkasuka opened the country in the 2nd century. But the successor of the king was weak, so the strong royal family succeeded the throne.

國人說,立國以來四百餘年,後嗣衰弱,王族有賢者,國人歸之

Possibly Langkasuka started the foreign trade in the 2nd century, and its ports for imports were Krabi, Phuket and Trang at the west coast of the Malay Peninsula.

2-6-2　Dvaravati（堕和羅鉢底）

The Mon people had founded their own kingdom around the Lower Burma and the inner Thailand and Peninsula, called Dun-Sun (頓遜＝Tenasserim), Lou-Yue (羅越) and Dvaravati (投和、獨和羅、堕和羅鉢底). Generally speaking they were rather independent from the Funanese direct rule.

In the kingdom of Dvaravati, Thaton was an important seaport on the Gulf of Martaban, for trade with India and Sri Lanka, and Tenasserim was one of major ports of the Mon people (Dvaravati). Around the 6th and the 7th century, several Mon states seem to have sent missions to China.

Photo 9: The Mon style terracotta images

According to the Chinese Chronicles, Tou-wa (投和) sent its envoy to the Chen (陳) Dynasty in 583, and Ratchaburi (加羅舍分) sent the missions to Sui (隋) in 608 and Tang in 662. Dvaravati (墮和羅、獨和羅、墮和羅鉢底) appeared in 627, 638, 640, 643 and 649. However, they stopped sending mission after the establishment of Shi-li-fo-shi (Srivijaya) before 670.

After Great General Fan Man of Funan had captured this place first in the 3rd century and Funan had dominated the region, but probably given some freedom for non-official trade with China.

From the 3rd century, Dun-Sun (頓遜=Tenasserim) seems to be one big territory which extends over the side of the Gulf of Thailand from Burma. Dun-Sun means 'five small kingdoms' in the old Mon language.

From the northern part of the Malay Peninsula to the Gulf of Martaban, the Mon people had dominated and lived. Prachoup Khiri Khan, Petchaburi, Ratchaburi, Nakhon Pathom and Lopburi

Photo 10: Buddha Footprint at Korat temple

in Thailand and the lower Burma had been tightly connected. They established unique style of the 'Dvaravati culture' which expanded into the mainland of Thailand, and arrived at Si Thep, Lamphun and Chiang Mai area. Many kinds of terracotta images are left and known as the symbol of the Dvaravati culture largely different from those of Funan and Khmer.

A lot of relics of those terracotta images were discovered from the Khu Bua ruins in the suburb of Ratchaburi. They were discovered all over Thailand.

After 649, what happened to Dvaravati is not recorded, however the Mon state was not absorbed by Srivijaya. The Mon people survived after the establishment of Srivijaya. Later Dvaravati had built a strong kingdom in Hariphunchai, Lamphun in the northern part of Thailand. The Haripunchai kingdom was established around

42   THE HISTORY OF SRIVIJAYA, ANGKOR and CHAMPA

750, and most of the central and northern Thailand had been under the rule of various Mon's city states, which had been eclipsed by the Angkor Dynasty step by step and in 1292 Hariphunchai was occupied by Mangrai of the Thai kingdom of Lanna.

The Mon people was wide spreading over present Thailand. Everywhere we can find the city or town named 'xx buri'. 'Buri' means 'City or Town 'in the Mon word. Specifically, the role of the Mons was very wide in agriculture, commerce and manufacturing. However, as for the whole history of the Mon people, many things are not clear.

They accepted since the early stage, Hinduism and Buddhism and made Buddha Footprint at their temples, as the certificate of the Buddhism worship in each village and town.

2-6-3   Kan-da-ri (干陀利), Chi-tu (赤土) and Srivijaya (室利佛逝)

Kedah had been convenient port to import western goods. So, Kedah started the tributary trade since the 5th century. In this case Kedah state used the ports on the east coast, for instance Songkhla and Kelantan.

In the Chinese annals, the name of Kalatan (呵羅單) had been recorded since 430, Kalatan was very civilized state and accepted Buddhism as early as the 5th century.

Kalatan sent tribute: in 430, 433, 434, 435, 436, 437, 441, 452, Kandari tribute; 453, 455, 502, 518, 520, 563. Tan-Tan sent envoys in 535, 571, 581, 585, 616. Chi-tu: 608, 609, 610. Possibly Kandari took over the position of Kalatan. But Kalatan changed its name as 'Tan-Tan' and continued sending mission.

The *Ming Shi* (明史) says that the old name of San fo chi is Kandari. 明史 「三佛齊,古名干陀利。」

This short sentence means "San fo-chi was Kandari (Kedah)". But many historians (followers of G.Cœdès) consider that San-fo-

2. Shi-li-fo-shi (Srivijaya)   43

chi is Srivijaya, so Kandari was located in Sumatra (Palembang). However, Kandari was Kedah. They have made miserable misunderstanding here.

In the San-fo-chi time, the negotiator with the west countries was Kedah, so Kedah had been known as San-fo-chi for foreign countries, especially for Arab and Chola (Tamil country, south India).

As above, the Kedah lines had continued the tributary missions from Kalatan, Kandari and Chi-tu. And finally, this export line was absorbed to Srivijaya (Shi-li-fo-shi) before 670.

2-6-4　Funan ⇒ Shi-li-fo-shi ⇒ Sailendra ⇒ San-fo-chi (三佛斉)

Many historians consider that San-fo-chi was Palembang or Jambi. Even M. Vickery follows the theory of G.Cœdès that Srivijaya was Palembang. Ming Dynasty says as above, "San-fo-chi was Kandari". The author of the *Ming shi* was better than G.Cœdès. 'San- fo-chi union regime' consists of Jambi, Kedah and Chaiya. San-fo-chi was the allied polity of major Srivijaya's big three states. So when San-fo-chi first visited the Tang Dynasty in 904 (天祐元年), Tang recorded that Fo-shi (Srivijaya) came to tribute and gave the ambassador Po Kho-su (蒲訶粟) the title of the Ning Yuan General　(寧遠將軍). (唐會要、the *Tang Hui Yao*). At that time, the official of Tang recognized they came from Shi-li-fo-shi (Srivijaya).

San Fo-Chi (三佛齊) means 'Three Vijayas'. Before San-fo-chi, Sailendra (new Kha-ling) had dominated the tribute mission of Srivijaya group. However, the Sailendra Dynasty of the central Jawa had lost hegemony after Maharaja Samaratunga (son of Panangkaran) died around 820. The crown prince Balaputradeva was defeated by Sanjaya prince Rakai Pikatan, whose wife was Balaputra's elder sister princess Pramodawarddhani. As the result Balaputra left the Jawa Island and fled to the old territory of Srivijaya (Sumatra and the Malay Peninsula). After the defeat in the central Jawa, the Srivijaya group had temporarily lost control of subordinate states. Jambi sent its own mission in 852 and 871. New

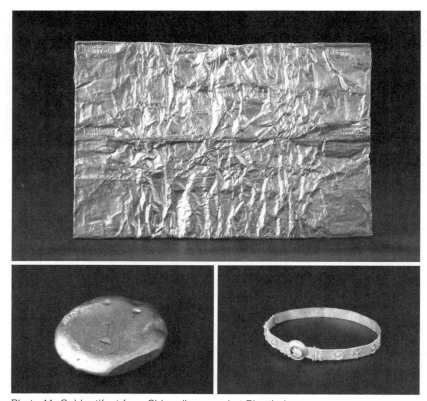

Photo 11: Gold artifact from China discovered at Phatthalung

Kha-ling (exiled Sailendra) also sent an envoy during 860-874 from the Malay Peninsula.

However, such kind of independent and separated activity was not profitable for every member state, so they decided to collaborate each other and formed a single allied polity ' San-fo-chi' at the end of the 9th century. Their method of trade is collecting the tribute goods from all of the Srivijaya group to Phatthalung (near Nakhon Si Thammarat) and transport them to Sathing Phra, then shipped to

2. Shi-li-fo-shi (Srivijaya) 45

China. So, Phatthalung was the distributing centre for San-fo-chi group and shipping port was Sathing Phra.

In 2014, occasionally big amount of gold products was discovered at Phatthalung. They were the evidence of Phatthalung's role as the distribution centre of the Srivijaya group. The officials of the Song Court had recognized 'Sathing Phra' was a part of Kha-ling.

Funan merged with Chi-tu (赤土國) in the first half of the 7th century. Before that, Chi-tu had been the largest state which sent tributary mission to the Sui Dynasty.

According to the *Sui-Shu*, Sui received Chi-tu envoys three times in 608, 609 and 610. The Emperor 'Yang-di (煬帝)' sent an ambassador Chang Jun (常駿) to Chi-tu. The real capital of Chi-tu was probably Kedah and on the east coast sub-capital was Songkhla (僧祇城). The ambassador Chang Jun recorded the itinerary and details on Chi-tu. However, the name of Chi-tu suddenly disappeared from the Chinese chronicles. The reason was not explained by any text, but probably Chi-tu was merged with the exiled Funan, at that time the Ban-Ban state. After integration of the Malay Peninsula, they established 'Srivijaya (室利佛逝, Shi-li-fo-shi)', and sent the first mission to the Tang Court, during 670-673. Probably it was in 670, because when Yi Jing left Kanton for India in 671, he had already recognized Srivijaya, which was the Buddhism flourishing state. After 20 days' journey, he arrived at Shi-li-fo-shi (Srivijaya), where he stayed for 6 months to study the grammar of the Sanskrit language. The king of Srivijaya warmly welcomed Yi Jing and sent him to Mulayu by his own ship, and probably sent him to Tamralipiti (Bengal port) via Kedah and the naked people's island.

The origin of name of 'Shi-li-fo-shi' probably came from 'Khao Si Wichai' located at Phun Pin. Khao Si Wichai (Srivijaya hill) is a small mountain and on the top of which there are Hindu temples and one Buddhism temple. A Vishnu image was unearthed from there, and now exhibited at the Bangkok National Museum.

THE HISTORY OF SRIVIJAYA, ANGKOR and CHAMPA

I agree with G.Cœdès that the founder of Srivijaya was former Funan rulers. However, G.Cœdès considered exiled Funan rulers had fled to the Jawa Island. It was the wrong direction. They could not have gone to the Jawa Island where Kha-ling, a strong kingdom already established stronghold. On the other hand, Ban-Ban had been a subordinate state of Funan since the 3rd century and in charge of the 'trans-peninsula trade route' for Funan and many times, had sent tributary missions on behalf of Funan since the middle of the 5th century.

Before founding Srivijaya, they had completely dominated Ban-Ban, and later merged with other major states in the Malay Peninsula. At the end of 670, only the name of Srivijaya remained in the middle of the Peninsula, which was recorded in Chinese history as a tributary country. Before 670, Chi-tu, Tan-Tan (丹丹) and Ban-Ban＝盤盤) had ceased sending envoys to the Tang Court. After absorbing Kedah, Srivijaya intended to control the whole Straits of Malacca. It was necessary for Srivijaya to control the Malacca Straits to procure (purchase) the western precious goods coming across the Bay of Bengal. In the middle of the seventh century, the presence of the western countries, Persia and Arab, increased in the Tang Court. This means comparative decrease of Srivijaya's status in the Tang Court. Historically Srivijaya had sent tribute of the western valuables to the Tang Dynasty as major items, so the increment of direct trade of the west countries with China means grave disadvantage for Srivijaya.

In the early 680s, Srivijaya sent an expeditionary navy to put Mulayu (末羅瑜), Jambi and Palembang under its control. After successful campaign, Srivijaya hurriedly had set up several inscriptions near Palembang and Jambi. The main purpose of these inscriptions was showing-off the existence of Srivijaya and threatening the local people to obey the authority of Srivijaya. Thereafter Srivijaya sent force in 686 from the base of the Bangka Island to Kha-ling (訶陵＝Sanjaya), located in the central Jawa. The

2. Shi-li-fo-shi (Srivijaya)

Map 4: The sea trade route of Srivijaya (6-7centuries)

48   THE HISTORY OF SRIVIJAYA, ANGKOR and CHAMPA

navy had successfully landed at Pekalongan, the major port of Kha-ling. In the central Jawa, where Srivijaya established the Sailendra kingdom. However Sailendra coexisted with the Kha-ling kingdom which was later identified as the kingdom of 'Sanjaya' or 'Mataram' in the central Jawa.

At the end of the 7th century, the territory of Srivijaya (Shi-li-fo-shi) became largest, covering the middle of the Malay Peninsula, the southeast coast of Sumatra and the central Jawa. At the same time, Srivijaya started to control the traffic of the Malacca Straits.

2-7 DISAPPEARANCE OF SHI-LI-FO-SHI AND EMERGENCE OF SAILENDRA

Around 745, Water Chenla (水眞臘, Cambodia) undoubtedly had attacked the capital of Srivijaya, and occupied Chaiya and Nakhon Si Thammarat. At the same time, the control of the Malacca Straits temporarily collapsed. However, nearly twenty years later, the Srivijaya group counter attacked Chenla and recovered the Chaiya area.

This event had not been explicitly recorded in any historical inscriptions or some other evidence, so it is a 'missing link'. However, some serious events had certainly happened around this region. The Ligor inscription dated in 755 and the sudden emergence of Sailendra suggest us a series of the unusual events.

This is the most important point to see the history of Srivijaya. If Srivijaya (Shi-li-fo-shi) was located at Palembang, there could not be a justifiable reason why Srivijaya suddenly ceased sending embassies after 741 and in 768 Sailendra (new Kha-ling) emerged as a tributary state instead of Srivijaya to the Tang Court.

Water Chenla had probably attacked and occupied around 745. Water Chenla sent mission to Tang in 750, but Srivijaya group counter attacked Water Chenla around 760 and retrieved Chaiya. At

2. Shi-li-fo-shi (Srivijaya)

that time the main force of Srivijaya group was the Sailendra navy. Thereafter Sailendra became the champion state of the Srivijaya group. The king of Sailendra, Panangkaran (Panamkaran) was later assigned 'Maharaja' of the Srivijaya group.

However, for many historians, the hypothesis that Chenla had attacked Chaiya and occupied there must be unacceptable. The reason is very simple because, as they suppose, Srivijaya (Shi-li-fo-shi) was located at Palembang, so Chenla could not have attacked Srivijaya. At the same time they cannot find the reason why Shi-li-fo-shi (室利佛逝) disappeared from the chronicles of the Tang Dynasty after 741. In 768, Sailendra appeared under the name of 'Kha-ling (訶陵)' in the Tang chronicles.

For many historians the nature of Sailendra is not clear, so they have continued long discussion, and concluded that San-fo-chi was dominated by Sailendra. This is not a correct answer at all. My discussion is that Sailendra had belonged to the Srivijayas after they had attacked the central Jawa, the commander Dapunta Selendra (Sailendra) became the king of Sailendra in 686. Later Water Chenla attacked Chaiya and the Srivijaya group counter attacked Water Chenla at the Bay of Ban Don. The main navy player, Sailendra king Panangkaran was given the title of 'Maharaja' of Srivijaya, and thereafter Sailendra became the leader of Srivijaya group. After the victory, the Srivijaya group, led by Panangkaran proceeded to the Mekong River and occupied major ports of Chenla. Around 770, Srivijaya sent big army to Cambodia to occupy the territory of Chenla, of which commander was Jayavarman II. He was probably a prince of Srivijaya's royal family member.

The victory monument of revenge war at Chaiya is 'Ligor inscription' dated 775. Thus Sailendra became the champion state of the Srivijaya group, but curiously Sailendra sent envoys to the Tang Court under the name of 'Kha-ling (訶陵)' same as former Sanjaya's. This seems quite mysterious for us. Of course there was a reason

50   THE HISTORY OF SRIVIJAYA, ANGKOR and CHAMPA

why Sailendra must use the name of 'Kha-ling (Ho-ling), because
the Tang Dynasty had never allowed conflict or quarrel among the
tributary states. In China, the emperor's subordinates were not
allowed to fight each other.

However the actual shipment of Sailendra's tribute to China had
been mostly dispatched from the east coast of the Malay Peninsula,
probably Sathing Phra, because where was the most convenient
place to gather commodities from the Srivijaya group.

Around 820, after Maharaja Samaratuṅga died, probably the
second Maharaja of Sailendra, his daughter Pramodawarddhani
might have succeeded him as 'Queen', but she had married with
Sanjaya prince Rakai Pikatan. As the result Samaratunga's son
Prince Balaputra had lost helm in the central Jawa and the kingship
of Sailendra. Later Balaputra was defeated by Rakai Pikatan
(Sanjaya prince), husband of Pramodawarddhani and was exiled
from Java. Rakai Pikatan assumed the kingship in 838, so Balaputra
might have left Jawa before that. At that time unity of Srivijaya once
collapsed, and Jambi sent envoys to Tang independently in 852 and
871. However, Jambi probably had realized a single state could not
make big profit, and at the end of the 9th century, big three states
of the Srivijaya group established a new polity, 'San-fo-chi (三佛齊).
San-fo-chi means three vijayas, namely Chaiya, Kedah and Jambi.
Chaiya and Tambralinga took care of the Gulf of Thailand and the
east region. Kedah took care of the north end of the Malacca Straits
and Jambi the south end of the Straits.

2-7-1   Ligor Inscription
Around 830, Prince Balaputra fled to Suwarnadvipa (Sumatra
and the Malay Peninsula) but he inherited the title of Maharaja
of Srivijaya. His final destination was probably Kedah. Jambi had
already the strongest economic power among the Srivijaya group
and the kingship was also unshakable, so Balaputra seemed to go
to Kedah. He also, probably became the ruler of Chaiya, old Shi-

li-fo-shi, and he possibly added some words on the back of Ligor inscription (face B).

This stele was found at first at Chaiya then removed to Ligor (Nakhon Si Thammarat), in the 13th century by Chandrabhanu, king of Tambralinga after collapse of the Srivijaya group. so it is called 'Ligor inscription'.

R.C. Majumdar says in his "Suvarnadvipa, The Sailendra Empire, pp149-150"

"The inscription A begins with eulogy of Sri-Vijayendra-raja, and then refer to the building of three brick temples for Buddhist gods by Sri-Vijayesvarabhupati. Jayanta, the royal priest (Rajasthavira), being ordered by the king, built three stupas. After Jayanta's death, his disciple and successor Adhimukhti built two brick caityas by the side of the three caityas (built by the king). In conclusion, it is said, that Srivijayanrpati, who resembled Devendra, built the stupas here in Saka 697 (775 AD).

The inscription B, engraved on the back of the stele of only one verse and a few letters of the second. It contains the eulogy of an emperor (Rajadhiraja) having the name Vishnu (Visnvakhyo). The last line is not clear. It seems to refer to a lord of the Sailendra Dynasty named Sri- Maharaja, and though probable, it is not absolutely certain, if this person is the same as Rajadhiraja having the name Vishnu."

Three 'stupas' mean 'Wat Wieng, Wat Long and Wat Kaeo'. Remains of Wat Long and Wat Kaeo are seen at Chaiya, near Wat

Photo 12: Ligor inscription A (Bangkok National Museum)

Photo 13: Bodhisattva image of Chaiya (now sxibited at the Bangkok National Museum)

Wieng.

Ligor A inscription tells about a Srivijayan king named Dharmasetu, the Maharaja, who built the Trisamaya caitya for Kajara. Dharmasetu's daughter princess Tara was said to be queen of Maharaja Samaratunga, son of Maharaja Panangkaran.

While the Ligor B inscription, dated 775 CE, contains the information about a king named Vishnu who holds the title Sri Maharaja, from Sailendravamśa hailed as Śesavvārimadavimathana (the slayer of arrogant enemies without any trace), who should be the commander of Sailenrdra navy, King Panagkaran. Panangkaran was assigned of Maharaja of Srivijaya, by Dharmasetu.

There are some different interpretations regarding the king mentioned in Ligor B inscription; some suggest that the king mentioned in this inscription was King Panangkaran while other argues that it was his successor, King Samaratunga. However, B inscription probably was written by Balaputra around 830s.

2. Shi-li-fo-shi (Srivijaya)

Anyway, this inscription suggests there was a fierce battle in this area (with the Water Chenla army), and many soldiers were killed.

2-8 SAILENDRA DYNASTY

Sailendra and Sanjaya co-existed (dual kingdoms).

The 'Kota Kapur' inscription of the Bangka Island dated 686 noticed that the Srivijaya force would attack the Jawa Island, where the Kha-ling kingdom had reigned.

The Srivijaya's navy directly attacked and occupied Pekalongan area. The Sojomerto inscription is a symbol of the victory monument of the Srivijaya force. Pekalongan was the major port of the central Jawa.

In the *Ling wei Tai-ta* (嶺外代答)' published in 1178, by Chou Ch'u-fei (周去非) wrote that She-Po (闍婆國) other name is Pekalongan (莆家龍). 「闍婆國, 又名莆家龍, 在海東南」. However, at least before the Tang Dynasty era, the concept of 'Java (She-po 闍婆)', had included the Malay Peninsula. In the early 5th century, high Buddhist priest Gnavarman (求那跋摩) said to have visited 'Java', but in his case he could not have visited the Jawa Island, because before the 5th century, Buddhism was not so popular there. He must have visited the Ban-Ban state (Chaiya) of the Malay Peninsula where Mahayana Buddhism had flourished already, and its king was a devotee of Buddhism. On the other hand, in the Java Island, the infrastructure of Buddhism was very scarce. Even a single ancient Buddha footprint did not exist there.

The Srivijaya Army defeated and captured the capital of central Javanese Sanjaya kingdom (Kha-ling) in 686. However, the Sailendra kingdom had not demolished the Sanjaya kingship. Both kingships had co-existed. The dual kingships (parallel kingship) continued.

If Srivijaya completely occupied the central Jawa, someday the Tang Dynasty would notice the fact, and Srivijaya should be

54   THE HISTORY OF SRIVIJAYA, ANGKOR and CHAMPA

penalized by the Tang Court. So, Srivijaya pretended the old Kha-
ling unchanged as if nothing had happened. Srivijaya's purpose
was to secure the major port of Jawa and monopolize the tribute to
Tang. Srivijaya's strategy was to 'monopolize' the tributary trade
with China, and had no intention to dominate the rural areas of the
Jawa Island to get the surplus agricultural products from farmers. It
is because, traditionally Funan and Srivijaya had no administrative
officials belonging to the kingdom. So Sailendra could not dominate
whole Jawa from the beginning. As the result, Sanjaya continued the
administration of inland Jawa and Sanjaya accumulated wealth and
the real political power and finally kicked out the Sailendra kingdom
from Jawa after the death of Maharaja Samaratunga around 830.
Sailendra had been satisfied with monopolizing the international
trade and navy.

(Misunderstanding of Cœdès)
After conquering Palembang and Jambi, next they attacked the
central Jawa Island. The Kota Kapur inscription of the Bangka
Island, wrote that Srivijaya wanted to attack the island of Jawa
because they refused to obey Srivijaya's policy on the tributary
trade. G.Cœdès said that the Srivijaya army went to attack the 'west
Jawa', not the central Jawa. In the west Jawa there was Taruma (多
羅摩, or 墮婆登＝Duo-po-deng) ,which sent tributary mission in 647.
(G.Cœdès, English, 1968, p83) G.Cœdès misunderstood Taruma
was a major competitor for Srivijaya. Srivijaya's rival was Kha-
ling (訶陵) located in the central Jawa and not Taruma, in the 'west
Jawa'. Kha-ling had sent the tributary missions many times in 640,
647, 648 and 666 and stopped suddenly after 666. Why G.Cœdès
avoided Kha-ling, it is because G.Cœdès thought Funan had fled
to the central Jawa from the Mekong Delta in the middle of the 6th
century. So, Srivijaya had no reason to attack Kha-ling. However
Duo-po-deng (墮婆登＝Taruma?) in the west Jawa was a small
country and could not be Srivijaya's rival.

2. Shi-li-fo-shi (Srivijaya)

G.Cœdès says: "The inscription of Bangka closes by mentioning the departure of an expedition against the unsubdued land of Java in 686. The land referred to, may have been the ancient kingdom of Taruma, on the other side of the Sunda Strait, which we do not have spoken again after its embassy to China in 666-69." (G.Cœdès, English, 1968, p83). However, the last mission of Duo-po-deng was in 647. Here again G.Cœdès made mistake or told a lie.

The Kha-ling sent the next tributary mission in 768, after 100 years' interval. This Kha-ling is apparently 'Sailendra (Srivijaya)'. If Duo-po-deng was Taruma as G.Cœdès says, it was not a strong rival for Srivijaya.

In the history of the Angkor Dynasty, the founder is Jayavarman II, who came to Cambodia from 'Java', but where was Java? M. Vickery says that Java is 'Cham' i.e. the 'Lin-yi' (Champa). In addition, M. Vickery thinks Sailendra (Dapunta Selendra) was originally a Javanese king and Sailendra has nothing to with Funan. This is because he is ignoring the historical development and establishment of Srivijaya. The 'Kota Kapur' inscription of the Bangka Island dated 686 clearly said that Srivijaya force would attack the Jawa Island, where the Kha-ling kingdom had reigned.

Kha-ling is divided into 'early' and 'latter'. The Early Kha-ling was Sanjaya and the 'Latter (new) Kha-ling' was Sailendra. Most historians do not understand the difference of the Kha-ling's tribute missions between Sanjaya and Sailendra. The Kha-ling of Sanajaya's mission stopped after 666 and the Sailendra's Kha-ling started tribute mission in 768. Sailendra started the tributary mission since 768. Because Sailendra was given authority to send mission to China, representing the Srivijaya Group, after the victory of war against Water Chenla at the Bay of Ban Don and the king of Sailendra (Panangkaran) had been given the title of 'Maharaja' of Srivijaya. Before that Sailendra was one of 14 subordinate states of the Srivijaya group.

The 'Sailendra Kha-ling' had broader business basis, because

56   THE HISTORY OF SRIVIJAYA, ANGKOR and CHAMPA

which was representing the whole Srivijaya group. And its shipping
port was changed to Sathing Phra (north of Songkhla) in the Malay
Peninsula. The 'Sanjaya Kha-ling' was limited its business base
within the central Jawa and its shipping port was Pekalongan.
Most historians do not understand this change. For instance,
Yumio Sakurai, Emeritus Professor of University of Tokyo says
that Srivijaya's tributary trade had been limited very small and
Srivijaya's contribution to the Tang Dynasty was only Buddhism.
(Southeast Asian history course Iwanami Vol No. 1, p143). This
is miserable mistake. The presence of Srivijaya to the Tang Court
was so big. Srivijaya stopped sending envoy after 741, and Sailendra
(New Kha-ling) succeeded Srivijaya's business. In the Song times,
San-fo-chi succeeded Sailendra business.

In the central Jawa Island, Sailendra controlled international trade
and navy. Sailendra's Kha-ling started tribute mission in 768, but the
actual business was handled in the Malay Peninsula, at Phatthalung
and Sathing Phra.

King Panangkaran, after he returned to the central Jawa, he unified
the Jawa island to the Sailendra Dynasty. Because he was assigned
to the Maharaja of Srivijaya. Maharaja Panangkaran had stripped of
'the delegacy' of the Sanjaya (former Kha-ling) royal family which
had been a co-ruler of the central Java for nearly 100 years.

The Sailendra Dynasty constructed the biggest Mahayana
Buddhism temple in the world, the 'Borobudur temple', as the
commemoration of the great victory over Chenla. At that time,
probably there were not so many Buddhists in Jawa. Buddhism
might be widely introduced into the Jawa Island after the occupation
by Srivijaya in 686.

However, the Sanjaya group, too, constructed the 'Prambanan
Siva temple' in the middle of the 9th century after Rakai Pikatan
had kicked out Prince Balaputra from Jawa (The Shiva-grha epitaph
of 856).

There is an opinion that the Borobudur temple had been naturally

2. Shi-li-fo-shi (Srivijaya)   57

buried by the eruption of the 'Merabi volcano', but it is difficult to believe. The Borobudur temple, possibly had been buried with earth by Sanjaya, as the result it could have fortunately survived under the earth.

Thanks to it, it will be possible to say that a state of good preservation had been maintained until the staff of Sir Stanford Raffles discovered it in the 19th century.

Both are the historic evidence how Sailendra and Sanjaya had co-existed near Jogjakarta since 686 until around 830.

Around 830, Crown Prince Balaputra of Sailendra was defeated at war, by Rakai Pikatan, prince of the Sanjaya family, and husband of Balaputra's elder sister, princess Pramodawarddhani. Soon after the death of their father Maharaja Samaratunga, the battle had started between Sailendra and Sanjaya. As the result, Balaputra was defeated and was driven out of the Jawa Island around 830 and the Sailendra kingdom in the Jawa Island disappeared forever.

The military activity of Sailendra must be remembered that during 760~830, Sailendra led the Srivijaya's expansion to Cambodia. After defeating 'Water Chenla' at the Chaiya region, the Sailendra navy proceeded to the Mekong Delta, and next to the sea-shore of Indochina, the territory of Lin-yi. The Sailendra navy probably destroyed the export facilities (including big merchant ships) of Lin-yi. So, Lin-yi had to stop sending the tributary mission to Tang after 749. The name of Lin-yi never appeared after 758 in the Chinese history.

After invading to Cambodia, the Srivijaya group tried to destroy the Chenla kingdom and established new polity, the Angkor Dynasty. This story is told later in the Chapter 4 "The Angkor Dynasty".

Before the 'New Kha-ling' sent its first tribute mission to Tang in 768, the Sailendra navy should have secured the Mekong Delta River mouth.

The story that Srivijaya broke into the Mekong River and invaded the coastal capital, killing the King, had prevailed among the Arab

58   THE HISTORY OF SRIVIJAYA, ANGKOR and CHAMPA

merchants, and an Arab scholar, Sulaiman wrote the similar story in 851. An ambitious Chenla King was anxious to attack the Maharaja of Srivijaya, but the Maharaja knew beforehand his intention and attacked Chenla. The Chenla king was beheaded by the Srivijaya army and his head was returned to the prince of Chenla king. But his name is unkwnown.

Q. Wales suggests that was Mahipativarman. However, he stayed throne during 780-788. King Sumbhuvarman reigned during 730-760, so he might be a killed king. But I cannot confirm his existence. Who were the kings of Water Chenla, after Queen Jayadevi? There is no record. The new king of the Angkor Kingdom, Jayavarman II was a prince from the Srivijaya group. Without doubt, he was strongly supported by the Sailendra navy. The Angkor Kingdom had been under control of the Srivijaya group for nearly 300 years.

Around 830, after being kicked out from Jawa, prince Balaputra first called in the Jambi state, but he could not have stayed there, because Jambi had established strong kingdom by themselves and probably had not accepted the authority of Balaputra. After all, he escaped to the Malay Peninsula and settled in Kedah and called himself the Maharaja of Sailendra (Srivijaya). He controlled Chaiya, too. At that time, Tambralinga had been half-independent and was busy to control the Angkor kingdom.

However, without Jambi there was no authority with him to command the whole Srivijaya group. The Jambi kingdom had sent independently its own mission to the Tang Court in 852 and 871. The independent behavior of Jambi might have given a big shock to the Srivijaya group. On the other hand, the Sailendra kingdom had continued sending the envoy to Tang, 2 times in 827-33 and in 860-874. In this case Sailedra might have shipped tribute from Sathing Phra. They had imported the western goods at Kedah.

On the other hand, the Sanjaya kingdom sent its mission 3 times in 820, 831 and 839. The Sanjaya mission used the name of 'Java (闍婆)'. So, Sanjaya might have recovered the reign of Jawa before

2. Shi-li-fo-shi (Srivijaya) 59

820 It is very funny why Sanjaya had not used their old name Kha-ling (訶陵)? The answer is obvious, if Sanjaya used the name of Kha-ling, the fact that Sanjaya had kicked out Sailendra after the battle would be revealed.

The Tang Court had strictly prohibited battle between the vassal states. Another question about the Sanjaya mission, why they sent envoy in 820, at that time Prince Balaputra was still active in Jawa. I suppose before 820, the Maharaja Samaratunga might have died and his daughter Pramodawarddhani declared the queen of Sailendra. But the other Srivijaya group might not have accepted her authority. Because she was a wife of Rakai Pikatan, a prince of Sanjaya. At first, Rakai Pikatan fought against Balaputra for the authority of his wife (queen), but after his victory, he assumed himself the king of Sanjaya kingdom and dominated the Jawa Island.

The Jambi kingdom, after sending the 2nd mission to the Tang Court in 871, might have realized that for a single state located at the bottom of the Malacca Straits, the trade benefit was limited, because Jambi could not procure sufficient western goods to tribute to the Tang Dynasty.

As the result, at the end of the 9th century, they formed the new polity of 'San-fo-chi (三佛齊)'. San-fo-chi means 'three Vijayas', namely,'Chaiya, Kedah and Jambi'. The biggest three states of the Srivijaya group formed a new polity for the tributary mission. Chaiya (and Tambralinga) covered the Gulf of Thailand and became the headquarters of San-fo-chi. Kedah supervised the Northern entrance of the Malacca Straits and Jambi covered the southern end of the Malacca Straits. San-fo-shi sent mission to Tang in 904. At that time, the Tang Court accepted San-fo-chi as 'Shi-li-fo-shi'.

The Karangtengah inscription dated 824 mentioned about the Maharaja Samaratunga. His daughter named Pramodawarddhani has inaugurated the Jinalaya, a sacred Buddhist sanctuary. The inscription also mentioned a sacred Buddhist building called the

Photo 14-1: Sailendra navy ship on the Borobudur relief

Venuvana to place the cremated ashes of King Indra (Samaratunga). The Tri Tepusan inscription dated 842 mentioned about the 'sima (tax free)' lands awarded by Sri Kahulunan (Pramodawarddhani, daughter of Samaratunga) to ensure the funding and maintenance of a Kamulan called Bhumisambhara (Borobudur). 'The mountain of combined virtues of the ten stages of Boddhisattvahood', was the original name of 'Borobudur'.

Borobudur is the largest Mahayana Buddhist structure in the world built by the Sailendra Dynasty under Samaratunga. The pictures of the Sailendra navy are left at the basement of Borobudur.

The Maharaja Samaratunga was the head of the Sailendra kingdom who ruled the central Jawa and the Srivijaya group in the 8th and the early 9th century. He was the successor of Maharaja Panangkaran, and his name was mentioned in the Karangtengah inscription dated 824, as the constructor of a sacred Buddhist building called Venuvana (Sanskrit: bamboo forest) to place the cremated ashes of his predecessor Maharaja Panangkaran of Sailendra. During his administration, he initiated the construction of a giant Buddhist

2. Shi-li-fo-shi (Srivijaya)

Photo 14-2: Sailendra war ship, supply boat

Photo 14-3: Sailendra soldier. (photos by Mr. Fairuz bin Kamrulzaman)

62   THE HISTORY OF SRIVIJAYA, ANGKOR and CHAMPA

monument Borobudur. Samaratunga married Dewi Tara, the princess of Srivijayan ruler Dharmasetu (former Maharaja). This marriage strengthened the authority of the Sailendra's family among Srivijaya group.

Samaratunga had one son by the name of Balaputra and one daughter Pramodawarddhani who was the elder sister of Balaputra. Pramodawarddhani married the Sivaite Rakai Pikatan from the Sanjaya kingdom. Rakai Pikatan managed to usurp Balaputra's authority over the central Jawa and forced the Sailendra to get out of Jawa.

Under the reign of Panangkaran, Jayavarman II was appointed as the governor of Indrapura (the Angkor kingdom) in the Mekong delta. According to the SKT inscription, Jayavarman II later pretended to have revoked his allegiance to the Sailedra and Srivijaya to form the Khmer Empire. In 813 and 814, Water Chenla (Angkor) sent tributary missions, but after then stopped sending envoys to Tang. Probably Srivijaya forced 'Water Chenla' to stop sending envoys to Tang. This Water Chenla was without doubt the Angkor Dynasty. In 1116, Suryavarman II resumed the tribute mission to China, after 300 years absence.

The role of Tambralinga (Nakhon Si Thammarat) which is situated the south of Chaiya, as the special headquarters, was to take care of the small states facing the Gulf of Thailand and collect the annual tributes (including tax) for Srivijaya (San-fo-chi). Furthermore, Tambarlinga took care of the Angkor, Khmer matters and supervised Lopburi where Srivijaya put the military base. Many military commanders of Angkor were dispatched by Tambralinga. Later the prince of Tambralinga, Suryavarman I directly took the throne of the Angkor Dynasty.

2. Shi-li-fo-shi (Srivijaya)   63

2-9 SAN-FO-CHI (三佛齊)

2-9-1 Function of San-fo-chi （三佛斉）

As for the trade window of China, Songkhla and later Sathing Phra were used as the shipping ports to China. In the time of Shi-li-fo-shi Chaiya and later Songkhla were mainly used, and in the 'new Kha-ling (Sailendra)' and San-fo-chi times, Sathing Phra was used and probably, was registered as the official port for China. The reason is this port was the most convenient to ship to China. In the San-fo-chi times, Phatthalung was used to collect the tributary goods from all of the Srivijaya states and the rewards of the Song Dynasty were redistributed there.

In 2014, huge amount of gold and gold artifacts were discovered at Phatthalung, which may be a part of the rewards from the Song Dynasty, perhaps secretly hidden by the officials of San-fo-chi.

San-fo-chi sent a mission to the Tang Dynasty in 904, so shortly before this mission, San-fo-chi was established. San-fo-chi had started activity after the establishment of the north Song Dynasty (in 960).

At the end of the Tang Dynasty, the officers of the Tang Court did not notice that shih-li-fo-shi (室利佛逝) and San-fo-chi (三佛齊) were different. Originally, both Shih-li-fo-shi and San-fo-chi were Srivijaya, but in the Tang times before 904, it was called as Shih-li-fo-shi and in the Song times as San-fo-chi.

However, some historians discuss that the Arabian merchants used to call the big trading country in the Malay Peninsula as Sribuza, Saboza or Zabag, so the name of San-fo-chi was recorded in the Chinese annals. But the name of Sribuza likely represented Shih-li-fo-shi.

A famous Japanese historian, Dr. Toyohachi Fujita believed

64   THE HISTORY OF SRIVIJAYA, ANGKOR and CHAMPA

simply that Shih-li-fo-shi (室利佛逝) and San-fo-chi (三佛齊) were the same Srivijaya. I agree with Dr. Fujita, but I suppose that the name of San-fo-chi came from 'three Srivijaya' states, namely Kedah, Jambi and Chaiya (not Palembang). The position of Palembang in Srivijaya was ambiguous and as an international port it was minor. Commercially and politically and culturally the position of Chaiya had been much stronger than Palembang through the history of Srivijaya.

Anyway, the two major players of San-fo-chi in the Malacca Strait were Jambi and Kedah. Chaiya was the centre of Srivijaya group on the east coast of the Malay Peninsula and controlled the Gulf of Thailand.

Chaiya had still functioned as a major international commercial port and at the same time the centre of Mahāyāna Buddhism. At the sea-shore of Laem Pho, Chaiya there are plenty of porcelain and ceramic shards of the Tang and Song age.

2-9-2 Chola's invasion (1025-1080?) and its influence

For San-fo-chi, the most important country of the West was Chola (Tamil). So, San-fo-chi had tried to keep good diplomatic relation with Chola.

San-fo-chi King Culamanivarmadeva (Kedah based), had constructed a temple at Nagapatam village in Chola and donated the temple to Chola. Later to maintain the temple Sri Maravijayottungavarman, son of Culamanivarmadeva donated villages in 1006. This is recorded in the 'great Leiden copper plate inscription'. The relation between San-fo-chi and Chola used to be very intimate and friendly. As above mentioned, Suryavarman I sent letter to the Chola King to ask for help his battle in the Chao Phraya basin.

However, the relation became suddenly bad after Chola sent tributary mission in 1015 to the North Song Dynasty. At that time, the mission of Chola took 1,150 days to arrive at Guangzhou. It was

2. Shi-li-fo-shi (Srivijaya)

unusually long journey. Usually it took less than one year. Probably some serious troubles on voyage during the Malacca Straits had happened.

San-fo-chi had controlling the whole Malacca Straits and forced all merchant-ships from western countries to sell one-third of their cargos. San-fo-chi probably wanted to enforce the same rule to the king's ship from Chola. The ambassador of Chola mission possibly resisted San-fo-chi. According to the *Zhu-fan-zhi* (諸蕃志, 1225), San-fo-chi required for the foreign ships to sell one third of their commodities before entering its port, otherwise they were attacked by the San-fo-chi navy. Chola probably got angry with the attitude of San-fo-chi and decided to attack San-fo-chi to secure the convenient trade route to China.

Chola had attacked San-fo-chi in 1025, and the main target was Kedah of the Malay Peninsula where was the entrance of the trans-peninsula route.

The following translation and list of the Tanjore inscription was made by RC. Majumdar: I add some comments on the list.

"And (who) (Rājendra Cola) having dispatched many ships in the midst of the rolling sea and having caught Saṅgrāma-Vijayottuṅgavarman, the king of Kadāram (Kedah), along with the rutting elephants of his army, (took) the large heap of treasures, which (that king) had rightfully accumulated; (captured) the (arch called) Vidyādhara-toraṇa at the "war gate" of the extensive city of the enemy; Śrī-Vijaya with "Jewel-gate", adorned with great splendor and the "gate of large jewels"; Paṇṇai, watered by the river; the ancient Malaiyŭr (with) a fort situated on a high hill; Māyirudiṅgam, surrounded by the deep sea (as) a moat; Ilaṅgāśogam undaunted (in) fierce battles; Māpapāḷam, having abundant (deep) waters as defense; Meviḷmbaṅgam, having fine walls as defense; Vaḷaipandūṟu, possessing (both) cultivated land (?) and jungle; Talaittakkolam,

66   THE HISTORY OF SRIVIJAYA, ANGKOR and CHAMPA

praised by great men (versed in) the sciences; Mādamāliṅgam, firm in great and fierce battles; Ilāmurideśam, whose fierce strength was subdued by a vehement (attack); Māṇakkavāram whose flower-gardens (resembled) the girdle (of the nymph) of the southern region; Kadāram, of fierce strength, which was protected by the neighboring sea."

① Śrī-Vijaya ⇒ Chaiya. But most historians believe it as Palembang. However, Palembang was not attractive for the Tamil kingdom.

② Paṇṇai ⇒ Panei on the east coast of Sumatra.

③ Malaiyŭr ⇒ Mulayu including Jambi.

④ Māyirudiṅgam ⇒ Majumdar comments that 'MĂ' means 'maha' in Sanskrit, so yirudiṅgam means 'Jerteh (日羅亭: near Kuala Besut)' which is also described by Chao Ju-kua (趙汝适) in the Zhu-fan-zhi. Concerning Jerteh there are many opinions. I suppose Jerteh locates south of Kota Bharu, near Kuala Busak. This port was probably connected with Kedah.

⑤ Ilaṅgāśogam ⇒ Belongs to the old territory of Langkasuka which was supposed to be Nakhon Si Thammarat. But the location of this Langkasuka is not exactly identified. Many people believe it located at Pattani. The Zhu-fan-zhi says Langkasuka was located six days' journey from Tambralinga (Nakhon Si Thammarat) by sea, but it is probably mistaken. Perhaps from "Tan-mei-ryu (丹眉流)".

⑥ Māpapāḷam ⇒ Probably Pahang.

⑦ Meviḷmbaṅgam ⇒ Kamalanka? Some say Kamalanka is the old Langkasuka located on the isthmus of Ligor, but no evidence.

⑧ Vaḷaipandūṛu ⇒ Panduranga (Phan Rang, Champa port)?

⑨ Talaittakkolam ⇒ Takola of Ptolemy. Takua Pa.

⑩ Mādamāliṅgamya ⇒ Tambralinga. Nakhon Si Tammarat.

⑪ Ilāmurideśam ⇒ Lamuri, Sumatra.

⑫ Māṇakkavāram ⇒ Nicobar Island.

⑬ Kadāram ⇒ Kedah

Plate 4, Bunga Emas, copy, Kuala Lumpure National Historical Museum

2. Shi-li-fo-shi (Srivijaya)

R.C. Majumdar did not put Sri-Vijaya in the above list. Sri-Vijaya is probably Chaiya but most historians believe it was Palembang. For Chola, Palembang was not important state, because Palembang was out of the trade course to go to China. But Chaiya was more important. Chola attacked Takua Pa, so Chola also should have captured Chaiya, because both states were strategic ports covering the Gulf of Thailand. For Chola, Kedah (Kadaram) was the most important target. Chola attacked major ports of San-fo-chi. Palembang was excluded, which was not so important as most of the contemporary historians convinced. Jambi kept relative independence, because Jambi was not so important for Chola, as the trade route to China.

Chola had no intention to occupy whole San-fo-chi, Chola wanted to dominate the shortest trade route to China. So, Chola occupied Kedah, but not intended to dominate the whole occupied area. In 1067, Chola received request from the King of Kedah to overcome the rebellion, after victory Chola returned the sovereign to the king of Kedah.

Jambi was one of the major states of San-fo-chi, but Chola had not occupied Jambi. Jambi sent tributary mission in 1079 and 1082, under the name of 'San-fo-chi Jambi '. Apparently, Jambi was one of 'Three Vijaya states'. So, the Northern Song Dynasty did not give 'rewards' to Jambi. The Song Court said that Song would give reward only to San-fo-chi, not to Jambi. The result is unknown, but the Song Court regarded Jambi as the major member of San-fo-shi together with Kedah and Chaiya, so Jambi had no reason to send the tributary mission independently. This incident clarified the nature and composition of San-fo-chi. San fo-chi was not a single state, but the allied polity of 'three major Srivijaya's states'.

In 1025, The Tamil's Chola navy attacked San-fo-chi and Kedah was occupied by Chola. The main purpose of Chola was the monopolistic use of the Malay Peninsula's crossing commerce

68   THE HISTORY OF SRIVIJAYA, ANGKOR and CHAMPA

road, which seemed of great merit for Chola. Chola attacked every important state (port), but it didn't aim to control all of them. The main objective of the Chola was to occupy Kedah and a part of Malay Peninsula to use exclusively on-land trade route. However, Chola could not use the route so often and returned it to San-fo-chi about 60 years later. Probably Chola had not sufficient commodities to send frequent tributes to China, on the other hand the maintenance cost to occupy the Peninsula was too high. After Chola retreated, San-fo-chi once again solidified unity and regained vitality.

The importance of existence of San-fo-chi faded away because the South Song Dynasty abolished the traditional tributary system at the end of the 12th century. The South Song Dynasty changed all the tributary trade system to the 'general commerce trade system' (市舶司) with the import duty, but reserved the right to purchase the most needed goods. The South Song government had to avoid the expensive traditional 'tribute and rewards' system due to the financial difficulty of the South Song Court.

San-fo-chi sent the last mission to the South Song Court in 1178, and then after nothing was heard about San-fo-chi. I suppose that San-fo-chi became extinct spontaneously soon after the end of the tributary system. The name of San-fo-chi remained in the mind and memory of local people.

In the 13th century, Chandrabhanu of the military chief of Tambralinga made proclamation of independence (1230) and places the territory of Srivijaya in the Malay Peninsula under his control.

However, the king Chandrabhanu had sent army to Ceylon two times and failed. At the end of the 13th century, the king Rama Khamheng of the Sukhothai kingdom put Tambralinga under his control.

At the beginning of the Ming Dynasty a mission came to the Ming Court from the Palembang state with the tribute, declaring that they came from 'San-fo-chi'. But, San-fo-chi had disappeared more than 200 years ago. So, their story was apparent lie from the beginning, but nobody of the Ming Court noticed their lie

The officials of the Ming knew nothing about San-fo-chi. Ma-Huan, in the Ming times, wrote this story in his book the "*Ying-yai Sheng-lan* (瀛涯勝覽)" without proper comment. In the Meiji times in Japan, some scholars took up this text and they believed that Palembang was San-fo-chi. Unfortunately, at first, no Japanese historian noticed this story of the Palembang was a mere lie.

CONCLUSION

Historically Funan, Srivijaya, Sailendra and San-fo-chi had lasted for nearly 1000 years, since the early 3rd century until the end of the 12th century.

What is the reason? I think the most important factor is the Srivijaya rulers had the rational strategy. They found first that the international business is the most profitable especially the tributary system with the Chinese Dynasties. So, Funan tried to monopolize the imports of the western goods, which would be presented to the Chinese Dynasties. The Chinese Emperors gave them very high rewards to the foreign 'vassals'. Moreover, the Chinese government was a major buyer. They also monopolized purchasing the precious imports. The trade was very simple and easy. However foreign mission had to perform very complicated ceremony to pay respect to the Emperor at the time. Some foreigners had to spend several months to master the protocol.

Long lasting Funan's strategy was invented by Great General 'Fan Man (范蔓)' in the 3rd century. He made a fleet of long rowing boats first and occupied the major ports of the Andaman seaside, where the west merchants stopped over and Funan monopolize to purchase the western goods there. Funan originally transported the goods to the Mekong River through on- land route. Funan accumulated them at the port of Oc Eo, and then shipped them to China and other

70   THE HISTORY OF SRIVIJAYA, ANGKOR and CHAMPA

destination.

Fan Man occupied Takua Pa at that time. Then Funan developed the trans-peninsula transportation of the imports to Chaiya, Surat Thani at the Bay of Bandon where had been the territory of the Mon rulers (Ban-Ban kingdom). Then Funan shifted shipping port from Oc Eo to Ban-Ban (Chaiya) gradually. When Chenla destroyed Funan in Cambodia, Funan could restart the whole trade business from Ban-Ban. It was very easy for Funan leaders. Funan integrated the middle Malay Peninsula after merged Chi-tu (赤土國) and formed Shi-li-fo-shi (Srivijaya). Srivijaya next tried to control the whole Malacca Straits and occupied Mulayu, Jambi and Palembang. Further Srivijaya conquered the central Jawa, Kha-ling (訶陵) kingdom (Sanjaya) in 686. There Sailendra kingdom was established but Srivijaya had no intention to dominate the whole Kha-ling (Sanjaya). Srivijaya (Shi-li-fo-shi) aimed to monopolize the international trade there.

Water Chenla occupied Ban-Ban (centre of Shi-li-fo-shi) around 745, but the Srivijaya group counter attacked Water Chenla at Chaiya. The major Srivijaya force was the Sailendra navy of Jawa. After the victory, the king of Sailendra (Panangkaran) was appointed as the Maharaja of Srivijaya. The Srivijaya group proceeded their navy to the Mekong River and occupied major cities. Then Jayavarman II was dispatched as the new ruler of Water Chenla. It was the beginning of the Angkor Dynasty. However, around 830, Sailendra prince Balaputra was defeated by Sanjaya prince Rakai Pikatan, and lost the reign of the Jawa Island. So Srivijaya set back to Sumatra and the Malay Peninsula, and later Srivijaya reorganized San-fo-chi, which is allied state of three major Srivijaya kingdoms, Jambi, Kedah and Chaiya. But San-fo-chi was invaded by the Tamil kingdom, Chola in 1025. Chola's purpose was to destroy Srivijaya's monopoly of the Malay Peninsula trade facility, but around 1080 Chola returned the reign to San-fo-chi. San-fo-chi regained the tributary right to China. However, the South Song finished the tributary system in 1178 due

2. Shi-li-fo-shi (Srivijaya)

to the financial difficulty. As the result, San-fo-chi disappeared naturally, and we have not heard its name after that.

In the 15th century, Palembang state appeared as 'the former San-fo-chi', but there was no ground to say that. Palembang was a small vassal state of San-fo-chi.

Anyway, the Srivijaya group had survived for nearly 1000 years, starting the Funan kingdom of the Mekong delta. Their strategy is to keep the strong position in the tributary system and maintained the strong navy consisted of fleets of rowing long boats.

CHAPTER
3
CHENLA AND PRE-ANGKOR KINGDOM

3 - 1 ORIGIN OF CHENLA AND FUNAN

Chenla was originally a subordinate state of Funan. Chenla had been a part of Funan which was in charge of the land-route transportation of the imported western commodities from the ports of the lower Myanmar (Burma) to the Oc Eo port in the Mekong Delta. At first Funan imported goods from India and Persia and unloaded at the ports of the lower Myanmar, such as Thaton, Moulmein, Tavoy and Tenasserim, and transported them on-land to the Mekong Delta. It was a very long journey and many people were engaged in the transportation. Funan had several deposit centres along the route. For example, Kanchanaburi, U Thong, Nakhon Sawan and Si Thep (Sri Deva) and these intermediary places had been developed as commercial cities by the Mon people from the ancient time. The Mons had controlled commercial activities of these regions from the prehistoric age.

Funan people (Indian origin) stayed these cities and gradually established leadership of the community. After long time, Funan people had become chiefs of the cities and kings of small local states. The most important city was Si Thep, where the boss became a ruler of the region. They gradually increased economic, political and military power.

According to the *Sui Shu* (隋書), Chenla was located at southwest of Lin-yi and originally a vassal state of Funan. Funan people controlled important market places on-land trade routes and the major river traffic routes. At the same time, they dominated vast rice paddy field area along the major rivers of northeast of Thailand and had strong economic and military power. This was the situation at the early stage of the 6th century.

Michael Vickery believes that Funan and Chenla were within one polity and could not be separated. Indeed, Funan's one section was Chenla in charge of stocking and transporting the imported western goods. However, their 'division of works' had been fixed for a long time, so the character of two groups had changed gradually. Funan group of the headquarters was located south and in charge of the direct international trade. On the other hand, Chenla group had been transporters but had dominated vast area of the northeast Thailand and upper part of the Mekong basin and became the great landlord, dominating enormous number of villages and farmers.

The last king of Funan was Rudravarman, there is the following description in the "*Liang Shu* (梁書)". Kaundinya Jayavarman (僑陳如闍邪) had sent missions in 511 and 514 to China. After his death in 514, Rudravarman, a son of the concubine killed his younger brother who was the child of the lawful wife, and claimed a regality to succeed the throne. Rudravarman was a typical usurper but he had real political power.

In case of such incident, the political strife usually happened among the rulers of Funan and royal family. Chenla group might have taken advantage of political change of Funan's regime. As the land-route controller, Chenla's position in the Funan group was declining since middle of the 4th century. Because Funan had developed another trade route in the Malay Peninsula. From Takua Pa to Chaiya, Funan transported the western imports and shipped them from Chaiya to Oc Eo or China directly. So, the importance of land transportation had decreased eventually.

However the economic power of Chenla had increased because Chenla became landlord in the northeast part of Thailand. They

3. Chenla and Pre-Angkor Kingdom

controlled Si-Thep and farm area. However, on the other hand, Funan was prosperous by international trade. The role of Ban-Ban state located at the Bandon Bay area increased instead of Si Thep and Oc-Eo line. So, the sentiment of the Chenla rulers became antagonistic toward Funan rulers who had neglected the land transportation. The conflict between the two groups was apparent after Rudravarman took the throne.

Rudravarman was a Buddhist and at the same time embraced Sivaism. The rulers of Chenla were all staunch believers in Sivaism, they hate Buddhism and even disliked Vishnu. Because Buddha was considered as the incarnation of Vishnu.

Rudravarman probably died in 540. He had sent 6 times tributary missions to China, in 517, 519, 520, 530, 535 and 539. The *Liang Shu* (梁書) says "the envoy of Funan paid tribute of rhinoceros, and in 539, Funan ambassador said in Funan they have Buddha's long hair twelve feet length. The emperor wanted the Buddha's hair and sent high rank priest Sri Yun Bao (釋雲寶) to receive the sacred hair. "

On the other hand, the rulers of Funan, anticipating Chenla's attack, they began preparation to shift headquarters to Ban-Ban (盤盤 = Pan Pan) at the Bay of Ban Don from the Mekong Delta.

Bhavavarman, after killing some of Funan's royal family or expelled them, claiming to be the first Chenla king, inheriting the throne after King Rudravarman around 550. Bhavavarman had clarified the point to identify himself as he belonged to the 'lunar line' of traditional Funan kingship. (Briggs, pp. 40)

Why Bhavavarman pretended he was on line with the Funan royal family? He simply wanted to declare to inherit the regal Funan kingship. On the other hand, in 803 Jayavarman II declared he belonged to the 'solar line (Chenla family)'. Anyway, both lines left no 'DNA' evidence.

Citrasena (later, king Mahendravarman), the younger brother of Bhavavarman was serving as the commander of the Chenla army.

One of his inscriptions is left at Si Thep. His connection with Si

76 THE HISTORY OF SRIVIJAYA, ANGKOR and CHAMPA

Thep seems so deep as he probably had come from there. Many historians believe they came from Wat Phu area, in Laos.

SI Thep had been the biggest city and centre of the Pa Sak river basin (Pa Sak Valley), in the paddy field rice-growing area in the north central part of Thailand.

Basically, land belonged to the community. The ruler of the community was a 'leader of the villagers' and took care after problems of the village. M. Vickery suggests that is the character of the society. (M. Vickery, Toyo, pp22-23). He adds that this type of organization was suitable for the pre-historic communities revealed by archaeology in northeastern Thailand, in which possibilities for concentration of wealth and territorial expansion were limited. In fact, villages were often separated by large areas of unoccupied and unowned land in the ancient time.

It is possible that leaders of Funan and Chenla had been in the brotherhood. But, the Chenla group in the inland area was engaged with the transportation of western goods at the same time they had controlled extensive rice paddy area. That means Chenla group had sufficient capability to amass large army. After Rudravarman's death, Chenla army proceeded to the south to take over the trade business of Funan, and finally kicked out the Funan rulers from the Mekong delta. Chenla had killed some princes of Funan, but most of the ruling class of Funan had fled to Ban-Ban with their navy. As the result Funan could have dominated the estuary of Mekong and the seashore of southern Indochina. Actually Chenla had no navy and no seafaring capability.

Chenla should have taken over the business of profitable trade from Funan, but miserably they had failed. Chenla started sending tributary mission to China in 616, but Chenla could not use the sea route which was dominated by the Funan's navy. M. Vickery made a serious misunderstanding that Funan was in decline, and no longer an attractive object for conquest (M. Vickery, Toyo, p79). However, Chenla had been eager to send tributary missions to China, as the

3. Chenla and Pre-Angkor Kingdom

Photo 15: Stupa Basement Si Thep

records shown later. Funan had been shifting its business centre to Ban-Ban since a long time ago. So Chenla could not take over the trade facility of Funan. Funan interfered Chenla's sea trade by blocking the estuary of the Mekong River.

Isanavarman sent to envoy to China together with Lin-yi using the sea route in October 628. At that time Chenla informed China that their state also called ' Khmer'. The origin of Chenla is not clear, so Chenla people preferred to be called 'Khmer'.

After Chenla's leaders had left Si-Thep for the administration of the new kingdom in Cambodia, the Mon people remained at Si Thep and they continued their business as usual. As the result, the culture of the Mons revived and flourished there. The establishment of Mahayana Buddhist temples and Buddha statues are observed. There are large remains of Buddhism at Si Thep. Today, there are large stupas of Dvaravati style and 'Dharma Chakra'. When Chenla leaders had stayed in Si Thep, they were keen Hinduists and

78   THE HISTORY OF SRIVIJAYA, ANGKOR and CHAMPA

basically rejected Buddhism.

U Thong was the second largest intermediary point of the Funan's land route. However, the size of U Thong was smaller than that of Si Thep. Major residents of the both cities were the Mon speaking people. They were flexible about religion, but later they worshiped mainly Buddhism.

According to the *Liang Shu*, the capital of Funan was located at 500 li (about 200km) from the river mouth, but it does not specify a city name.

The *Xin Tang Shu* (新唐書) noted that the Funan had transferred the capital to 'the Na-fu-na (那弗那)' from 'Te-mu-city (特牧城)' which was attacked at first by Chenla. Na-fu-na is not identified yet, but it seems to be Navanakar, Kampot provine which used to be the important port and naval base of Funan. 'Te-mu' is not identified yet, but which may be 'Takeo', including Angkor Borei and Phnom Da.

Coedes supposes that 'Te-mu city' was Vyadhapura, near Ba Phnom, but Ba Phnom had no direct access to the canal network to the Oc Eo port and the Mekong River. (M.Vickery, Toyo, p61).

Considering the plenty of historical remains, Angkor Borei (including Phnom Da) was the most suitable capital of Funan, and Takeo (including Angkor Borei) may fit for 'Te-mu city'. Then the location of Na-fu-na' is the next problem. Pelliot suggests it was 'Navanakar', Kampot province. Kampot area may be a probable candidate, where directly faces sea and had the port facility. Kampot had been a traditional port of Funan and there is inscription of Jayavarman I who donated there. (M. Vickery, Toyo, p41)

For short term, Funan shifted its capital to 'Na-fu-na', but Isanavrman did not allow Funan to stay in Cambodia. He finally expelled Funan until 630.

For the Funan people, 'Navanakar' was the easiest place to evacuate in case of danger.

3. Chenla and Pre-Angkor Kingdom

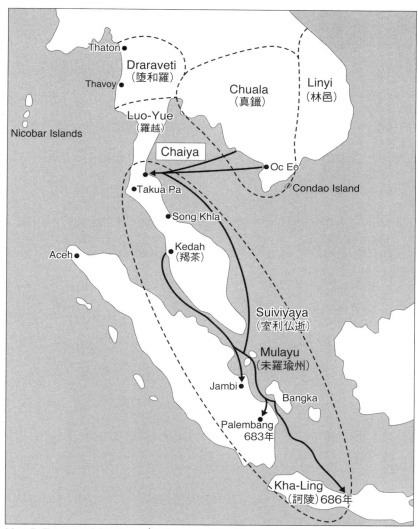

Map 5: Territory of Srivijaya (At the end of the 7th century)

Photo 16: Angkor Borei Museum

Photo 17-1: Vishnu image, excavated from Phnom Da, near Angkor Borei, exhibited now at Phnom Penh National Museum

Photo 17-2: Big tower of Phnom Da

3-2 SI THEP AS THE ORIGINAL BASE OF CHENLA

The dominating area of Chenla was the land-route of Funan, starting from Si-Thep, connecting to the Chi River, the Mun River, Ubon Ratchathani and Champasak (Wat Phu). Chenla could not have accumulated enough military force at Wat Phu to attack Funan, because Wat Phu area is too narrow. Chenla's economic and political base had been located in wider place, the north of the Dangrek mountains area.

Si Thep was the commercial centre of the Mons from the ancient times where Indian merchants came later, settled and established hegemony in the city. The contribution of Indian people to the residents was significant. They taught many things to the Mons and Khmer people other than religion how to cultivate paddy field, how to manufacture iron products and sold them a part of their imports from the West. At the same time, Indian imported Hinduism and spread among the local people. There are many Hindu images of deities. Many Surya, Krishna, Siva and Vishnu images were discovered at Si Thep and some of them are exhibited at the Bangkok National Museum. Q. Wales says there is similar Siva image at Bhumara temple in India. Probably the original images were imported from India, but local craft men made simplified the original images and made many copies. So, Vishnu images spread to the Malay Peninsula and other vicinities.

The first king Bhavavarman had not a son of the succession, so after his death, Citrasena (Mahendravarman, Bhavavarman's younger brother) succeeded the throne. C. Jacques says they were sons of Vivavarman.

C. Jacques says that the brothers came from the south of the Dangrek Range and the north of Cambodia. Perhaps he wanted to say they came from Wat Phu area. Cœdès had a similar opinion. However, I suppose they came from Si Thep or the north of the Dangrek Mountains area, because Wat Phu (Champasak) is too

Photo 18: Surya, Krisna, Shiva, Vishnu (From Left)

narrow to gather a big army. At least their family might have lived at Si Thep where was the commercial centre of the region and was surrounded by vast paddy field with many farmers. The farmers were source of large army. Champasak (Wat Phu) was the intermediary point of the land-route of Funan. The north of the Dangrek Range was from the economic point of view, very rich and prosperous at that time. There were iron, copper and salt making facilities and broad paddy field. Chenla group might have economic and military superiority from the beginning of the conflict with Funan.

The movement of Chenla's military action was recognized by Funan's rulers and many of them had fled away beforehand to Ban-Ban (盤盤 = Pan Pan). For Funan rulers, Ban-Ban was sufficient to conduct trade, because the most of western commodities were unloaded at Takua Pa, and directly shipped to China from Chaiya. M. Vickery did not recognize this special advantage of Funan, and ignored its 'exiled' story and the function of Ban-Ban state. He believes that due to decrease of international trade, Funan group

3. Chenla and Pre-Angkor Kingdom 83

demised naturally within Cambodia. However, Funan's trade with China had never decreased, but increased significantly including Ban-Ban's export.

After kicked out Funan rulers, Bhavavarman I set up his capital at Sambor Prei Kuk (30-40km the north of Kompong Thom), where later became Isanapura, the capital of Isanavarman. This place keeps some distance (30km) from the Mekong River to avoid sudden attack of the Funan navy. Funan maintained a strong navy and was controlling the estuary of the Mekong River and the South China Sea.

M. Vickery says: "The inscriptions which name him (Bhavavarman I) do not permit certainly that he ever went north beyond the Dangrek mountains, and indicate that his territory was not very large, between the Tonle Sap and the Mekong River. His death would have been around 600CE. (M. Vickery, Toyo. p330)

The inscriptions of Citrasena exist in northeast Thailand, the Pasak valley, Korat (Nakhon Ratchasima), Ubon Ratchathani, Phimai, Surin, Ta Praya (Sa Kaeo province) and in Cambodia at Kratie. The range of his activities had greatly extended in the northern part of the Dangrek mountains. The inscriptions of Bhavavarman exist at Si Thep, Battambang, Stung Treng (Cambodian territory) and Wat Phu (Vat Phou). The two brothers are a genealogy of the rulers of the land transportation of Funan and their stronghold was in the northeast of Thailand.

Cœdès says that Wat Phu, Laos was the first Chenla stronghold, but his view is not reasonable as above mentioned.

Cœdès named Srutavarman and Sresthavarman as kings of the early Wat Phu district (Cœdès, 1968 English, p66). M. Vickery points out that the two old time kings were named for the first time in the inscription of Jayavarman VII period (12th century). (M. Vickery, Toyo, p42).

He says that these two kings were not known their exact position of 600 years ago. This method is a typical approach of Cœdès.

84   THE HISTORY OF SRIVIJAYA, ANGKOR and CHAMPA

It was probably impossible for Chenla to conquer Funan with the small army, amassed from Champasak area. Champasak and Wat Phu had not so large rice field and the population was relatively small, compared with that of Funan's dominating area. The large army of Chenla probably had been mobilized from the vast farmland of the Pasak Valley and the northeast of Thailand.

On the other hand, Funan was the international trading country, and promoted the development of a rational international trade route. Finally, Takua Pa (Ko Koh Khao) and Chaiya in the Malay Peninsula were selected. From Takua Pa to Chaiya, Funan could carry their west goods within a week or ten days, so the cross Peninsula on-land route was fixed as their regular course. They used the small rivers, the Klong Sok and Phum Dung River. Further from Ban-Ban Funan directly sailed to China, under the name of Funan and sometimes under the name of Ban-Ban. Funan used two trade names to China since the middle of the 5th century, including from Oc Eo port in the Mekong delta and from Chaiya to China.

The Funan's mainstream of trade, since the middle of the 5th century, gradually changed 'from Oc Eo to Ban-Ban', to China. They moved their navy to the Bandon Bay, together with craftsmen, sculptors in advance. For instance, we can see the similar Vishnu images of Angkor Borei, at Chaiya, Surat Thani district.

The *Xin* (*New*) *Tang Shu* says that in Shi-li-fo-shi (室利佛逝、 Srivijaya), there are too many men (males). This suggests Srivijaya maintained many navy soldiers. It is unreasonable of M. Vickery's saying that foreign trade is facing the loss, so Funan has made 'natural demise'.

3-3 PRE-ANGKOR KINGDOM

C. Jacques says, "King Bhavavarman I was a prince from the region of Wat Phu in southern Laos. He had not been chosen to successor to the throne of his father's small state and decided, nevertheless,

3. Chenla and Pre-Angkor Kingdom

to establish a kingdom of his own. After having conquered of the main part of what is now Cambodia, he had set up his capital some 30 kilometers from the town now called Kompong Thom. The precise location of his city, near or on the site of Smbor Prei Kuk, has not yet been identified." (C. Jacques, pp56). C. Jacques says that Bhavavarman was too ambitious to inherit his father's small kingdom and he independently expanded his territory. His intention to take over Funan's business was very clear from the beginning. Furthermore, it is not sure that he was a prince of the Wat Phu kingdom. Bhavavarman extended his kingdom for northwest town of Battambang, where he left inscription. Why Battambang? There was vast paddy field and on the nearest route to the Chantaburi port which is the shortest trade route to the Malay Peninsula. From where Water Chenla could have attacked Ban-Ban (Chaiya) in the middle of the 8th century.

On the other hand, according to C. Jacques, his 'less ambitious' younger brother Citrasena, had inherited small kingdom of Wat Phu from his father. However, his activity as the commander of Chenla army had been very striking. He left many inscriptions as above mentioned. The brothers had established their base at Wat Phu and Stung Treng, along the Mekong River, which were not their home town.

Two inscriptions related Citrasena were discovered at Ubon Ratchathani (K.496-497) and another (K.363) was discovered at Champasak in Laos. These are written the name of Citrasena, also named Mahendravarman, younger brother of Bhavavarman, sons of Vivavarman'. In another inscription (K.508), a word, 'grandson of Svabhauma', is added (M.Vickery, pp74).

Photo 19: Inscription of Citrasena, Ubon Ratchatanee Museum.

3-3-1 Isanavarman

Some more inscriptions of Citrasena are at Khon Kaen, Nakhon Ratchasima, Phimai, Surin, and Ta Praya. These inscriptions were in the north side (today's northeast area of Thailand) of the Dangrek mountains where were his main activity area. At that time, the northeast Thailand (Isaan) had been very prosperous with various kind of industries. So, Chenla had to confirm these area under its control.

M. Vickery says that the 'Dangrek' inscriptions should be regarded as records of exploratory probes rather than enduring conquests, with little, if any, permanent effect (in the words of Cœdès about K. 213, a 'simple cry of victory' not implying a permanent occupation of the country) and I would not interpret Mahendravarman's inscriptions as 'delimiting' any kingdom, either his father's or his

3. Chenla and Pre-Angkor Kingdom   87

own. (M. Vickery, Toyo, p79).

Indeed,' simple cry of victory 'would not elaborate their family relation. Si Thep had been their 'home town' and not conquered area, because the local people celebrated their success.

About the reign dates of the kings of Chenla are not identified exactly. M. Vickery says that Mahendravarman's reign, no fixed date is available.

After Mahendravarman's death Isanavarman (616?-635?) succeeded him. He placed his capital at Isanapura (Siva city). Within the city wall more than 20,000 families resided.

Isanavarman established his capital 30km north of Kompong Tom, soon after he took the throne, around 618. There are about 170 ruins of Hindu temples, government houses and a large king' palace.

Siva was enshrined in the temple. In this time Harihara appeared for the first time, combining Siva and Vishnu. But Siva faith was the most valued as the religion of the Chenla Kingdom.

Isanavarman promoted administrative reform and invited many scholars and Brahmans from India. Isanapura is located about 30 km from the Mekong River. That is because probably he also avoided the sudden assault of former Funan. If at all Chenla integrated Funan peacefully, as M. Vickery says, Chenla could have sent tribute by the sea smoothly. However, Chenla continued sending tribute to the Tang dynasty mainly using the land route. The navy of Funan and Shi-li-fo-shi had been heavy obstacle for Chenla.

On the death of King Isanavarman I in 635, his younger son succeeded under the name of Bhavavarman II. M. Vickery says that his original name was Bhavakumara and later became king (M. Vickery, p24). But Briggs says that he was not a son of Isanavarman, and his reign was very short. (Briggs, p52-53). He was far from having the prestige of Isanavarman, and failed to maintain the unity of the Chenla kingdom. The local chiefs regained their independence. Later, Jayavarman I tried to rebuild the empire of Isanavarman I.

As M. Vickery says that the irrigation system had been introduced between Funan and Chenla times, but the scale of the artificial ponds was small and carried out at the level of the local communities and no remains of large hydraulic works have been discovered. (M.Vickery, Toyo, p306)

As for the expansion of rice field, they had done only a little, and neglected the large size expansion of irrigation system. Through pre-Angkor time, economic development was limited. As the result, the pre-Angkor kingdom declined gradually without the trade profit.

The *Sui Shu* says that Citrasena expelled Funan rulers, but some Funan people might have remained in the south part of Cambodia (Navanakar?). In Isanapura, there is a big hall in which king practiced usual administration. There are 30 big cities near the capital, and each city has several thousand families living and has army. The officials ' titles are same as those of Ling-yi.

Isanavarman's reign is supposed as 616-635, which have been based on a Chinese record of a Cambodian mission.

Isanavarman was the most powerful king of the pre-Angkor era. He assigned many local governors (kings). However, they often claimed some degree of local autonomy. (M. Vickery, Toyo, p25)

Probably he did not aware that his policy would be the cause of disunity of Chenla in the future.

It is remarkable that the administration system of Chenla and Lin-yi seemed similar. Isanavarman's daughter married with a prince of Lin-yi. His daughter Sri Sarvani married to the prince of Cham, Jagaddharma. However, he lived at Bhavapura of Chenla, after involved with some trouble. They had a prince, named Prakasadharma (諸葛地), and he mounted the throne of Champa in 635, as Vikrantavarman (Briggs, p52). This is recorded in the inscription in My-son and in the Chinese annals.

The *Xin Tang Shu* writes that Isanavarman completely expelled Funan at the early time of the ' Zhen Guan (貞觀. 627-649) era and integrated Cambodia.

Judging from this description, Funan might have maintained some

3. Chenla and Pre-Angkor Kingdom

small territory in Cambodia until around 630. However, their main staff had migrated and settled at Chaiya.

Isanavarman was 'protector of the Master Siva' and succeeded his father, Mahendravarman. More than a dozen inscriptions are attributed to the reign of Isanavarman.

According to the inscriptions and monuments, the territory of Chenla of Bhvavarman and Mahendravarman was not so wide. From the lower valley of the Mun River, it seems to include a strip along both sides of the Mekong River, and including the Tonle Sap basin, perhaps to the Great Lake. However, Chenla put under its control the northern part of the Dangrek mountains, which was accomplished by Citrasena as inscriptions showed.

Briggs says "Funan, at the South, seems to have enjoyed a degree of autonomy and may still at the beginning of Isanavarman reign, have exercised some control over the coast of the Bay of Camranth (Panduranga) and have had the loyalty of some of its maritime colonies." (Briggs, pp47)

However, the most of Funan rulers fled away to the Bay of Bandon area (Ban-Ban state), because Bhavavarman had killed some princes of Funan, and there was no safe place to stay in Cambodia after the victory of Chenla. Antagonism between Chenla and Funan was very severe, so Chenla could not have sent tributary mission to China through the sea route. For a short time, Funan group could have survived at the sea-shore area, for instance in Kampot, but they were probably attacked by Chenla and could not have stayed for a long time. Chenla could not have merged Funan peacefully, as M. Vickery suggested.

Isanavarman had two sons, and their mother (Sakaramanjari) was from the Adhyapura family. The elder brother was Sivadatta and younger brother was Bhavakumara, later King Bhavavarman II. Sivadatta was ruler of several cities (pura), Bhavapura, Adhyapura and Jyestjhapura. Sivaddata also left inscription at Prachinburi, near the Gulf of Thailand. Sivadatta might have become a member of the

90   THE HISTORY OF SRIVIJAYA, ANGKOR and CHAMPA

Adhyapura family which was the most influential clan. M. Vickery says that Sivadatta's mother must have been sister of Dharmadeva, ruler of Adhyapura family. (M. Vickery, Toyo, P371).

Bhavavarman II may have been recognized as the king of Chenla after 637 and until the mid-650s, although only two dates 637, 639 and or 644, are associated with his reign in contemporary inscriptions. Although he was called 'Maharaja', his real territory might have been same as Bhavavarman I's and he was the king of part of the South and of the Nortwest. (M. Vickery, Toyo, p331). On the other hand, Sivadatta, as the ruler of the Adhyapura family governed the important part of South Cambodia. Actually, Sivadatta seemes to have stronger political and economic power than his younger brother, Bhavavarman II.

What means the separation of two brothers? While Isanavarman was alive, there might be little problems. Isanavarman tried to pull together local leaders under his arm to centralize political power. However, after his death, serious problems might have occurred within Cambodia.

Here, the territory of Bavavaruman II seems to be 'Land Chenla' and Sivadatta's territory 'Water Chenla' in the future.

The successor of Bhavavarman II is Jayavarman I, and his reign date is similarly controversial, and he probably reigned roughly from 655/657 to 680/81.

Only one date is recorded for Queen Jayadevi, 713, and then there is no more date associated with the names of rulers until the first inscriptions of Jayavarman II in 770 and 781" (M. Vickery, Toyo, p22).

However, there must be some rulers of Water Chenla after her death. As M. Vickery says after Queen Jayadevi, Chenla was sufficiently at peace and unified for its rulers to extract enough wealth to invest in more and larger temples than had been built in

3. Chenla and Pre-Angkor Kingdom 91

the seventh century, with the exception of the city of Isanapura, capital of Isanavarman and Bhavavarman II. (M. Vickery, "What and Where was Chenla?" 1994, p15)

M. Vickery says that a more forceful policy of centralization was instituted by Jayavarman I (657? -681?), who may also, through his mother, had been in a line of descent from Isanavarman, and who does not appear of the Adhyapura family, although he was in a way adopted by them retrospectively, meaning that he probably married into their group". (M. Vickery, Toyo, p25)

3-3-2 Adhyapura family

This Adhyapura family had progressive idea, and influenced Jayavarman 1 (655-681?) and probably the Angkor Dynasty later.

Usually Jayavarman I is said to be a son of Bhavavarman II (Cœdès) but there is a different opinion that Jayavarman I was born as the son of Candravarman of the local lord in Kompong Thom by Soma royal family. Directly, he had nothing to do with this Adhyapura family, but his wife came from the Adhyapura family. (Briggs, p54). He had strong support from the Adhyapura family.

The capital of Jayavarman I was said to be Purandrapura, but not identified, however he did not settle in Isanapura nor Bhavaputra as his capital. He mainly dominated southern part of Cambodia (later Water Chenla).

The beginning kings, Bhavavarman, Mahendravarman and Isanavarman, are known as staunch Sivaists and suppressed Buddhism. Economically they failed to promote international trade by sea, especially the tributary trade to China. So, they could not have increased their wealth as expected. Jayavarman I seemed a little flexible about religion and economy.

At first, the centre of Chenla government was located at northern part of Kompong Tom, Sombor Prei Kok area (Isanapura), but the centre of commercial activity was located in the southern area.

Briggs says as following: "To the west of the Mekong, Aninditapura-

92   THE HISTORY OF SRIVIJAYA, ANGKOR and CHAMPA

at this time, probably called Baladityapura seems to have occupied the valley of the Sung Sen, a tributary of the Tonle Sap parallel to the Mekong and the territory to the west, to the line running from the eastern end of the Great Lake, roughly corresponding to the present Kompong Thom".

As above mentioned, Isanavarman's wife came from Aninditapura family. Adhyapura (rich town) was located near Ba Phnom.

(Sacred Mountain and Pyramid)

Cœdès says that the Mountain 'Lingaparvata (陵伽鉢婆山)' written in the *Sui Shu* is the high mountain of Wat Phu. Of which the peak shaped huge natural lingam. M. Vickery considers that judging from the context of the *Sui Shu* this mountain (Mt. Meru) should be close to the capital of Isanavarman, and it was probably 'Phnom Suntuk' 30 km away from the capital. The sacred mountain should be near capital. The sacred mountain was considered as the centre of the universe, that is the basic idea at that time. Lingaparvata of Wat Phu is located too far away as the sacred mountain of Isanavarman. Later, in the Angkor kingdom, many kings constructed pyramid style towers and the tallest tower was considered as the sacred Mt. Meru where the king's linga was set up.

Brahmanism took a very unusual form, apparently for the first time in Cambodia, during the reign of Isanavarman. This was the worship of Harihara — Vishnu and Siva combined in one body. (Briggs, p51). This harihara became popular in Chenla.

3-3-3   Jayavarman I and the decline of Pre-Angkor

Yi Jing wrote in the "*Nan Hui*" at the end of the 7th century:

義淨「西南一月。至跋南國。舊扶南。先是裸國。人多事天。後乃佛法盛流。惡王今竝除滅。無僧衆。外道雜居。」

"After one month's journey to the southwest, there is Funan country. In the past Funan was a naked people's country.

3. Chenla and Pre-Angkor Kingdom   93

Nowadays many people believe in Hinduism. Once in Funan, the law of Buddha prospered and spread, but the wicked kings (of Chenla) destroyed it and there are no more monks, and non-Buddhism (Hindu) prevails."

After Funan was kicked out, Chenla rulers worshipped Hinduism and suppressed Buddhism. So, once Buddhist monk disappeared from Cambodia. However, in the 2nd half of the 7th century, a little different type of king appeared, whose name is Jayavarman I. In the time of Jayavarman I, inscriptions related Buddhism began to appear. M. Vickery says," It is an edict by Jayavarman I, confirming possession of a large Buddhist establishment (personnel, animals, rice fields, plantations) in the third generation of the family which had founded it." (M. Vickery, Toyo, p352). He was apparently tolerant of Buddhism, and himself is regarded even as a Buddhist.

Jayavarman I's inscription which attached the title of Maharaja (k 1059) have been found. Certainly, he integrated whole Cambodia. However, Jayavarman I, despite its outward success, the unity of Cambodia was going into cracks. (C. Jacques. p57). He has sent army for the first time throughout Cambodia and confirmed unity, then he sent troops to upper Laos and Yunnan Province in China.

Vyadhapura (Prei Veng) is Kompong Cham, in the South. Some say here was the old capital city of Funan, but M. Vickery denies it. However, this area used to be the centre of commercial activities and flourished. Jayavarman I seemed to love this region. The old capital city to the north of Kompong Thom (Isanapura) was in the defensive position and unsuitable place for economic activity. Jayavarman I tried to unite Cambodia, but his intention was unsuccessful by the division of the country. Jayavarman II later selected this area as a starting point to control the whole Cambodia.

Jayavarman I left many inscriptions during the reign. Among them he has been hailed as the warrior. He had stretched the forces to Siem Reap, Wat Phu, Battambang, Chantaburi (Thailand), Prey

94   THE HISTORY OF SRIVIJAYA, ANGKOR and CHAMPA

Veng, Takeo (Phnom Bayang), Thailand border Preah Vihear and Kompong Thom's Han Cheikara. Expedition to the northern central Laos is also recorded (Briggs, p54). Chantaburi is the nearest port to the Malay Peninsula, where is as the most important port to access the Bay of Ban Don (Chaiya). Around 745, Water Chenla probably had sent navy from Chantaburi and occupied Chaiya area.

Anyway, he managed to maintain unity by the military force, but he gained only nominal and superficial unity. Jayavarman 1 directly controlled the territory of Kompong Thom and Kompong Cham in the centre of Cambodia. His capital was supposed located at Purandarapura where is unidentified yet. Briggs supposes his city 'Banteay Prei Nokor', 1.2 km southeast from Kompong Cham. (Briggs, pp54-57).

M. Vickery says: "Jayavarman I, is shown making real efforts to exert central control. Not only is he more frequently named in inscriptions, and over a slightly wider area than his predecessors, but he issued direct royal orders concerning foundations, occasionally ordering or forbidding their unification, and indicating who should have local control over them". (M. Vickery, Toyo, p367)

M. Vickery says that the dates and locations of pre-Angkor and early Angkor inscriptions indicate a gradual shift northward of the political and economic centre of the Cambodian polity during the 7th-8th century, from the Takeo and Kampot→Prey Veng→Kompong Cham→Kompong Tom region, to just north of the Tonle Sap where Angkor was established. (M. Vickery, Toyo, p315). During the Funan times, Takeo and Kampot were important economic bases, but in the Angkor time economic centre moved to Kompong Cham and the north of Tonle Sap (Siem Reap) area. This means the economy of Pre-Angkor (Chenla) began to emphasize the importance of agriculture, because the weight of the international trade decreased drastically in Chenla times.

More than 120 years later, since the reign of Jayavarman II, the

3. Chenla and Pre-Angkor Kingdom   95

Angkor Kingdom, the central administration was restored. It was beginning of the Angkor Dynasty. Even though Jyavarman II pretended as Sivaist, but the Mahayana Buddhism became rapidly popular in Cambodia. The Mahayana Buddhism was the symbolic religion of Srivijaya group.

After the death of Jayavarman I in 681, until the declaration of independence by Jayavarman II in 802, for more than 120 years, the central administration of Cambodia had not officially existed.

On the other hand, local governments (chiefdom) had developed steadily, getting stable tax-income of rice farming and became rich and strong. Stable income of local government was obstacles to establish the powerful central government.

Jayavarman 1's successor (son-in-law) was weak. His daughter, Jayadevi's husband Nripaditya succeeded to the throne but he had done nothing for the unity. Local chiefs had already stronger power. Finally, Jayadevi took over the throne as the Queen. However, the territories were divided. Her power was limited in the South (Water Chela), and lost the 'central control'. Jayadevi also lamented the division of political power. Cœdès says that Jayavarman 1 had no male successor, and Queen Jayadevi could not maintain the unity of Chenla. M. Vickery says that Cambodia was not patrilineal heritage society. However, after the death of Queen Jayadevi Water Chenla did some important action against Srivijaya, during 745-760. Water Chenla attacked Srivijaya and occupied Chaiya and Nakhon Si Thammrat area. But they were crushed by the Sailendra navy at the first half of 760s. These incidents were not recorded in any document, but certainly happened. The Ligor inscription dated 775, recorded about these incidents. Soon after the battle at Chaiya area, probably the invasion of Srivijaya to the Mekong River area happened. This invasion was the beginning of the Angkor Dynasty. At the same time, the Srivijaya navy led by the Sailendra king Panangkaran probably attacked Lin-yi and destroyed export facilities.

96   THE HISTORY OF SRIVIJAYA, ANGKOR and CHAMPA

3-3-4   Division of Chenla

The *Jiu Tang Shu*（舊唐書）says in 'Shen Long（神龍）2nd year' 706 , Chenla was separated by two states, the northern part with many mountains and deep grass, called 'Land Chenla' and the southern part, near sea and plenty of water, called 'Water Chela'. Water Chela has width of 800 li, the King's palace is located at Baladityapura（婆羅提拔城）.The same story is written in the *Xin Tang Shu*, which added that Land Chenla was called 'Wen-dan（文單). Wen-dan was probably 'Vientiane', and a subordinate state of Land Chenla, which often sent tributary missions by land-route. With one or two exceptions, the Land Chenla had sent mission to Tang via on-land route.

Water Chela governed commercial area of the central part of Cambodia, around Kompong Cham area was predominant in economy. This area included Aninditapura region, and Jayavarman 1 possibly put the capital there. C. Jacques does not fix the location of Anindithapura, but the name appears in the inscription of the Angkor period. C. Jacques says the location was Purandarapura. However, Purandarapura itself is not identified. That is approximately the same as Anindithapura, where would be slightly South of Kompong Cham. The area near the Tonle Sap Lake, located in the basin of the Mekong River, is famous for its commercial activities, regional economic development was observed or the most prosperous region. Jayavarman I seemed to have placed his capital in this area.

On the other hand, Land Chenla was located in the northern part of Cambodia and the northeast of Thailand. Kratié of the Mekong River was the centre of Land Chenla. Geographically Land Chenla was inland and basically agricultural area. In the Pre- Angkor Cambodia, new economic development could not be expected so much. M. Vickery says that economic activities recorded in the 7th-century inscriptions are agriculture, wet rice, fruit-growing, animal husbandry and crafts such as weaving and leaf-sewing, probably for

3. Chenla and Pre-Angkor Kingdom   97

thatch, and metal works to produce the articles of jewelry sometimes
recorded. (M. Vickery, Toyo. pp27)

M. Vickery is suspicious about the description (division of
Chenla) of the *Xin* (*Jiu*) *Tang* Shu. However, high-ranking Chinese
official unlikely to tell easy lie about such an important matter. The
Xin Tang Shu was compiled under the supervision of Ou Yang Xiu
(歐陽修). The written records on the Chinese annals are mostly
based on the information of the envoys of 'Land Chenla', which had
often sent small tributary missions to Tang. Chenla could not enjoy
the trade advantage of Funan after the victory over Funan. So, the
economic power of Chenla kings did not seem to expand remarkably.
The economic activity of Land Chenla had been dull, so it became
conservative. The separation of Land Chenla from Water Chela
might be the biggest factor for the declining of the Chenla kingdom.
    Land Chenla had continued sending mission to Tang, 10 times
during the 8th century. However, the mission of Wen-dan (文單)
after 753 was by the instruction of Land Chenla or by Wen-dan's
initiative was quite dubious.
    The Srivijaya group regained control over the South India Sea
after 760. Probably the army (navy) of Srivijaya (Sailendra) landed
'Water Chela's territory' south of Cambodia before 770. In 768, new
'Kha-ling (Sailendra)' started sending envoy to Tang, that meant
Srivijaya had recovered hegemony in the South China Sea before
that. The commander of the Srivijaya army which conquered inland
Cambodia was Jayavarman II who left inscription dated 770 at the
Kompong Cham district.

3-3-5　Tributary missions of Chenla
    M. Vickery says the international trade of Funan had declined and
had lost the significance, however Chenla sent missions many times
as following.
    (Chenla to Sui) in 616. (Chenla toTang) in 623, 625, 628 (Chenla

98   THE HISTORY OF SRIVIJAYA, ANGKOR and CHAMPA

with Lin-yi), 635, 651, 682 ,697, 707, 710, 717 (Wen-dan = Land Chenla), 750 (Water Chela?), 753 (Wen-dan), 755 (Wen-dan), (Wen-dan) 767, 771 (Wen-dan), 780 (Chenla), 798 (Wen-dan), 813 (Water Chenla), 814 (Water Chenla).

In the Angkor times, 1116 (Suryavarman II), 1120, 1155 (with Lopburi), 1200 (Jayavarman VII).

Chenla sent the tribute for the first time to Sui in 616. The first mission to Tang was in 623, and after that continued sending mission. In 628. Chenla sent an envoy together with Lin-yi by sea. In 628, Isanavarman asked Lin-yi to send mission to Tang by Lin-yi's ship. The both states visited Tang at the same time, the October 628. At the time Tang's Emperor Tai-zong (太宗) was very delighted and said that Chenla's effort was highly appreciated, coming 'on-land and by sea' and gave large award to Chenla. Especially neighboring states' friendly relation was most favorable for the Tang Dynasty. Chenla apparently had sent mission before through on-land route, using the upper Mekong River and entered Yunan, then to the capital of Tang.

However, Chenla could not use the sea-route anymore, because the activity of Funan's navy became stronger after Funan was exiled from the Mekon Delta around 530. And in 643, Lin-yi appealed to Tai-zong (Tang) to stop Funan's harassment at sea. Lin-yi also feared activity of Funan's navy.

In 750, Chenla sent mission with its tribute 'alive Rhino' which is difficult to transport on-land. This mission might have visited by ship, if so, this 'Chenla' was 'Water Chela' which occupied Chaiya area and temporary gained the freedom of sea-faring from Srivijaya. This is historical guess, but Water Chela might have attacked Chaiya around 745, and got maritime freedom. Who was the king of Water Chela at that time? After Jayadevi, king's name of Water Chenla is unknown. But around 760, the king of Water Chela was beheaded by Srivijaya.

In 813 and 814, Tang recorded that 'Water Chela' missions came, but they were probably 'Angkor mission'. However, Jayavarman II

3. Chenla and Pre-Angkor Kingdom 99

might have been prohibited by Srivijaya to send anymore envoy to Tang. Angkor resumed to send mission after more than 300 years later in 1116 (Angkor, under Suryavarman II), 1120 (Angkor), 1155 (Angkor and Lopburi), 1200 (under Jayavarman VII, Angkor). Suryavarman II had no relation with Srivijaya, so he sent mission freely to Song. After the invasion by Chola (1025), Srivijaya seems to have lost control over the South China sea.

The *Jiu Tang Shu* (舊唐書) writes about Water Chenla;

"Water Chenla occupied the flourishing area of south.; The border, east-west-south-north 800 li (320km), east faces Panduranga (Phan Rang), west faces Dvaravati, south faces sea and north faces Land Chenla. The capital is called Baladityapura (婆羅提跋)".

The location of 'Baladityapura' is not identified yet. C. Jacques says it was Purandarapura and M. Vickery says it was City of Indrapura. Then where was Indrapura? Judging from inscription (k.105 and k.325), it is said that 'Banteay Prei Nokor' south of Kompong Cham, might be the most suitable place.

3-4 THE END OF PRE-ANGKOR (CHENLA)

After the death of Jayavarman I in 680-681, the throne was succeeded by his son-in-law Nripaditya. But he could not govern the kingdom, so Jayavarman's daughter Jayadevi became the queen of the kingdom. Her inscription dated 713 was left in the Angkor area, and her title was '*vrah kamuratan an*' which meant the Khmer royal title and her inscription exists at 'Ak Yom', western end of West Baray.

Queen Jayadevi governed the Water Chela, and she seems so far respected by local chiefs. But she could not maintain the national

100   THE HISTORY OF SRIVIJAYA, ANGKOR and CHAMPA

unity, and her dominion was said to be limited around Aninditapura (exact location unspecified), and stayed in the area. In the 8th century no central government existed. But Water Chela maintained strong power in the southern half of the Cambodia. Water Chela, as above mentioned, probably had some navy to attack Srivijaya around 745 and temporarily occupied Chaiya for nearly 20 years.

If Water Chela had sent the mission to Tang in 750. Water Chela should have attacked Chaiya area in the 740s, and they had succeeded to occupy Chaiya, the capital of Srivijaya. In 750, 'Chenla' presented 'alive rehinoceros' which could be transported by sea. Only Water Chela could do such invasion, which had enough strong navy force to attack the headquarters of Srivijaya. Within 20 years, the Srivijaya group, main force was the Sailendra navy (led by king Panagkaran) of Jawa, counter attacked the Water Chela army at Chaiya, and destroyed the army of Chenla completely. Furthermore, the main force of Srivijaya's navy advanced further to the Mekong River area and occupied the main ports of Water Chela and probably the capital of Land Chenla, Kratie was also occupied in the early 760s. At that time pre-Angkor Chenla was destroyed basically. The inland of Cambodia was still not attacked, so at the end of 760s, Srivijaya deployed troops led by the commander Jayavarman II, whose troops conquered the remaining area.

The remaining forces of Chenla were divided locally and which had been defeated one by one by Jayavaramn II.

About this revenge war, no record was left, but the Ligor inscription dated in 775, suggests the fatal victory of Srivijaya over Chenla, at the same time why Srivijaya stopped sending tributary mission after 742 could be explained.

According to Briggs, when Chenla attacked Baladityapura area (Funan) in the middle of the 6th century, then Aninditapura rulers first surrendered to Chenla. The rulers of this region, came from the blood line of Kaundinya-Soma (柳葉), in other words they are blood group of traditional Funan line. Of course, it is dubious, but they

3. Chenla and Pre-Angkor Kingdom

wanted to say they were different from Chenla group. However, they had been probably not included in the main family of Funan and stayed in the neutral position.

The *Xin Tang Shu* says the capital of Water Chela was 'Baladeva (婆羅提拔)', so it might be 'Baladityapura.' Originally, there was King Baladitya in the past. But the location of 'Baladityapura' is not identified. C. Jacques says it may be Purandarapura where is also, unclear. M. Vickery suggests it might be Indrapura. (M. Vickery, Toyo, p355). But Indrapura's location is also unidentified exactly. Inscription K.105 and K.325 tell us it is in the South of Kompong Cham, Nokor (Banteay Prei Nokor). In the 7-10th centuries, Indrapura might have been from Kompong Cham to Kompong Thom area, (M. Vickery, Toyo, p356).

However, after long time, Indrapura might be narrowed, and Kompong Cham was the major city in the South. Perhaps King Jayavarman I had put his capital there.

Water Chela's territory was the lower basin of the Mekong River, which leads to the Tonle Sap Lake area. It was in the heart of the economy of later 'Angkor'.

'Land Chenla' had the two big cities along the Mekong River, Sambor (Sambhupura) and Kratié, however economic activity was dull.

Briggs says: "At first, Sambhupura may have included the Khmer settlements beyond the mouth of the Se Mun (Mun River), including what later became Upper (Land) Chenla in what is believed to have been the vassal state of Bhavapura. The first ruler of Sambhupura mentioned in the inscriptions is a female, presumed a daughter of the supposititious Sambhuvarman. This daughter married Pushakaraksha, son of Nripatindravarman of Aninditapura, and he thus became king of Sambhupura." (Briggs, p58)

However, M. Vickery completely denies this story. He says that stories related Pushakaraksha is all Cœdès fiction. (M. Vickery,

102   THE HISTORY OF SRIVIJAYA, ANGKOR and CHAMPA

Cœdès ' Histories of Cambodia, p18, 2-7 reference). His point is important when we study the history of the Chenla Kingdom.

Why Chenla became weak within 200 years? The first reason is that Chenla had failed to develop its economy. Chenla could not increase the agricultural production so much, especially rice. The second reason is Chenla failed to take over the international trade benefit from Funan. The third reason was that Chenla was divided politically by local chiefs, who had no idea of the integrity of Chenla.

3-5 Theoretical Problems of Michael Vickery

3-5-1   Michael Vickery criticizes Cœdès
Here I must check the theory of Dr. Michael Vickery. He acquired Ph.D. at Yale University in the United States. He spent most of his time in Southeast Asia, had lived mainly in Cambodia, and passed away 29 June 2017 at Battambang, West of Cambodia. He has published many excellent papers and books on Khmer and Champa. Many of M. Vickery's works are in his blog, but unfortunately in his main work "Society, Economics and Politics in Pre-Angkor Cambodia: The 7th-8th Centuries. Centre for East Asian Cultural Studies for UNESCO, The Toyo Bunko, Tokyo 1998". (Toyo Bunko published) is excluded.

M. Vickery pointed out many of misunderstanding and exaggeration of Cœdès in the Southeast Asian history. M. Vickery clarified many important points, but many historians seem to ignore him unfortunately.

In the following, M. Vickery tries to clarify the misunderstanding and inadequate methodology of Cœdès. One of the papers are housed in a collection of his blog, which is "Cœdès ' Histories of Cambodia" in Silpakorn University International Journal (Bangkok) Volume1, January-June 2000, p61-108.

Many historians insist that "The Indianized States of Southeast Asia" 1968 Edition (The original France language) should be called as the 'masterpiece of Cœdès'.

Cœdès has many followers, and one of them is American scholar O. W. Wolters. He says that no course on earlier Southeast Asia history should be taught anywhere for foreseeable time without frequent reference to Cœdès' book .

In addition, renowned as an authority on the history of the Thailand, David K. Wyatt even says the similar tone. He says that Cœdès is 'standard textbook' required reading for the student to learn the history of Southeast Asia.

In fact, Cœdès' books had been treated as both scholars say the 'world standard'. But I read them often and know they contain many terrible mistakes as M. Vickery says. Especially in the theory of Srivijaya, Cœdès wrote a lot of mistakes and lies from the beginning. Wyatt was a Cornell University professor of Thai history, and Wolters was a specialist of history of Indonesia (early Indonesian commerce) and Srivijaya history etc. In Wolters' books on the phenomena of ancient Indonesia seemed to be without written firm evidence.

I have written these basic mistakes of Cœdès in my book "The History of Srivijaya", Tokyo, Mekong Publishing Co., 2012.

M. Vickery suggests you should read the Cœdès carefully and not swallow the ridiculous things. I also think the books of Cœdès should be read carefully because there are several 'land mines' which are hidden in various places, full of danger. Where hidden lies and mistakes, the amateur cannot find them out easily. M. Vickery says that Cœdès, in his books, did not write as a scientist. These books are not high-standard scholarship. They are intellectual entertainment for well-read 'dilettante'. They are monuments to uncritical synthesization, some of which belongs in historical

104   THE HISTORY OF SRIVIJAYA, ANGKOR and CHAMPA

romance, not in history ".

M. Vickery adds "Cœdès a great synthesizer-indeed that may have been his greatest talent when functioning as writer of historic accounts; and he had to find, or imagine a connection every detail and some other detail in another time or place " and Cœdès is like the history narrative authors rolling up stories, to the trivial fact of it here and there without thinking of time.

Certainly, on Palembang, in the Kedukan Bukit Inscription, Cœdès found the word Srivijaya. But Cœdès decided Palembang was Srivijaya itself. However, Palembang is Palembang, one of subordinate states of Srivijaya.

Cœdès had found out Srivijaya was Shi-li-fo-shi. Shi-li-fo-shi （室利佛逝） in the Chinese text was difficult how to read, but it is certainly Srivijaya. Even, Dr. Takakusu could not read it, and he wrote as 'Sri Bhoga'.

After finding the word 'Srivijaya', he derailed from the real history of Srivijaya. He misunderstood ' Palembang was the capital of Srivijaya and the newly assigned king Jayanasa was the Maharaja of Srivijaya.' In fact, Palembang was newly 'occupied by Srivijaya' and became one of the subordinate states of Srivijaya since 683. The Kedukan Bukit Inscription is a 'vitory momument' in nature, and not the monument of the founding 'Srivijaya kingdom'. Srivijaya had already sent the first mission to Tang, between 670-673.

The Kedukan Bukit inscription at Palembang should have been considered more carefully by scholars. This inscription is basically the 'victory monument of the Srivijayan army' against the local kingdom. However, Cœdès jumped to the conclusion that in 683, the 'Srivijaya kingdom was established at Palembang'. Actually, the army of Srivijaya invaded Palembang from the Malay Peninsula with big navy force, and they were like modern 'marine' and the crew fought on land. Their number was recorded as 1.312 persons.

Cœdès had made grave mistake from the very beginning and the

3. Chenla and Pre-Angkor Kingdom 105

Srivijaya history had been distorted to the terrible direction. After him most historians have followed the Palembang theory, so they could not have explained what had happened in this area properly.

The *Xin Tang Shu* (new history of Tang,) says that Srivijaya had 14 subordinate states and the west of Shi-li-fo-shi is Lang-po-lo-si (郎婆露斯), the Nicobar Islands. So, the location of Srivijaya is on the Malay Peninsula, not Sumatra. This is the firm fact.

Cœdès decided the king of Palembang, Jayanasa as the Maharaja of Srivijaya group. But Jayanasa was Dapunta Hyang, and the commander of Srivijaya troops which attacked the Southeast Sumatra Island.

The first tributary of Srivijaya to China was recorded as 'between 670-673', however when Yi Jing left Kanton in 671, he already knew 'Shi-li-fo-shi'. So, the ambassador of Shu-li-fo-shi came to Chaina in 670. But Cœdès says the first tribute of Srivijaya was in 695. This year is the Tang court decided to provide food for the returning tributary missions. In fact, Shi-li-fo-shi had not visited China in 695. This is only a simple fiction of Cœdès. Cœdès thought Shi-li-fo-shi had been established in 683 (the Kedukan Bukit Inscription) so, Shi-li-fo-shi should have sent an envoy later than that. So Cœdès decided, the first Shi-li-fo-shi mission was in 695. There is no evidence at all to support the fabrication of Cœdès, but it is simple contradiction. He should have read the original Chinese text first.

No historian in the world has pointed out this kind of apparent misunderstanding (or lie) of Cœdès. At least Japanese historians can read Chinese text directly, so they should have noticed the distortion of Cœdès.

M. Vickery appreciated the capability of Cœdès as reader of the ancient inscriptions. However, M. Vickery criticizes Cœdès' method to make his historical framework and unscientific understanding of the history. Cœdès often did not respect the historical facts and neglected historical scientific analysis. M. Vickery says that his book should be called 'novel'.

After reading the analysis of M. Vickery, many complicated facts are well clarified.

It goes without saying that Cambodia's ancient history researchers should make more research on many aspects. Many of them also depend upon the hypotheses of Cœdès. History of Cambodia should be paid more attention to the relation with Srivijaya, especially about the Angkor Dynasty.

We also need go beyond M. Vickery's view about the history of Khmer. M. Vickery's book features, lots of new things revealed from the inscriptions.

The aspect of the inner economy of Chenla regime is not so clear. About land ownership of paddy field, farmers seem they had only cultivation rights. The land ownership belonged to temples and local chiefs. There are many inscriptions concerning about donations of land.

No money as a medium of daily exchange, was used. As the exchange-tools, silver bullion and clothing and rice were frequently used. Basically, barter trade was practiced for daily life. Without international trade, money system was not necessary.

Inadequate formation of centralized government did not have a common currency, and the underdeveloped commodity economy need not currency. However, under the Funan regime, some amount of coins prevailed, because Funan traded internationally they needed money. The coins became the measure of value, and in the medium of trade. It is not, however, a barter economy in the domestic rural areas, people seldom used these coins.

M. Vickery's achievement in the decipherment of the ancient Khmer inscription, and correcting predecessors such as Cœdès' mistranslation or misunderstanding must be highly evaluated first. But he also has some serious misconceptions. The main points are described below.

3-5-2　Michael Vickery's misunderstanding

M. Vickery also made misunderstanding that Chenla had not stretched forces in the territory of Funan and merged Funan. The reason is Funan had lost economic power due to the decline of foreign trade, and Funan surrendered to the Chenla naturally and was absorbed peacefully and was not annexed by the armed forces of Chenla.

This is a serious misunderstanding. If so, Chenla had not tried desperately to send the tributary mission to China after integration of Funan. Moreover, Chenla developed the land routes to send mission because Funan intercepted by naval force the sea route of Chenla.

M. Vickery ignores the importance of Funan's foreign trade. However, from the beginning of domination, Chenla's tributary trade-oriented policy is clear. But for Chenla it was unexpected that Funan fled with navy and increased the navy force in the Gulf of Thailand and the South Sea. Therefore, unavoidably Chenla had to develop the land route from the upper Mekong River to Yunnan province. Tribute by land was responsible for the small subordinate state 'Wen-dan（文單）', which is supposed Vientiane, Laos.

Also, Chenla tried to use the trade ship of Lin-yi to multiply the tribute by the sea. In 628, Chenla（King Isanavarman）sent mission to the Tang Court with Lin-yi as above mentioned.

However such a method had not lasted long after the death of Isanavarman, and there happened the political confusion in the Lin-yi side.

M. Vickery understands Cham is 'Java'. Certainly, the Cham tribe is a family of Austronesian languages and Cham tribe is skillful in sailing.

The problem here is in 802, Jayavarman II had declared

108   THE HISTORY OF SRIVIJAYA, ANGKOR and CHAMPA

independence from 'Java', according to the SKT inscription. Cœdès believed Funan fled away to the Jawa Island and here M. Vickery believes this 'Java' is Champa. Unfortunately, Cœdès and M. Vickery are both wrong. There is no inscription in Champa that Jayavarman II amassed huge troops to invade Chenla. In this case 'Java' should be regarded as Srivijaya located in the Malay Peninsula, Chaiya or Nakhon Si Thammarate (as the military base).

King Jayavarman II was probably born in the royal family of the Srivijaya in Chaiya area where he grew up. Jayavarman II's background of parents and ancestors are not known, but M. Vickery says Jayendra-dhipativarman is his relative on his mother side, but the name of Jayavarman II's parent is unknown.

Angkor had not sent the tribute mission to China from 814 until 1116 for 300 years. It is mystery why Angkor had not sent tribute to China for long time. M. Vickery should have noticed this fact.

M. Vickery had no notion of Srivijaya, especially the relation with Funan and Srivijaya. So, his understanding of Sailendra is too simple that Sailendra was a native kingdom of the Jawa Island. So, he did not understand the development of Srivijaya at all and the meaning of the Ligor inscription. He looked like a follower of Cœdès in this point.

3-6 SUMMARY OF THE HISTORY OF CHENLA

After the death of Jayavarman I in 681, Chenla significantly lost its political power. The unity of Chenla had collapsed in the early 8th century. According to the Chinese chronicles (the *Xin Tang Shu*), Chenla was divided between Water Chenla (south) and Land Chenla (north). From the economic point of view Water Chela was more active and prosperous than Land Chenla.

The Chenla kingdom had centralized system in the early stage, they improved the economic situation a little, but could not enjoy the

3. Chenla and Pre-Angkor Kingdom 109

profit of the international trade. On the other hand, the local chiefs enjoyed autonomy and increased wealth and power, as the result the central government could not control them. The central government had lost the authority to control local chiefs.

The politics of the central authority of Sivaism could not control and influence people's mind.

Siva faith is ultimately King's religion and did not get the support of farmers who had experienced Mahayana Buddhism in the Funan regime.

Rulers of Funan went into exile to the Ban-Ban state and unified the central Malay Peninsula. Finally, before in 670 they established Shi-li-fo-shi (Srivijaya), which had the strong economic power to monopolize the tributary mission of the Malay Peninsula to the Tang dynasty.

In 680s, they put 'Melayu' in front of Singapore, Jambi, Palembang under control, and finally in 686, Srivijaya conquered Kha-ling (訶 陵, Sanjaya) in the central Jawa. As the result Srivijaya completely controlled the sea-lane of the Malacca Straits. So, Chenla was blocked from the trade with west countries. Srivijaya had monopolized purchasing the west goods at the Malacca Straits.

Probably Water Chenla invaded the Chaiya district around 745, but the Srivijaya group (mainly Sailendra navy) counter attacked around 760. The war between Funan and Chenla was moved to the sea and the Sailendra navy (Srivijaya army) overwhelmed Chenla finally at the Bay of Bandon and further Chenla lost the river side ports of the Mekong River. As the result, Water Chenla was occupied by Srivijaya and Jayavarman II, the commander of Srivijaya force landed at Kompong Cham area before 770. He overwhelmed Chenla finally and intergrated Chenla before 802.

Lin-yi (Champa) was probably attacked by the Sailendra navy, but escaped the occupation. However, Lin-yi had stopped sending

110   THE HISTORY OF SRIVIJAYA, ANGKOR and CHAMPA

the tribute mission after 749. Perhaps, Sailendra had destroyed the shipping facilities of Lin-yi around 760. The collapse of Water Chenla and Lin-yi occurred almost at the same time.

Jayavarman II was dispatched from Srivijaya as the commander, and almost 30 years later he pretended to achieve the full independence from 'Java' and wiped out the old Chenla power from Cambodia. However, the relation between Srivijaya and Angkor had not changed for 300 years.

Chenla had been economically confined within simple reproduction of rice and could not find the source of wealth in the international trade. Chenla rulers prohibited Mahayana Buddhism to the common people, while Sivaism was enforced. The religious restriction by the Chenla kings accelerated the spiritual division between the rulers and farmers.

3. Chenla and Pre-Angkor Kingdom

Table1. Chenla Kings

	King names	Reign	
1	Bhavavarman I	550-600 ?	Son of Virvavarman
2	Citrasena	600-611 ?	Bhavavarman's younger brother, Mahendravarman, His father is Virvavarman
3	Isanavarman	611 ? -635?	Isanavarman had been strategic ruler who integrated Khmer kingdom and wiped out Funan completely from Cambodia.
4	Bhavavarman II	635 ? -655 / 7	Isanavarman's youngest son.
5	Jayavarman I	655/7-681 ?	Spread the Chenla territory widest.
6	Queen Jayadevi	681-713	Jayavarman I's daughter. Mourn the disunity of Chenla. Her successors are unknown.
	Samnhuvarman	713-716	The following is not a King of united Chenla, (Wikipedia)
	Pushkaraksha	716-730	
	Samhuvarman	730-760	Killed by Sailendra?
	Rajendravarman I	760-780	Was the ruler of the coastal regions? (Briggs p105)
	Mahipativarman	780-788	Son of Rajendravarman

CHAPTER
4
ANGKOR DYNASTY

4-1 SRIVIJAYA GROUP PROCEEDED TO CAMBODIA

Cœdès mentioned that Jayavarman II (the first king of Angkor) returned from the Jawa Island when 'Sailendra declined'. But his story is most unlikely, because around 770, Sailendra was the sun-rising country. Why he made such an explanation is mysterious.

In 768 the 'latter (new) Kha-ling (Sailendra)' after 100 years' interval, resumed tribute to Tang, Sailendra used the name of Kha-ling (訶陵)which was the original name of conquered Sanjaya of the central Jawa kingdom. Why Sailendra used the former name of 'Kha-ling', it was because Sailendra wanted to hide the fact that Srivijaya had conquered Sanjaya kingdom in 686. The reason is that the Tang Dynasty had strictly prohibited the conflict and war among its subordinate states. Therefore, Sailendra had to use the name of 'Kha-ling' for the tribute missions to Tang.

About Jayavarman II, a British archaeologist Quaritch Wales in his book "Towards Angkor 1937, p221)" said as following:

"'This great king (Jayavarman II) had ruled for sixty-seven years (actual official period on the throne was 32 years: 802-834,) from the time when, in his extreme youth, he was sent by the King of the Mountain to occupy the Khmer throne."

' The King of the Mountain ' means without doubt the Maharaja of Srivijaya (at that time Sailendra Panangkaran or his predecessor Dharmasetu). The Srivijaya group probably wanted to retake the old

114   THE HISTORY OF SRIVIJAYA, ANGKOR and CHAMPA

Funan places.

I agree with Q. Wales. However, most scholars ignore this fact. C. Jacques and M. Vickery say nothing about this theory. Former Pre-Angkor (Chenla) and the Angkor (after Jayavarman II) Dynasty were clearly different, considering the wide spread of Mahayana Buddhism and big irrigation reservoir construction in the Angkor times. And most historians do not touch the problem that Angkor had not sent the tribute missions to China for nearly 300 years (814-1116).

In the past, Srivijaya adopted the 'marines' (navy soldiers) tactics for war. For instance, in 683 Dapunta Hyang used navy to occupy Palembang, and left there the victory monument called the 'Keducan Bukit' inscription dated 683. Dapunta Hyang was later appointed to the king of Palembang (King Jayanasa). He was a Mahayana Buddhist with tantrism, who left the 'Talang Tuwo' inscription dated in 684. Mahayana Buddhism was the main religion of Srivijaya group. In 686, Dapunta Selendra (Sailendra) attacked Kha-ling (the central Jawa) with huge fleet. Around 760, Srivijaya occupied the major ports of Chenla with the navy of Sailendra. The commander was probably King Panangkaran of Sailendra. Few years later Jayavarman II was sent to Cambodia to conquer the whole Cambodia, and in 802 declared 'independence from 'Java'. But, he did not really achieve independence from Srivijaya. He just pretended independence for the Chenla chiefs and people.

Since the declaration of Jayavarman II's throne of Kambu in 802, the Angkor Dynasty had officially started. It lasted until the middle of the 15th century.

The most remarkable matter is that the Angkor Dynasty had ceased sending the tributary mission to China during 814 until 1116 for nearly 300 years. Another problem is Angkor itself had no strong navy. So, the Angkor kings could not have ignored Srivjaya's instruction until Suryavarman II. This means Angkor had given up foreign trade. On the other hand, Angkor had started giant

4. Angkor Dynasty 115

irrigation projects. That means Angkor government had strategy to increase the production of rice more efficiently. The rulers might have economic philosophy that farmers and vast paddy fields are the resources of wealth.

Jayavarman II made up the grand design of the Angkor Kingdom's development while he had stayed at Phnom Kulen. Jayavarman II probably had stayed Phnom Kulen for nearly 20 years, because recently, the ruins of a big ancient city were discovered at the foot of Phnom Kulen, now covered with jangle. Judging from this huge ruin of the city, Kulen must have had longer history than we suppose today.

The first, most striking different point of the Angkor Dynasty from the Chenla (pre-Angkor) Dynasty is the production method of the wet-rice. Angkor increased rice production drastically with the construction of the big irrigation system reservoir (Baray). By Baray, the Khmer farmer could plant wet-rice in the dry season.

The Second point is the expansion of Mahayana Buddhism. The economic life of the farmers, too, seems to have improved rapidly with the development of irrigation system. There was an effect to make the inner life of the farmers to be stable with the worship of Mahayana Buddhism. Basically, Sivaism is the religion of kings and rulers, and had nothing to do with farmers. Mahayana Buddhism is the religion of the common people. Through Mahayana Buddhism, the communication between rulers and farmers became easier and frequent.

The third point is the construction of numerous giant stone temples and castles, such as Angkor Wat, Bayon, Phimai, etc. The rulers had accumulated huge wealth, and they spent wealth on the construction of huge temples and palaces.

For the Angkor kingdom, the tributary mission to China had been prohibited by Srivijaya, and the outer economic development of the Angkor Dynasty was limited. As the result, the development of

116   THE HISTORY OF SRIVIJAYA, ANGKOR and CHAMPA

Angkor was in a sense, of 'inward' tendency, even though Angkor wanted to expand its influence in Champa and some kings invaded Laos and Yun-nan.

4-2 JAYAVARMAN II

Jayavarman II was the first king of the Angkor Dynasty.

Jayavarman II had left very few inscriptions and had not been recorded by the Chinese chronicles so we have little evidence about him. Only the Sdok Kak Thom inscription (SKT = K235) dated 1053 in the reign of Udayādityavarman II, tells us his history however it was made nearly 200 years later after his death. M. Vickery says the SKT inscription is fictitious. However, this inscription gives a list of royal succession from Jayavarman II to Udayadityavarman II and all the names of the high priests of tutelary deities of Kambuja with a catalog of pious work, religious foundation and so on (Sharan, p256).

The SKT inscription recounts that on the top of the Kulen mountain, Jayavarman II instructed Brahman, Hiranhadama to conduct a religious ceremony as the cult of the 'Devaraja' which placed him as a 'Chakravatin', universal monarch. In 802, he declared independence from 'Java.' But no other inscription was left to record this event.

Jayavarman II is said to have returned from 'Java' around 770, but not sure and his exact age was unknown, but he left his inscription dated in 770 at Kompong Cham and in 781 at Kratie. Another inscription of the early 10th century is recently found at Tbang Khmum, Kompong Cham. On which Yasovarman left his name in the lineage of Yasovarman's family. (below, Prof. T.S. Maxwell translated 8th May 2014).

'Java', in this case means the Malay Peninsula (Srivijaya), probably Chaiya area, and not the 'Jawa Island'. Jayavarman II died in 834, so he must have landed at early 20 years old.

4. Angkor Dynasty   117

Moreover, he could not have 'returned' alone, because he had started conquering the whole Cambodia. Without doubt he had been supported by Sailendra (Srivijaya) army. That means he was probably a member of royal family of Srivijaya and was assigned the commander of Srivijaya (Sailendra) army.

Jayavarman II had left no inscription of these incidents for nearly 200 years, so probably he had little local roots and back ground, and had come from outside of Cambodia. He probably came from 'Java', but it meant the Malay Peninsula. However, he seems to have some connection with Aninditapura family, because he got staunch support from them. Jayavarman II picked up two young generals, Sivakaivalya and Sivavinduka brothers as the leaders of army. The sister of them, Svamini Hyang Amrita became his wife, who were from Aninditapura family, but major troops were from Srivijaya (Sailendra). Rudravarman (not the king of Funan), who worked at Roluos with Jayavarman II was a member of Aninditapura family and a remote relative of Jayavarman II. However, the names of Jayavarman's parents are unknown.

In the past Srivijaya had assigned as the commanders of invading force from their royal families, for instance 'Dapunta Hyang ' in case of Palembang and ' Dapunta Selendra' in case of Pekalongan (the central Jawa).

Before invading Cambodia, as mentioned above, several important events happened in this region, but almost everything is not recorded and left as 'missing link'.

After the victory of the Chaiya area against the invader from Water Chenla around 760, the Srivijaya (Sailendra) navy had proceeded to the Mekong River and killed a Chenla king. Srivijaya sent back his skull to the prince of Chenla. The similar story is written by Sulaiman as quoted its translation by Q. Wales ("Towards Angkor", p175-178):

"An Arab merchant, Sulaiman by name, who travelled

118   THE HISTORY OF SRIVIJAYA, ANGKOR and CHAMPA

through the empire of Zabag (Srivijaya) around 851, has handed down to us the following account which tells us exactly how the matter came out, and is of such lively interest that I shall quote it below. In this case the Cambodian king brought the trouble upon himself, though one can well imagine that the King of the Mountain, or Maharaja as he is termed by the Arab writer, was not averse to taking advantage of the opportunity offered. As we know from other sources, these events took place in the last half of the eighth century, following quickly on Sailendra's southern conquests."

"They say that formerly there was a Khmer king who was young and rash. One day he was sitting in his palace which overlooked a river resembling the Tigris (from the palace to the sea the distance was a day's journey), and his minister was with him. He was discussing with his minister the grandeur of the kingdom of the Maharaja of Zabag and of its immense population, and of the enormous number of islands which it comprised. "I have a desire, said the king, that I should like to satisfy." The minister, who was sincerely devoted to his sovereign, and who knew with what rashness he often made up his mind, replied, "What is your Majesty's desire?" The latter answered, "I wish to see the head of the Maharaja, King of Zabag and before me on a plate." The minister understood that it was jealousy that had suggested this to his sovereign, and said, "I do not like it, your Majesty, to hear my sovereign express such a desire. The peoples of Cambodia and Zabag have as yet shown each other no hatred, and Zabag has done us no harm. It is a distant land, and its king has shown no wish to attack us. No one must hear about this desire, and it must never be repeated.

The Khmer king was angry with his minister, and ignoring the advice of his wise and loyal counsellor, repeated the proposal before the generals and courtiers who were present.

4. Angkor Dynasty   119

The idea spread from mouth to mouth, until it reached the knowledge of the Maharaja of Zabag himself. The latter was energetic and experienced monarch, who had then reached a mature age. He called his minister and informed him of what he had heard, adding, "After the proposal that the foolish Khmer king has made in public concerning a desire which is born of his youth, I must take steps in the matter. To take no notice of these insults would be no humble myself before him. The King ordered his minister to keep this conversation secret, and to go and prepare a thousand ships of moderate size, to equip them. And put on board arms as many valiant troops as possible. To explain the situation, it was given out that the Maharaja intended to make a tour among islands of his kingdom; and he wrote to the governors to warn them of the tour that he was going to make. The news spread everywhere, and the governors of each island prepared to receive the Maharaja.

When the king's orders had been executed and the preparations were finished he embarked, and with his fleet set sail for Cambodia. The Khmer king had no suspicion of what was going on until the Maharaja had arrived at the river which led to the capital and had landed his troops. These invested the capital by surprise, surrounded the palace, and seized the king. The people fled before the invaders. But the Maharaja proclaimed by public criers that he guaranteed the safety of everybody; and then he seated himself on the Khmer king's throne and ordered the captive monarch to be brought before him. He said to the Khmer king, "Why did you formulate a desire which was not in your power to satisfy, which could not have done you any good if it had been satisfied, and which would not even have been justified if it had been possible?" The Khmer king did not reply, and the Maharaja continued: "You wished to see my head before you on a plate. If you had similarly desired to seize my kingdom or to ravage part of it I should have done the same to Cambodia, but as

120   THE HISTORY OF SRIVIJAYA, ANGKOR and CHAMPA

you only wished to see my head cut off I shall return to my own country without taking anything from Cambodia of value great or small. My victory will serve as a lesson to your successors, so that no one will be tempted in future to undertake a task beyond his powers, or to desire more than fate has in store for him. He then had the Khmer king beheaded, and addressing the Khmer minister, said, "I am going to recompense you for the good that you tried to do as minister, since I know well that you had wisely advised your master. What a pity for him that he did not listen! Now seek somebody who can be a good king after this madman and put him on the throne instead. "

The Maharaja left at once for his own country, and neither he nor his followers took anything away from the Khmer country. When he returned to his own kingdom he seated himself on his throne, which looked over a lake, and he had the Khmer king's head placed before him on a plate. Then he called together the dignitaries of his kingdom. And told them what had happened and why he had undertaken this expedition against the Khmer king. On learning this, the people of Zabag prayed for blessings to be bestowed upon their ruler. The Maharaja then had the Khmer king's head washed and embalmed, and placing it in a vase and had it sent to the new Khmer king, together with a letter to the following effect: "I was obliged to act as I did because of the hatred that the former king manifested against me, and we have chastised him to serve as a lesson to those who might wish to imitate him." When the news of these events reached the kings of India and China the Maharaja rose in their estimation. Since that time the kings of Cambodia every morning turn their faces towards Zabag and bow to the earth to do homage to the Maharaja."

This original script was from G. Ferrand in his work *"L'Empire Sumatranais de Çrivijaya, in Journal Asiatique (1922) "*

4. Angkor Dynasty   121

Selaiman's story does not necessarily coincide with the actual incident. But it is sure that similar rumor was well known among Arab merchants.

My hypotheses are as following; Khmer (Water Chenla) invaded Chaiya, the capital of Srivijaya and occupied there around 745, then the allied army of Srivijaya counter attacked Khmer soon, around 760. The main force was the navy of Sailendra from the central Jawa Island. After the victory of revenge war in the Malay Peninsula, the Srivijaya invaded Cambodia along the Mekong River and killed a king of Water Chenla and occupied some important ports. Then Srivijaya made the strategy to occupy the whole Cambodia and as the commander, young Jayavarman II had been assigned. At that time, he was early 20 years old. He was probably a prince of the royal family of former Funan. He is said to have landed Cambodia around 770. Within less than 20 years, the political map of this region changed drastically. Cambodia was unified again by the Srivijaya group militarily.

4-2-1   Jayavarman II conquered Cambodia

Claude Jacques says in his "Angkor cities and temples, 1997, River Books Co., Ltd" as follows.

"In 790, a young prince became king, taking the name of Jayavarman II. He was a descendant of the great family of Khmer kings whose lineage went back to the princes of Aninditapura. He came from 'Java' where he is assumed to have been 'held prisoner' with his family. It may have lain in the region of present-day Malaysia, but it was probably not the island of Java itself. Jayavarman II assumed power in the kingdom Vyadhapura in the general area of the town now called Prei Veng in south-east Cambodia". (C. Jacques, p61)

122   THE HISTORY OF SRIVIJAYA, ANGKOR and CHAMPA

However, a prince of Aninditapura had no reason to go to Malaysia. Aninditapura family had no reason to be captured by Srivijaya.

M. Vickery says Vyadhapura had included Ba Phnom and its mountain. Vydhapura was important in the Angkor royal genealogies because it was the original chiefdom of Angkor's founder (M. Vickery, Toyo, p398)

Probably he was a prince of the royal family of former Funan. In Cambodia, the Srivijaya (Sailendra) navy may have occupied Vyadhapura (Prei Veng) beforehand and where would become the front base of Srivijaya (Jayavarman II).

C. Jacques continues; "Jayavarman II seized the kingdom of Sambhupura, today's Sambor, south of Kratie. As his capital, he chose Indrapura, present day Banteay Prei Nokor, although not rich in monuments it is marked out by a two and half kilometer-square earth bank, which in fact lies at the presumed frontier between the two kingdoms about 40 km south-east of Kompong Cham town." (C. Jacques, p61)

At first, Srivijaya's strategy was to occupy the major ports of the Mekong River, then Jayavarman II might have proceeded to conquer the whole Cambodia. By using a strong navy, to occupy the ports along the Mekong River was easy job for Jayavarman II. His problem was how to invade the centre of Cambodia, especially the north of the lake Tonle Sap and Battambang area.

C.Jacques considers that pursuing his conquests northwards he reached Wat Phu in the southern Laos, where was a big shrine. He then made his way along the southern part of the Dangrek Ranges and finally took the kingdom of Aninditapura, setting in its capital Hariharalaya somewhere in the region of Roluos. (C. Jacques, p61)

M. Vickery has different thinking that Jayavarman II occupied Bhavarapura first, 30Km from Kompong Thom. Bhavapura used to be the capital of pre-Angkor kingdom before Jayavarman I, which had maintained the political influence among the Chenla group, even though the capital of 'Land Chenla' moved to Kratie and Sambor on the Mekong River. Thereafter Jayavarman II proceeded into the Thonle Sap Lake by fleet of long boats and went westwards to occupy Battambang area and came back to the Angkor area, northern part of the Tonle Sap and settled at Phnom Kulen. He finally moved to Roluos (Hariharalaya) to construct the new capital.

Jayavarman II went to Battambang, like Isanavarman and Jayavarman I, to control that outlet to the Gulf of Siam, and the area was rich rice-growing region. Jayavarman II brought people from Vyadhapura to settle at Amoghapura in Battambang. (M. Vickery, Toyo, p396)

Cœdès says he found a reference to the Siva of Vyadhapura on the mountain in an inscription near Ba Phnom, and concluded Vyadhapura had been the capital of Funan (特牧城、Te-mu) (Cœdès, 1968, p68). M. Vickery adds that Vyadhapura was important in Angkor royal genealogies because it was the original chiefdom of Angkor's founder (M. Vickery,Toyo, p398).

I think the hypothesis of M. Vickery has some reasons, because for a big army, it was difficult to take on land route due to the logistics problem and traffics.

Concerning the origin of Jayavarman II, both scholars are not correct. The reason why Jayavarman II conquered whole Cambodia with big army was not properly explained. Another point is why he could not have sent the tributary mission to Tang after 814, was not explained at all. Both scholars deny the influence of Srivijaya over the Angkor Dynasty.

After Jayavarman II had set up the first military base at Kompong Cham area, he mainly used river and lake for moving his soldiers. He had conquered many small kingdoms and chiefdoms. His principality in Cambodia was to unify them into a single 'Angkor Dynasty'.

It is strange to say the personal history of Jayavarman II is only recorded in the inscription of Sdok Kak Thom (SKT) near Aranyaprathet far from Angkor dated in 1053, more than 200 years

124   THE HISTORY OF SRIVIJAYA, ANGKOR and CHAMPA

after his death.

Other inscriptions of Jayavarman II are dated 770 and 781 which are very simple and nominal.

The inscription dated 770 was discovered at Preah Theat Preah Srei in Tboung Khmum prefecture in the Kompong Cham district and only 'Jayavarman's name is written who funded donation.

If the name of Jayavarman in this inscription meant Jayavarman II, he might have made there the military base, after landing at Kompong Cham. Kompong Cham was economically the most developed area and the territory of Adhyapura family. Probably Jayavarman I also had lived here, but he died nearly one century before.

Sailendra (new Kha-ling) began the tribute in 768. Within 2 years later, Sailenrda (Srivijaya) began to take the military action in Cambodia. Before this action, Srivijaya had already retaken Chaiya area from Water Chenla, and probably proceeded to the Mekong River and occupied some important cities. However, Wen-dan (文 單、Land Chenla's subordinate) had sent tribute in 767 and 769 to the Tang Court. Land Chenla continued sending mission afterwards in 780 and 798. Judging from the tributary record, the northern part of Land Chenla had survived until early 9th century in the northern Dangrek Ranges. Probably Jayavarman II could not have sent army so fast to the northern part, because his main force was navy.

Jayavarman II seems to have arrived at Phnom Kulen much earlier than 802, and constructed his capital there. At Phnom Kulen area he made his capital with many residents. Recently ruins of the big capital city were found by 'aero-razor survey'.

In 802, He made declaration of independence from 'Java'. It is the outline to have become the initiator of the Angkor Dynasty as the world king 'Chacravartin' and he erected a symbol of king, a linga named' Kamaraten jagat ta raja ' as a Sivaite king, meaning 'God King'. The king who has such a title was the first in Cambodia.

All authority was centered on this king, so to speak. This was the declaration of centralization of power. It is certain that the old Chenla rulers in the south of the Dangrek Ranges surrendered to Jayavarman II, but some rulers in the northern area might not be conquered at that time.

Above ceremony is described in the SKT inscription. But this contains some fictitious matters. Jayavarman II behaved as a 'Sivaite' king same as the former Chenla kings. However, Mahayana Buddhism spread rapidly during the early stage of the Angkor time. Had he really declared independence from 'Java' or Srivijaya? Practically, he needed some kinds of political gesture as a 'real Cambodian king' to appease the local people and chieftains.

M. Vickery says the SKT inscription is fiction. At least there may be some distortion and exaggeration of facts. Inscription is usually good evidence, but the SKT inscription was made after 200 years of Jayavarman II's death. There is no other evidence to support the contents of the SKT inscription. Jayavarman II is said to have returned from Java, but where is Java? Cœdès thought he was involved internal power struggle of Chenla, and he had fled to the island of Jawa, then the Sailendra Dynasty 'declined', so he returned to Cambodia. But around 770, Sailendra had just entered the 'golden age' after the victory against Water Chenla. Sailendra started construction of the Borobudur Temple, the world biggest Mahayana Buddhism temple. Cœdès also says that he was only distantly related to the ancient dynasties of pre-Angkorian Cambodia: he was the great-grandnephew through the female line of Pushkaraksha, the prince of Aninditapura who became the king of Sambhupura (Sambor), and Jayavarman II was the nephew of a King Jayendradhipativarman about whom we know nothing. (Cœdès,1968, p97) This story is also doubtful. Nobody knows the parent of Jayavarman II.

The inscription of 'Prasart Kandol Dom (North)' says Indravarman I was the grandson of Jayendradhipativarman, who was the maternal uncle of Jayavarman II. But Briggs doubts the fact. (Briggs, p64)

126   THE HISTORY OF SRIVIJAYA, ANGKOR and CHAMPA

Jayavarman II landed with strong navy, near Kompong Cham at the centre of Water Chenla. Jayavarman II established the first capital of Vydhapura which was occupied by Srivijaya and proceeded to the Land Chenla's capital Kratie slightly north of Sambor, where was governed by a queen. However, Jayavarman II's intention was to conquer the whole Cambodia. C. Jacques said that he attacked and occupied Wat Phu area. However, Wat Phu had not strategic importance at the end of the 8th century. He settled down first 'Banteay Prei Nokor' where was probably the capital of Water Chenla, thereafter he cleared along the Mekong River side such as Kratie and finally went forward to the west.

Jayavarman II had to proceed through the Tonle Sap Lake to the western area, Battambang where he destroyed the strong enemy. Jayavarman II probably used mainly navy, which was traditional force of Srivijaya. The rowers of boats fought in case of battle like 'modern marines'. Land battalions for long-distance march on land had not been appropriate, considering road and climate conditions. Jayavarman II finally occupied the area of Siem Reap (Angkor)

M. Vickery points out that Jayavarman II really came back from 'Java' but this 'Java' was 'Champa'. He says in Cambodia language, 'Java/Chvea and the Cham' is the common. (M. Vickery, Toyo, p29)

M. Vickery's theory is unrealistic in this case. A lonely prince could not have organised a strong army in the neighboring land, and he could not have mobilized a big army to conquer Chenla. Only Srivijaya had strong military force to conquer Chenla.

Q. Wales considers: "Still more important is a Cambodian inscription which tells us that in 802 a king named Jayavarman, who came from 'Java,' ascended the Khmer throne. The use of 'Java' in these inscriptions does not necessarily mean the modern island of Java, but any part of the empire Javaka (mainly the Malay Peninsula), especially its capital." (Q. Wales, 1937, p179) Q. Wales is a rare historian who knew the real meaning of 'Java'.

From the beginning of the (South, Liu) Song Dynasty, 'Java'

4. Angkor Dynasty

(She-po=闍婆) in many cases means the Malay Peninsula. However, many historians often consider 'Java' is simply the Jawa Island. This is the starting point of 'misguided history'.

At Phnom Kulen, Jayavarman II had made up the future strategy how to develop the country. He had decided to move to Hariharajaya, Roluos 15 km the north of the Tonle Sap Lake. Then he started to construct the big irrigation system (Baray), to increase productivity of rice. The big reservoir could supply enough water to the paddy field in the dry season, Roluos became his final capital. His basic economic policy was to increase production of rice as much as possible by constructing the giant irrigation reservoir.

Jayavarman II had to gather many staff for the construction of 'Baray', and his remote relative, Rudravarman from Aninditapura came to Roluos and supported his works. Probably Rudravarman's family had supported Jayavarman II from the beginning.

Hence after the choice of Hariharalaya (Roluos), Jayavarman II designed and constructed the giant irrigation project. That policy was practiced continually by successive kings. It was the basic philosophy of the Angkor Dynasty that farmers' labor was a sole source of wealth, because Angkor could not rely upon the international trade like Funan. Sufficient water was available for the irrigation of Angkor area, and water was supplied by the rivers from Phnom Kulen mountain side.

It should be called 'national projects' of the Angkor Dynasty. Of course, the Pre-Angkor Chenla made irrigation ponds at many places, but all of them were small-scale, so they could not have increased rice production so much and the Pre-Angkor Chenla could not have large centralized political power. On the contrary, many of small local rulers had gained economic and political independence all over Cambodia.

Jayavarman II picked up two young generals, Sivakaivalya and Sivakinduka brothers as the leaders of army from the family member of Aninditapura, to which Rudravarman belonged.

128   THE HISTORY OF SRIVIJAYA, ANGKOR and CHAMPA

The chief of staff, Prithivinarendra said 'burning like fire the enemy troops'. At Malyang (south of Battambang), the resistance might have been strong. Malyang was the nearest place to Chantaburi, port of the Gulf of Thailand, which is nearest port to Chaiya and Nakhon Si Thammarat (Ligor).

After this war, above two brothers were given the conquered lands. (Briggs, p83) Sivakaivalya was given the position of purohita (chief priest) of Devaraja cult later, and his family had maintained its position until 1053 after the death of Suryavarman I. In Cambodia, these priests were supposed to be the mediators between the king and the God. At the same time, they might keep record about what had happened in the court.

About the religion of Funan, according to the *South Ji Shu* (南齊 書), Funan king Kaundinya Jayavarman in 484 sent an envoy Indian Brahman Nagasena to the court , and he explained about the religion of Funan, that people worshiped together with the king, 'Maheshvara (Siva God)'. And the God guaranteed people 'peace and prosperity' so they worshiped the God. The king was considered as divine. His 'ego' or 'will' was preserved and it was not allowed to diminish or extinguish after his death.

The people of Ban-Ban worshiped Buddhism and many Funan staff staying there also accepted Buddhism. So, naturally Buddhism began to spread into Funan and finally Buddhism became the religion of Funan (later Srivijaya). So, the rulers of Funan had knowledge of Buddhism and the number of Buddhists increased rapidly in the middle of the 6th century.

During the Pre-Angkor (Chenla) times, Siva and linga had been worshiped by the kings and their subordinates and people were probably prohibited officially to worship Buddhism as Yi Jing wrote. The Wat Prei Van stone inscription of Jayavarman I dated 687, located in Ba Phnom (probably the oldest Buddhist inscription of Cambodia), mentions about Buddhism. However, the inscription of Buddhism was very rare in the Pre-Angkor Chenla. It appears

4. Angkor Dynasty 129

that during this period Buddhism was subjected to some sort of apathy by the administration (Sharan, p280-281).

However, at the Angkor Dynasty, the attitude for Buddhism changed largely. The Kok Sambhor inscription of the reign of Rajendravarman II (944-968) gives a description of complementary attitude towards the Sangha, Lord Buddha and Buddhism. (Sharan, p281).

Hynayana entered Kambuja after Mahayana. Only one inscription related to Hynayana sect of Buddhism has been found at Lopburi (Thailand). It is dated in the Saka Samvat 944-947 (about 1025 CE), when Suryavarman I was on the throne (Sharan, p282). Hynayana Buddhism believed brought by the Mon people from Burma, Thaton area.

Among the Hindus there had been some cults in Cambodia, which were Sivaism, Vishnuism and Brahmanism. There was a case one sect constructed temples and installed status of gods belonging to other sects. Bhavavarman installed a linga of Siva, he allowed also established the statues of Durga, Sambhu and Vishnu. He granted donations to the shrines of Siva and Vishnu, but Buddhism was rejected. However, among the common people, Buddhism survived in the part of the lower Mekong region, and Mahayana Bodhisattva images dated from this period were often found. (History of Buddhism in Cambodia, Wikipedia.)

Jayavarman II established the cult of 'Devaraja' as the official religion of the Angkor Dynasty. In the Angkor period (802-1432), the Devaraja cult seems to have been the basic religion. It is generally believed to have been introduced in Cambodia by Jayavarman II. It is called 'Kamaraten Jagat ta Raja' in Khmer language. These words were found in the Sdok Kak Thom inscription (SKT=K235) dated 1053. Some scholars point out that the only new thing what Jayavarman II did, was the installation of royal linga whose names are initially associated with the names of the founders. Before him, since the second Kaundinya, it seems the official religion of Funan and

130   THE HISTORY OF SRIVIJAYA, ANGKOR and CHAMPA

Chenla had been the worship of a Sivalinga as 'Maheshvara', which was set up in a temple on a mountain in the capital. Such a mountain was regarded as 'Mt. Meru (sacred mountain)'. Jayavarman II had changed the identity of the king with Siva (Briggs, p90).

When Jayavarman II assumed a king, he became a 'Chackravartin Raja', and he invited a Brahman named Hiranyadama from Bharatavasra (India) for teaching Tantra Vidya to his royal priest Sivakaivalya. In religious terms, the priest Sivakaivalya (Guru = spiritual guide), at the ceremony crowned as 'king'. Sivakayvalya family held the hereditary position of hotar (royal chaplain) and purohita (chief priest) of the Devaraja for two and half centuries, from 802 to 1053. (Briggs, p82). Sivakaivalya family had maintained the top position of the chief priest of Devaraja from the coronation of Jayavarman II (in 802) until the death of Suryavarman I (in 1050). The worship of the newly installed Devaraja will not be performed by any Brahman other than those belonging to the family of descendant of Sivakaivalya. And as per this decision the post of Rajapurohita remained with this family for about 250 years (Sharan, p259).

The family of Sivakaivalya came originally from the sruk (village) of Satagrama in Aninditapura. The kurung (king) of Bhavapura had given them a piece of land in Indrapura and there they had founded the sruk of Bhadrayogi and erected a Sivalinga (Briggs, p82).

Hiranyadama, Brahman skilled in witchcraft (magic technology) came from Jayapada, because Jayavarman II invited him to perform a ceremony that would declare independence from 'Java'. By this ceremony Kambujadesa was said to be free from 'Java' (Srivijaya). Hiranyadama taught Saivakaivalya how to prepare the ritual to create a new Devaraja (King of the earth).

The purohita of the Devaraja was also a hotar; but there were other hotar (Briggs, p90). At the same time, Devaraja has become the established faith and the official religion of the Angkor kingdom. It can be said that the religion is 'the deification of the king'. On the

4. Angkor Dynasty   131

other hand, Mahayana Buddhism as a religion in public widespread, and the adoption to the ruler maintains the connection with the people. Kirttivarman was the minister of Jayavarman II. It was because of him that Buddhism could come out of very troublesome days. Along with the Hindu gods and goddesses, many images of Buddha and Buddhist gods of Mahayana school have been found. The Khmer monuments contain images of the Buddha at various places (Sharan, p283).

However, in a recent study, there is a theory that Jayavarman II ruled the mundane world, but chief priest such as high priest Sivakaivalya (purohita) reigned in the world of God as a God-king.

Jayavarman II was friendly to and sponsored Buddhist officially, throughout his kingdom. Especially Guanyin Bodhisattva (觀音菩薩) was worshiped widely as symbols of Mahayana Buddhism in Cambodia. There might be relation with the religious policy of the rulers of Srivijaya who had faith in Mahayana Buddhism. Ordinary people had been friendly with Mahayana Buddhism since Funan period and Jayavarman II was supporter of Mahayana Buddhism. When Jayavarman II died in 834, he was given posthumous name 'Paramesvara=Siva incarnate or Supreme Lord'.

Anyway, we cannot solve the mystery of history only depending on the Sdok Kak Thom Inscription. The story of Jayavarman II after 200 years without any evidence cannot be exact. The Sdok Kak Thom inscription would have to be interpreted with hidden political purpose. It is unclear how during the previous 200 years they had kept the records. Probably the top priests had kept records about them.

If this inscription was placed at Angkor, it might have been destroyed easily. In the 13th century, Siva fanatic Jayavarman VIII had destroyed many inscriptions of the Buddhists' kings, especially the 'Phimeanakas inscription', and Buddhism images and temples especially Jayavarman VII had built. Jayavarman VIII seems to have had a special hostility to Buddhism and Jayavarman VII.

132   THE HISTORY OF SRIVIJAYA, ANGKOR and CHAMPA

The inscriptions on Jayavarman VII are very rare in Cambodia. Probably they were destroyed by Jayavarman VIII and his followers. If important inscriptions were destroyed, we could not trace the history.

The word 'Kambuja' appeared for the first time in the inscription of Champa, Po Nagar (Po Nagar-Nha Trang City) inscription dated 817 says the Senapati Par ravaged some cities of the Kambuja. But the word 'Kambujalaksimi' (queen of Jayavarman II) was known in the early 9th century.

Jayavarman II's successors called him, 'the guardian of the honor of the 'Solar race (Chenla group)' of Sri Kambu.' Yasovarman called his capital Yasodharapura as Kambupuri (Briggs, p88). Jayavarman II probably had pretended he belonged to the 'Solar race' to hide the origin of his 'Lunar race' (=Funan kingdom). The SKT inscription's Angkor Dynasty history should not be accepted at face value.

Before or at the time of Jayavarman II's war in Cambodia, the Sailendra navy seems to have attacked the southern part of Champa. The Po Nagar Temple Inscription (dated 774) tells us that 'terribly dark, skinny' people attacked, robbed the lingam. Also, the inscription of Pang Hang (dated 787) west of Panduranga Temple tells they were attacked by 'Java.' After these incidents (attack by Srivijaya), Lin-yi stopped the tribute to Tang.

Huan Wang (環王) was another Champa state (different from Lin-yi), which sent the mission to Tang. Two times in 'Wu-di (武德) period (618-622) and in Zheng-Guan period (貞觀＝627-649) and far later in 793.

When the North Song Dynasty (China) started in 960, at the same time Champa (占城) started sending the tributary missions very frequently until 1168. Da Shi (大食, Arab) later joined Champa mission since the beginning of the 11th century.

4. Angkor Dynasty   133

4-2-2 Jayavarman II' s capital of Roluos

Jayavarman II's name is very rarely seen in inscription, however it appeared in an unexpected way. Roluos, Hariharajaya is located 15km away from east of Angkor. There is a temple called Preah Ko (Ko means Nandi, the sacred Bull, Siva's vehicle). The temple consists of 6 towers of which the front row 3 towers from left to right are for Rudravarman (Rudresvara), Jayavarman II (Paramesvara) and Prithivindravarman (Prithivindresvara, father of Indravarman I). In the rear towers, three images of the devi (= Pravati, wife of Siva) represented the wives of three kings, namely Prthivindradevi, mother of Indravarman; Dharanindradevi, wife of Jayavarman II: and the wife of Rudravarman, who was Indravarman's maternal grandmother

The centre tower belongs to Jayavarman II (Paramesvara), but without any inscription. The left one is dedicated for king Rudravarman, who was a father of Indravarman I's mother, but nothing to do with the last king of Funan. The right tower is dedicated for Indravarman's father Prithivindravarman and his wife whose maternal grandfather was king Nripatindravarman. This temple was built by Indravarman 1 (reign; 877-889 years).

4-3 Yasovarman's Inscription of Práḥ Thãt Khtom

(Brief Introduction and Translation by Prof. T. S. Maxwell, Siem Reap, 8th May 2014)

King Yaśovarman I ascended the throne as the paramount ruler of Cambodia in the Śaka year 811 (=889 CE). In that same year, he established numerous āśramas (monasteries) near already-established Hindu temples in the borderlands of his kingdom. These were located particularly across the north, in the south and southeast, and at both ends of the Tonle Sap (in the modern provinces of Banteay Meanchey), Preah Vihear, Prei Veng, Kampot,

134   THE HISTORY OF SRIVIJAYA, ANGKOR and CHAMPA

Siem Reap and Kompong Cham, as well as in the northeast Thailand and the southern Laos. An āśrama was usually attached to a temple, but maintained its own discipline and functioned autonomously under the direction of a superior called the kulādhyakṣa or kulapati, himself a religious ascetic, who lived on the premises. The connection between a temple and āśrama was often mentioned in donors' inscriptions on the temple or on stone slabs (steles).

Yasovarman (889-910) made long inscription (K.0110) at Kompong Cham province the Tboung Khmum district, Preah Theat Prof. T.S. Maxwell made English translation and comment. As follows;

" (1)   There was a descendant of the royal line of Aninditapura called Sri Pushkaraksa (Lotus – Eyed) who obtained the kingship of Sambhupura (Siva's City). Firm in battle, he was the maternal uncle of the maternal uncle of the mother of the king who made his residence on the summit of Mount Mahendra (Kulen = Jayavarman II).

(2)   Rajendravarman (I) was a descendant of the latter's lineage, and had the succession of the great kings of Vyadhapura in his mother's lineage. He combined all the good qualities, and he too obtained the kingship in Sambhupura

(3)   His renown was pure as a clear ray of moonlight. By (Queen) Nrpatinfradevi he had a son, namely King Mahipativarman, who was the foremost of warriors in battle, a Garuda to the serpent kings who were his arrogant enemies.

(4)   Now a twice-born (= Brahmin), Agastya by name, who stemmed from Aryadesa (= India) and knew the Vedas and Vedangas (= the holiest scriptures of orthodox Hinduism), and his noble queen of glittering lineage, celebrated by the famous as Yasomti 'The famous', had a son named Sri-Narendravarman, who was impetuous in battle and the best of kings. That king had a laksmi, as it were, for a daughter, and she was named

4. Angkor Dynasty

Narendralaksmi.

(5) To her and King Rajapativarman-who in battle was a lion against the lordly elephants who were his enemies-was born (the princess) Rajendradevi, who seemed a child of the gods, and whose unblemished renown spread in all directions.

(6) To ensure the generation of a line of lion-like kings, King Mahipativarman fathered on her Queen Indradevi, of unusurped physical beauty and whose fame was pure as the Milk Ocean, just as the sun fathered Tapati.

(7) Then, to Sri-Jayavarman (Jayaraman II), who made his residence on Mount Mahendra and whose feet were honored by the most eminent kings, a son with the splendor of the sun and complete valor was born.

(8) Lord of the earth (mahipati), he was a sovereign by birth, the prompter of fortune and victory, who was called Sri-Jayavardhana, but having assumed kingship he took the name Sri-Jayavarman, and his feet were placed on the heads of great kings.

(9) The younger brother of that paramount king's (=Jayavarman II's) grandmother, [a man] of conquering power, whose only thoughts were Rudra, who performed the feats of Rudra in battle, and whose nature was pure, was called Sri-Rudravarman.

(10) His (=Rudravarman's) nephew (sister's son), like an ocean containing virtues instead of treasures, intelligent and clever at extracting the earth's treasures, just like Prthu ('Far-and-Wide', the mythical king who milked the earth as if it were a cow), and worthy of being praised by the lords of the earth – he as king, was named Sri-Prthivindravarman.

(11) [Meanwhile] the daughter of King Sri-Rudravarman was born like a crescent moon in the sky of this ruling lineage, a virtuous queen, like a maiden of the gods, whose mother was the daughter of Sri-Nrpathindravarman.

(12) They (Sri-Prthivindravarman and Sri-Rudravarman's

136   THE HISTORY OF SRIVIJAYA, ANGKOR and CHAMPA

daughter) had a son-prince who was as a lion against the lordly elephants who were his enemies, worthy of praise by lion-like men and proud was as the Man-Lion himself (incarnation of Vishnu), whose perpetual fame reverberates around horizon-and he, Sri-Indravarman, bore all the world [that is. he became the paramount king] (Indravarman reigned 877-889).

(13) In a building made of stone (=Bakong) he (Sri-Indravarman) established a Linga of Siva named Sri-Indresvara, and six images of Siva and the Goddess all together (in Preah Ko), and he dug the superb lake Sri-Indratataka (the lake of Lolei).

(14) Just as Karttikeya (God of War) was fathered by the Destroyer of Strongholds (purabhida = Siva) on the Daughter the Mountain, so His Majesty Sri-Yasovarman-a mass of fiery energy wielding the spear (like Karttikeya) to destroy the multitudes of his enemies-was fathered by that king whose fame extended in all directions on his chief queen, Sri-Indradevi.The physical birth of the king compared to the divine birth of the war god, again emphasizing Yasovarman's warlike nature. Yasovarman reigned from 889-910."

As above mentioned, Pushkarakusa, of the Aninditapura family, was the maternal uncle of the maternal uncle of the mother of Jayavarman II.

However, M. Vickery says that Jayavarman II's a distant ancestor of Pushkarakusa is too vague and uncertain.

Jayavarman II's grandmother's younger brother was King Rudravarman. Jayavarman II had mobilized many army officers during battle and government officials to promote the big project of a large irrigation pond. Some of major staff were the Rudravarman's people including Indravarman I. Probably Indrvarman I was a chief staff of the project.

M. Vickery, quoting the theory of Dupont, adds above Rajendravarman (not Rajendravarman II), whom the official genealogies list the grandfather of Indradevi, queen of Indravarman I, is said to be a king of Sambhupura, and to have married Nripatindradevi. (M. Vickery, Toyo, p399)

Bgriggs made following explanation about the wives of Jayavarman II;

"Jayavarman II's queen was a niece of Rudravarman, who was ruling Dviradapura near Lovek in the latter part of the 8th century, and according to the inscription of Baksei Changkrong she was the paternal aunt of Indravarman I, who dedicated a funerary tower to her at Preah Ko, under the name of Dharanindradevi.

According to the inscription of Palhal, Jayavarman II seems to have married the Svamini Hyang Amrita, called also Nripendradevi, younger sister of the Sivakaivalya who helped Prithivinarendra to subdue the country. A mutilated stele-inscription says Jayavarman II married Kambujalakshmi, called also Prana. A pillar inscription says his principal queen was Hyang Pavitra of Haripura and from her was descended Sivacarya, purohita of Jayavarman V and Suryavarman I. Another pillar inscription says his wife was Bhas-svamini and that from her was descended Yogisvarapandita, guru of Suryavarman I" (Briggs, p90).

King Jayavarman II's successor is his son, Jayavarman III's name was not directory mentioned in above inscription and temple. He left his name on some other inscriptions. It is something unnatural, because Jayavarman III was supposed on the throne during 834-877. During his reign, the major projects including the construction of the Bakong tower and the big irrigation lake were started. But his name was erased from the history. Probably earlier than 877, he must be killed. The beneficiary was Indravarman, and who ascended the throne of the Angkor Dynasty. Jayavarman III was the first Vaisnavite king (Vishnu) of the Angkor Dynasty, and the

138   THE HISTORY OF SRIVIJAYA, ANGKOR and CHAMPA

second king was Suryavarman II who embraced this sect.

In the Srivijaya group, around 830, the Sailendra kingship (Prince Balaputra) had been expelled from the Jawa Island by Sanjaya family. The control of Srivijaya group was temporarily collapsed during the 2nd half of the 9th century. For instance, the Jambi kingdom sent its own mission to Tang in 852 and 871. But at the end of the 9th century, the Srivijaya group formed the new polity 'San-fo-chi (三佛齊)', which sent its first mission to Tang in 904. During this period around 850-890, the Srivijaya group possibly could not have controlled the Angkor Dynasty.

In the latter half of the 9th century Indravarman family got some degree of independence from Srivijaya. But Indravarman I and Yasovarman could not have dominated everything, because they also could not be entirely free from the influence of Srivijaya. And religious chief Sivakaivalya family also stayed at Angkor. Although Sivakaivalya died at Hariharalaya during the reign of Jayavarman II, he was succeeded by his sister's son, Sukshmavindu who served as purohita of the royal linga during the reign of Jayavarman III (Briggs, p94).

Later Pranavatman, Sikasanti and Kesavabhatta and others succeeded purohita, but the function of purohita was reserved exclusively to the family of Sivakaivalya (Briggs, p95).

Indravarman I succeeded to get throne formally in 877. However, he seems to be a kind of usurper. He ignored Jayavarman III and Buddhism.

Jayavarman III's, inscriptions speak of him as having conquered his enemies and as having ruled his people wisely. Several inscriptions speak of him as a great elephant hunter and he seems to have lost his life in chase of elephants. (Briggs, p97).

But when Jayavarman III was killed? Nothing tells us truth. Indravarman I seems to have been a cousin of Jayavarman III or an inscription of the 10th century says Indravarman I was a nephew of the queen of Jayavarman II (Briggs, p97).

Indravarman I had grasped all the power and led the construction of the Preah Ko which is the mausoleum for his family. He also left his linga at the Bakong Tower. Jayavarman III was a Vishnu devotee and was only given his posthumous name 'Visnuloka.

Even the Yasovarman's inscription (above mentioned) tells nothing about Jayavarman III. Indavarman's family seems to have been indifferent to Buddhism, and they acted as if they were 'Chenla' kings.

Preah Ko was completed in 879, and the Bakong high tower was completed in 881, where Indravarman I set Siva lingam of himself. At his death in 889 Indravarman I received posthumous name Isvaraloka. Indravarman 1 succeeded the construction of giant irrigation reservoir, and during the dry season rice cultivation became possible, to increase rice productivity. This basic policy was also succeeded by Yasovarman, who moved to the Angkor area, Yasodharapura. Yasovarman built his castle at Phnom Bakheng. The central linga of which bore the name of Yasodharesvara. In 889, after a bitter power struggle with his brothers, Yasovarman succeeded throne. His mother was Queen Indradevi who was a descendant of the ancient royal family of Vyadhapura, Sambhupura and Aninditapura. His teacher was Brahman Vamasiva, who belonged to the powerful priestly family assigned by Jayavarman II to the cult of the Devaraja.

The Angkor Dynasty forces expanded into the northeast areas of Thailand (northern Dangrek Ranges). From there Chenla had secured the trade routes to Yunnan province in China. In the north and northeast Thailand, historically the Mons had lived and engaged in commerce, manufacturing and agriculture. They were comparatively rich and developped their own culture (Dvaravati style).

140   THE HISTORY OF SRIVIJAYA, ANGKOR and CHAMPA

4-4 FROM ROLUOS TO ANGKOR DISTRICT

Jayavarman II and his successor Jayavarman III (835-877?) and Indravarman I (877-889) lived at Hariharajaya (Roluos), their capital. They made irrigation agriculture policy and constructed large reservoir, owing to the reservoir during the dry season wet-rice cultivation became possible. This strategy was a growth model for the Angkor Dynasty, constructing giant irrigation facilities. Later Yasovarman I left Roluos and went to Angkor (Siem Reap) area 15 km away to find new irrigation land. From here a new history of the Angkor Dynasty began.

In the same Roluos area, there are Preah Ko and pyramid-shaped pagoda (Bakong) were constructed, and at Lolei in which the island was made in the irrigation pond, on the opposite side of Roluos, which Yasovarman constructed a mausoleum for their ancestors (893, completed). Yasovarman had took over the throne after Indravarman I. It is said also there was a succession struggle among his brothers.

The Bakong Tower, which Jayavarman III had started construction and was completed in 881 after his death. The height of tower is 15m, and this tower assumed 'Mt. Meru', and became a model for many towers of the Angkor times. However, the linga was of Indravarman I. Here also the name of King Jayavarman III was neglected by Indravarman I.

Indravarman I completed the large reservoir for irrigation 'Indratataka', and later the Angkor Dynasty had completed several giant irrigation reservoirs which stocked excess water during the rainy season and in dry season rice was cultivated. Indratataka is 3.8km length and 800m width.

4. Angkor Dynasty

Photo 20: Preah Ko temple (built in 877)

Photo 21: Bakong Tower (built in 881)

142   THE HISTORY OF SRIVIJAYA, ANGKOR and CHAMPA

4-4-1   Yasovarman transferred capital to Angkor

Yasovarman (889-910) moved to his capital named Yasodharapura, 15 km from Hariharajaya, and constructed as his castle Phnom Bakheng at the Angkor capital, which is a Siva temple and palace. He started the agricultural development project (construction of irrigation reservoirs, etc.).

Angkor Wat and Angkor Thom (great city) and its vast irrigation reservoirs were completed later by Suryavarman II (1113 - 1149?) and Jayavarman VII (1181-1218).

On the South side of West Baray, there was the remain of 'AK Yom' (Prasat Ak Yom). This is Cambodia's oldest pyramid-temple, which was constructed by Queen Jayadevi and completed by Jayavarman II. Here is the inscription of Jayadevi who had owned this area, dated in 713. She inherited this area from her father Jayavarman I.

On the top of Phnom Bakheng, there are remains of linga and small towers. At the foot of the stairs of the pyramid there is a Nandi (sacred cow for Siva ride). On the East side of Phnom Bakheng, there is Yasodharatataka of length 7.5 km, width 1.38 km, depth 4-5 m of a huge irrigation reservoir called the 'East Baray'. There is an island in the middle of the pond known as the 'East Mebon' on which there is a temple. The temple is dedicated to Siva, Vishnu and Buddha. He had built many temples in other places, such as the Preah Vihear temple at the border with Thailand. The number of farmers under Yasovarman's reign increased significantly owing to the expansion of the paddy field along irrigation. There were many officials of his administration to support development. Yasovarman had powerful army and expanded territory. But Yasovarman is said to be killed at the battle of Champa or he died of leper, so later no king wanted to inherit his name. 'Yasovarman II' appeared in 1160 but killed in 1165 by his minister. Yasovarman I received the posthumous Sivaite name of 'Paramasivaloka'.

4. Angkor Dynasty

Photo 22-1: Top of Phnom Bakheng

Photo 22-2: Phnom Bakheng Holy Bull (Nandi)

144   THE HISTORY OF SRIVIJAYA, ANGKOR and CHAMPA

After his death, 2 sons Harshavarman I (910-922) and Isanavarman II (922-928) succeeded. Yasovarman I had married a daughter of his maternal uncle.

4-4-2   Jayavarman IV transferred capital to Koh Ker

Jayavarman IV (928-941), who probably had been Isanabarman II's vassal and had, since 921 at the latest, reigned at 'Koh Ker', the capital of a small kingdom some 100km northeast of Angkor. It is not known how the succession came about, but Jayavarman IV was an uncle by marriage of the preceding kings. (C. Jacques, p91). He was a son of Indravarman I's daughter, Mahendradevi.

According to the Baksei Chamkrong inscription Jayavarman IV married a half-sister of Yasovarman. He had to wait for the death of Isanavarman II (928), and took the throne by force. (Bgiggs, p 116).

He had some trouble to live in Yasodharapura, because he was regarded as the 'usurper', then he had moved his capital to Koh Ker with the Devaraja (Chok Gargyar). At Koh Ker, he started construction of a new irrigation pond and temples. (Briggs, p 90). Koh Ker was called 'Lingapura'. He never took care of Buddhism.

From Siem Reap to Koh Ker, with 100 km distance connected inconveniently, but from Koh Ker to Preah Vihear is nearer. Koh Ker is good for defense against enemy from the Mekong River, like Isanapura. He seems to have evaded the influence of Srivijaya.

He developed the culture there, such as Hindu deity images known as Koh Ker style. The scale of the ruins of Koh Ker is considerably immense.

This city might have been planned much earlier and the irrigation facilities have been constructed long before.   According to C. Jacques, Jayavarman IV has a career as a feudal vassal state since 921, as lord of the land of Koh Ker. As an irrigation pond length 1200 m, wide 560 m of the Rahal Baray is small size due to the hard rock. So, at Koh Ker, the further development of irrigation was impossible. Koh Ker was facing dead rock.

Jayavarman IV built here the 7 stories, height 35 m of the pyramid-temple,'Prasat Thom'. Lingam and Devaraja were enshrined at the top. His is given posthumous name 'Paramasivapada'. In the main Meru mountain was assumed as the centre of the world. For the pyramid sandstone was used in abundance. It seems that large volume of iron was used in cutting sandstone.

Iron production in the Northeast Thailand (Isaan) made it possible to cut large volume of sandstone. Professor Eiji Nitta, Kagoshima University made archaeological excavation work at Ban Dong Phlong Ruins, Buriram Province, in the Northeast Thailand. He discovered that since ancient times, iron making and salt making had been very active throughout the northeastern Thailand.

After the death of Jayavarman IV, his son succeeded him as Harshavarman II (941-944), who seems to be forced abdication or killed by his cousin, Rajendravarman II, who moved the capital back to Yasodharapura. Harshavarman II died in 944 and received the posthumous name of Brahmaloka.

Since Indravarman I (877-) to the end of Harshavarman II (-944), Buddhism had been neglected and they behaved like former Chenla kings. Especially Jayavarman IV moved the capital to Koh Ker from Angkor. the Srivijaya group had quietly watched their reigns, but finally might have taken an action.

4-5 RAJENDRAVARMAN II AND JAYAVARMAN V

Rajendravarman II (944-968) is said to be a son of Yasovarman's elder sister (Mahendradevi). M. Vickery says that Mahendradevi's parents are not clear, and added a Khmer inscription indicated that on her mother's side she must have been daughter or granddaughter of Jayavarman III (M. Vickery, 1994, P13). Rajendravarman II succeeded his father King Mahendravarman several years before, decided to help his cousin Harshavarman II to mount and retain the supreme throne. He was not personally entitled to the succession

146   THE HISTORY OF SRIVIJAYA, ANGKOR and CHAMPA

but the struggle for his matrilineal ancestry incited him to seize the supreme throne on the death of his cousin in 944 (C. Jacques, p94). He changed the preceding regime of the 'Hinduist' Angkor Dynasty (877-944) drastically. They were ardent Hinduists (worshipped Siva and Vishnu). He redesigned the Angkor Dynasty. Rajendravarman II was said to be a great admirer of Yasovarman I and shifted his capital to Angkor from Koh Ker. At first Rajendravarman II lived at Bhavaputra, he built a palace in 953 at Angkor. He was considered an intruder and was evidently unwelcome from the outset. Throughout his reign, he had to face numerous rebellions from Khmer chieftains. (C. Jacques, p95).

Briggs wrote about Rajendravarman II as follows;

> "The inscription of Baksei Chamkrong, at the foot of Phnom Bakheng, Angkor, in Sanskrit, dated 946, gives the genealogy of Rajendravarman II (944-968). It mentions first the eponymous ancestor, Kambu Svayambhuva, and the apsaras Mera and their descendants 'who have Srutavavarman for root'. Then comes the race having for chief of branch the King Sri Rudravarman (Funan) drawing their origin from Sri Kaundinya and the daughter of Soma. The first king of the family mentioned, after Rudravarman, was Jayavarman II, who is called 'guardian of the honor of the solar race of Sri Kambu'.

As to Indravarman I, the inscription simply says that he was the son of the maternal uncle of Jayavarman III". (Briggs, p62).

So, Indravarman I's line had not been so strong as the kings of Anggkor Dynasty.

The above descriptions suggested Rajendravarman II had been supported by the Srivijaya group. The regime between Indravarman I and Harshavarman II seems to be somewhat unpleasant for the Srivijaya group. Those kings excessively worshipped Hinduism (Siva and Vishnu) like kings of 'Chenla' and neglected Buddhism,

4. Angkor Dynasty 147

and they behaved as if they were kings of Chenla.

In the inscriptions of Rajendravarman II, the words of Buddhism began to appear;

1) The Bat Chum Inscription (960), dedicates that sanctuary to the Buddha and the Bodhisattva, Vjarapani, and Prajnaparamita.

2) the Mebon Inscription (962) referred to 'burning the city of Champa and his study of the Buddhist doctrine.

Briggs adds: "The inscription of Mebon, in the East Baray of Angkor Thom dated 952, says Rajendravarman II was of the Kaudinya-Soma line and that his mother was a descendant of Sarasvati (niece of Baladitya), and who married a brahman, Visvarupa."

"The Pre Rup inscription (dated 961), says Saravasti was the daughter of the sister of Baladitya, that King Nripatindravarman was a descendant of Sarasvati and King Pushkaraksha was a son of Nripatindravarman and uncle of the uncle of the mother of Jayavarman II" (Briggs, p62).

This inscription wanted to say that Jayavarman II is a remote relative of Aninditapura (Baladitya) family. Despite these inscriptions, the origin of Jayavarman II is still not clear.

At Pre Rup, he restored the nearby temple of Baksei Chamkrong, a Siva temple. At the East Baray he built a small island, called the 'East Mebon' and on which Rajendravarman II built 5 towers over the 3 stories basement. It was dedicated to Yasovarman by his son, King Harshavarman I. The temple was completed by Rajendravarman II.

Rajendravarman II's Buddhist chief minister, and architect Kavindrarimathan made many Buddhist foundations, as well as many works dedicated to Siva, had supervised the construction of the capital and its public buildings.

C. Jacques adds; "There was no linga, but a golden statue called 'Paramesvara' (Jayavarman II) was erected in 947, Wednesday 23 February. From then on the temple was also the seat of the 'spirits' of all previous Khmer kings who are invoked in a splendid inscription

148   THE HISTORY OF SRIVIJAYA, ANGKOR and CHAMPA

which covers the whole of the tower's gate-jambs. Thanks to this inscription we have a clue as to how the Khmers would rewrite their history at the time." (C. Jacques, p94)

In the Angkor area at Phimeanakas he built a new pyramid temple and his palace there. Phimeanakas or the Prasat Phimeanakas is a relatively small temple pyramid, 35 m long and 28 m wide and 12 m high, within the compound of the Royal Palace in Angkor Thom. The construction of Phimeanakas was started by Rajendravarman II, but subsequent kings made alterations to it, especially the long-reigning Suryavarman I. But Jayavarman VII completed it and erected the 'Phimeanakas Inscription'. It is predominantly a laterite structure, with some sandstone elements. There is an inscription on a door jamb, reused from an older temple of a minister of Yasovarman I.

Rajendravarman II attacked Champa in 946, and captured Po Nagar (Nha Trang) from where he took a Golden Goddess (Bhagavati) image. He constructed the Banteay Srei temple with red sand stone near the Phnom Kulen.

M. Vickery says that Rajendravarman II had established the real central government and solid administration system.

After Jayavarman II until Rajendravarman II, all the kings seemed to ignore Buddhism. For instance, 'Koh Ker' is the city of 'Sivaism', without relics of Buddhism. Rajendravarman II made effort to foster Buddhism in Cambodia.

Rajendravarman II died in 968, his son Jayavarman V (968-1000) succeeded his father at the age of 10 years old. His relatives, ministers and scholars supported him. Jayavarman V sometimes ran into battle and threatened Champa. Harshavarman l's grandchildren Yajnyanavaraha and some other people who are familiar with medicine and astrology, an eminent Buddhist scholar undertook teaching of the young King. The most politically influential person was Saptadevakula from Northern India. He was Dr. (Bhatta) and married Jayavarman V's younger sister Indralakshmi. His group

4. Angkor Dynasty

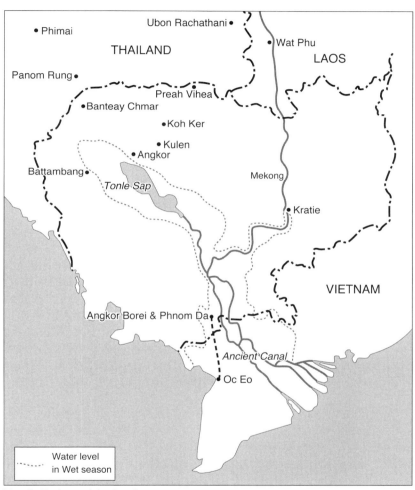

Map 6: Territory of Angkor Dynasty

150   THE HISTORY OF SRIVIJAYA, ANGKOR and CHAMPA

was said to support Suryavarman 1 to take the throne as King of Angkor.

Rajendravarman II studied Buddhism intensely. Although he decided to remain a Sivaist, but he appointed a Buddhist, Kavindrarimathana, as the chief minister. Kavindrarimathana built shrines of Buddha and Siva. Jayavarman V remained a devotee of Siva. However, he permitted his own chief Buddhist minister, Kirrtipandita, to foster Mahayana Buddhism. He imported one hundred thousand texts of Buddhism.

During Rajendravarman II and Jayavarman V reign, Buddhism was raised to a level of Sivaism by dressing Buddha's images in Sivaic forms and its rites performed in the same forms as Sivaism and through Sivaite agencies (Sharan, p229).

Why both most important ministers selected by kings were Buddhists? I think there is a shadow of Srivijaya behind them. When Rajendravarman shifted the capital from Koh Ker to Siem Reap, there might be serious resistance. In Angkor, he faced many enemies against him. He got victory over many enemies, because probably he had strong power, or army. The resource of his army might be support from Srivijaya. After he took the throne, he propagated Mahayana Buddhism, before him all the kings were devotees of Siva and Vishnu, like Chenla kings. Rajendravarman II certainly fulfilled a religious revolution in the Angkor Dynasty.

Rajendravarman II died in 968 in battle with Champa. His posthumous name is Sivaloka. Jayavarman V took the throne immediately. In this year the Banteay Srei with red sandstone near Phnom Kulen was completed, which was called the 'Temple of women'. Also, Jayavarman V started construction of the Preah Vihear temple (completed by Suryavarman 1) near Thai border. He officially worshiped Sivaism, but Mahayana Buddhism became prevailed in his era. The minister of Buddhist Kirtipandita was ordered to spread Buddhism.

4. Angkor Dynasty 151

Photo 23: Banteay Srei

In his time, many scriptures and documents related to Buddhism were imported in vast quantities. Bodhisattva statues were made in large numbers, which housed in many temples. Vishnu worship was also popular to the masses at that time, and enshrined around the temples.

Jayavarman V renovated Phnom Bakheng (Yasovarman built). In nearby there, at Takeo (Angkor) he launched construction of the temple in 975. This is called Hemasringagiri (Golden-toped Mountain) and meant 'Meru Mountain'. He moved his troops to the northeastern part of Thailand, but in his reign Cambodia was mostly at peace. However, after his death, within 10 years, 3 kings took thrones. The last one is Suryavarman I.

152   THE HISTORY OF SRIVIJAYA, ANGKOR and CHAMPA

4-6 SURYAVARMAN I

Jayavarman V had no male heir and Udayadityavarman I succeeded him first for a transient ruler, the next is Jayaviravarman and the third is Suryavarman I (1002-1050) who reigned until 1050. Jayaviravarman was certainly on the throne in 1003. But he is supposed to have reigned during 1002-1006. The inscriptions show there is no definite date on which the name Jayaviravarman ends and that of Suryavarman begins. The geographical distribution of the inscriptions shows that, while Jayaviravarman ruled at Angkor, Suryavarman began in the east and gradually moved toward the capital. (Briggs, p145).

However, there are some inscriptions which mention about Suryavarman I.

1) the Prasat Trapam Run (Kompong Svay) dated saka 924 (or 934).
2) the Tuol Ta Pec (Kompong Thom) inscription refers to a war of 9 years by Suryavarman who became king in Saka 924 (1002). There are also inscriptions related to Jayaviravarman. 1) The Stun Crap Inscription; this is recorded that in Saka 925 (1003), Vap Bramaputra made a petition to king Sri Jayaviravarman. 2) The Tuol Prasat Inscription (Kompong Svay) dated Saka 925 (1003). About the land property, made decision by King Jayaviravarman.

The name of Jayaviravarman is not in the SKT (Sdok Kak Thom) inscription, so he was doubted he really got the throne. Probably Suryavarman I might have instructed the author to delete his name from the list of SKT inscription's kings. Jayaviravarman worshiped Vishnu, so he was different from Suryavarman I (Buddhist, who rejected the Devaraja).

The inscription of Preah Vihear, dated 1028, says Suryavarman I was of the line of Indravarman and that his queen Viralakshmi, was of the line of Harshavarman and Isanavarman. But Suryavarman I's throne had nothing to do with remote ancestor. His father's marriage

4. Angkor Dynasty

to a princess of the family of Saptadevakula brought him the support of that powerful family. His own marriage to a princess of the line of Yasovarman strengthened his position against claimants of the line of Harshavarman II or Rajendravarman II, of which Udayadityavarman I certainly — and Jayaviravarman probably— claimed (Briggs, p148-149).

The family of Saptadevakula rose into prominence during his reign. At its head was the distinguished scholar and poet, Kavisvarapandita, who had served as preceptor for Jayavarman V (Briggs, p149). However, Suryavarman I had been supported by his strong army from Tambralinga (the Srivijaya group).

These three kings'conflicts looked like the power struggle among relatives. But they had known each other connected in Tambralinga (Nakhon Si Thammarat). According to some inscriptions, Suryavarman I defeated his rivals, so there might have been some battle at the final stage. Notably all of them came from Tambralinga as military generals. It means that Srivijaya had sent military to the Angkor kingdom, and their advanced military base was located at Lopburi. M. Vickery and C. Jacque strongly deny the theory of Tambralinga. They deny also that Srivijaya (former Funan) had controlled the Angkor Dynasty. But they are wrong. From the beginning, the Angkor Dynasty had been supported and supervised by the Srivijaya group. The Angkor Dynasty could not have sent tributary mission for 300 years, probably because the Srivijaya group had prohibited Angkor to send mission to China. Another problem of Suryavarman I is that he rejected the tradition of Devaraja cult. Suryavarman I had not accepted the worship of Devaraja to identify himself with Siva in a linga as his predecessors had done. (Sharan, p264)

In fact, Suryavarman I was a revolutionary Buddhist king. Even Jayavarman VII believed in this Devaraja cult and had constructed and established lingas.

154   THE HISTORY OF SRIVIJAYA, ANGKOR and CHAMPA

Udayadityavarman I was a son of Jayavarman V's wife's elder sister. According to the Inscription Prasat-Khna his mother came from Sreshthapura family. The temple of Prasat Khna seems to have been dedicated to Vishnu in the form of Krishna, the first in Cambodia. (Briggs, p166-167). Angkor Wat is also dedicated to Vishnu by Suryavarman II.

Udayadityavarman1's reign was very short, only for 2 years. Upon the death of Jayavarman V, Suryavarman I claimed that he had the right to get the throne. He was a son of the ruler of the king of Tambralinga and his mother was from Indravarman 1's matriarchal lineage. He led the navy and landed in eastern Cambodia and began advancing toward the capital. According to the Robang Romeas Inscription, In Saka 923 year (1001-1002) he got to the throne, and the Wat Thipdei Inscription and the Takeo Inscription say that in 1002 he went to the throne. Udayadityavarman 1 had no record when he left the throne, and when Jayaviravarman took the throne unclear. One thing is clear that he reigned in 1003, but when he lost kingship was not known (Briggs, p144-145).

Jayaviravarman had no special justification to succeed the throne of Jayavarman V. There is an inscription saying Suryavarman I became the king in 1002. However, there is a theory that Jayaviravarman occupied the capital, on the other hand, Suryavarman I led his troops into the Mekong River and dominated the eastern part. Suryavarman I made ceremony of coronation at Sambhupura. There is no evidence that both armies had faced for 9 years with hostilities. According to the Dambok Khpos Inscription saying in 1005, Suryavarman I had dominated the Kompong Tom district (Briggs, p146).

The power of ministers and priests was strong in the reign of Jayavarman V. They had been longtime at Jayavarman V's service, and holding substantial administrative and religious power. Saptadevakula is the direct descendant of queen of Rajendravarman II and the most powerful person during the Jayavarman V's reign.

4. Angkor Dynasty   155

The Saptadevakula clan claimed victory (Briggs, p146). Also without doubt, Tambralinga, the headquarters of the Srivijaya Group had supported Suryavarman I.

4-6-1   Influence of Srivijaya through Tambralinga and Lopburi
In the ancient time, Lopburi had been founded by the Mon people, as a commercial city state, and was one of the major kingdoms of Dvaravati group. Srivijaya used Lopburi as the military base to supervise Angkor from there, and at the same time watched the Menam Chao Praya basin area. The former king of Lopburi, after kicked out of Lopburi, went away in North Lampung, and later founded the kingdom of Hariphunchai. In the 8th century, there is a legend that Princess Cham Devi, from Lopburi went to the Lampung Kingdom and married the king.

The authenticity of this story aside, Jayaviravarman was a nephew of Rajendravarman II, and became King of Angkor. On the other hand, Suryavarman 1 might be 'No. 2 King (Obyuvaraja) of Angkor until he took throne. Udayadityavarman I (Udayaraja) was the commander of Jayavarman V's army (Obraja) and he took the throne first. In fact, these 3 persons were in acquaintance relationship beforehand as the generals from Tambralinga. In this time, Tambralinga was the headquarters of the Srivijaya Army, and supervised the Angkor Dynasty. Jayaviravarman and Udayadityavarman I are brothers, and were in the Palace of Lopburi which was surrounded by high walls. Briggs says 'Suryavarman was the royal family of Tambralinga, whose sovereigns had been given the title, Sri Dharmaraja (King of the Law). There are reasons to think that he may have gone further in the establishment of Buddhism in Kambubujadesa than has been generally recognized.' (Briggs, p167)

The Ta Praya Inscription was made in 962, during Rajendravarman II's reign. Jayaviravarman was still in the position of Army Commander, and his step-brother.

The Prasart Trapan Run (dated 1006) speaks of Jayaviravarman

156   THE HISTORY OF SRIVIJAYA, ANGKOR and CHAMPA

as residing at the Palace of the Caturvara (Four Doors) at
Yasodharapura. Another inscription, of the same year (the Phnom
Sanke Kong, dated 1006), speaks of Suryavarman 1 as King of the
Caturdvara (Angkor Capital) (Briggs, p140). In 1006, at the same
time both kings were in Angkor.

The Angkor Dynasty, until Suryavarman 1 era had been under the
control of Srivijaya since Jayavarman II. Srivijaya had maintained
a huge military force at Lopburi. However, some historians believe
that 'the Angkor Dynasty ruled Tambralinga and Malay Peninsula',
but it is on the contrary. The Angkor Dynasty could not control San-
fo-chi or Tambralinga, unless Angkor had exceeding naval force.
Historians often misunderstand the relationship among Southeast
Asian countries.

At the beginning, Cœdès made a decisive mistake that Srivijaya
was based at Palembang. Most historians had blindly followed him.
In considering the relationship between the Srivijaya and the Angkor
Dynasty, the rulers of Tambralinga and Lopburi were commanding
Angkor army. At the same time, the Srivijaya group had dominated
the Mekong River and the coastal region of south Indo-china. So
Suryavarman I brought a large navy force and landed near Kratie,
while Jayaviravarman was staying at Angkor.

M. Vickery and C. Jacques ignore the political and military
influence of the Srivijaya group, so they do not understand the
origin of Jayavarman II and the influence of Srivijaya group in the
Angkor Dynasty.

In the above inscriptions dated 1002, Jayaviravarman and
Suryavarman 1 could have once coexisted. There is possibility
that Jayaviravarman reigned at Angkor as 'No. 1 King' and
Suryavarman I might have dominated the eastern half as 'No. 2
King'. Jayaviravarman in fact had secured the capital, Suryavarman
1 came up from the East toward the Angkor and was gradually
stretched forces (Briggs, p146).

Udayadityavarman 1, in the inscription of Koh Ker dated in 1002,

4. Angkor Dynasty

157

was written by royal decree as a king (C. Jacques, p123). However, probably he was to be deposed in that year.

C. Jacques says that Jayaviravarman had set up in Angkor himself, apparently in the palace of Jayavarman V, and carried on building of Ta Keo (Angkor). He was a self-styled descendant of the (legendary) 'line of Kaundinya and Soma', which once again suggests that his rights were insecurely linked to ancient legend and his accession based on violent conquest. (C. Jacques, p124). He had dominated Angkor and Battambang area.

Suryavarman 1 took the throne in 1002. But Jayaviravarman was also on the throne until 1006. In the second half of 1006 Suryavarman I probably seized Angkor. The Phimeanakas temple was built by Rajendravarman II, but completed by Suryavarman I.

The Phimeanakas inscription says Suryavarman I was stayed in Sri Dharmaraja (= Tambralinga) in 1002. This description is also important, and certainly he was born in the Srivijaya group. Since Jayavarman II, Angkor had been historically put under the supervision of Tambralinga. Angkor had been the formal Kingdom of Cambodia, and Tambralinga's position seems to 'assist the King of Angkor (Obyuraja = Viceroyalty)', but the real power had belonged to Tambralinga. In realty the political and military power of Tambralinga was higher than those of the Angkor Dynasty.

Suryavarman 1's reign had been generally at peace in the country. But, his residence was surrounded with walls. Also, to Yasodharapura, he gathered 4,000 top military brass and local chiefs who swore his allegiance to Suryavarman I. He is said to have siphoned off the wealth from local rulers, preventing them from gathering mighty power and wealth. These measures were required to maintain political 'centralization'. His power was fully consolidated by 1011, and after his long reign was devoted to construction and expansion.

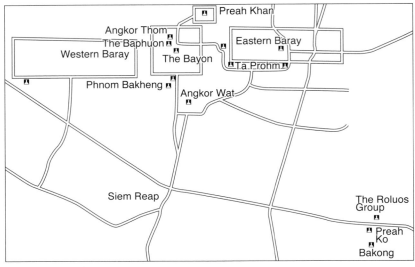

Map 7: Angkor Centre

4. Angkor Dynasty   159

The Phimai Hindu temple located in the Khorat plateau was completed during Suryavarman I's time. Some say it was constructed by Jayavarman VI, but the temple was at first built as a Buddhist temple. The Angkor Dynasty had widely dominated northeast Thailand (Isaan), where remains many Khmer temples. In Thailand, Isaan area had rich archaeological sites to prove there was economic and industrial prosperity. As the Angkor Dynasty had been prohibited by Srivijaya to send tribute to China, Angkor economic energy was concentrated on nation-building, driven by domestic demand. Especially in Jayavarman VII's time, the royal roads were built from Angkor to Phimai and also extended to Vijaya of Champa.

The Phimeanakas temple at Angkor Thom was constructed by Rajendravarman II at first as a Hindu temple, and completed by Suryavarman 1. Later Jayavarman VII lived there and left an inscription which was probably destroyed by Jayavarman VIII. It has 40 m height on the pyramid with laterite, which was simulated Mt. Meru. It is known as 'Royal Palace of Elephant Commander'. Upper structure is lost, now remains a basic part. The residence of the King had been described as 'Gold Tower' by Zhou Daguan (周達觀).

Suryavarman I at Angkor started construction of the West Baray, which was succeeded by Udayadityavarman II. The west Baray is located on the West side of Angkor Thom, length from East -West 8 km, width North-South 2.1km, the largest reservoir of Angkor. There is a small island with a temple in the Central West Mebon and a bronze statue of reclining Vishnu. The size is 4 m long. Now the upper body with a head is displayed at the Phnom Penh National Museum.

Zhou Daguan (周達觀) wrote at the end of the 13th century; "A copper Buddha in the middle of the pond (East Mebon) pagoda is laying down in the Tower and spouting water at all times from the

Photo 24: Declining Vishnu (By T. Suzuki)

navel."
The copper 'Buddha' was a bronze 'Vishnu' and its location was at the West Mebon (not East Mebon). At the end of the 13th century, a reclining Vishnu was active.

C. Jacques says that according to the inscription Suryavarman 1, at Sambhupura -Mekong basin, simply raised his coronation, but not a detailed description was found. Suryavarman 1 had sent a letter to King Rajaraja Chola (985-1016) in 1012 asking for military help to overcome enemies in the Chao Praya basin. The enemies of the Chao Phraya were probably the Mons states. However, this story was never realized. Suryavarman 1 was certainly belonged to the clan of the royal house of the Srivijaya group, considering the communication with the Chola king.

However, the good relation collapsed after Chola occupied Kedah in 1025. Probably the officials of San-fo-chi had interfered with the mission of Chola to the North Song Dynasty in 1015. (see, Chapter

4. Angkor Dynasty   161

2)
    During Suryavarman I's reign of 1002?-1050, the most inconvenient
incident was the invasion of Chola in 1025. Kedah had been occupied
by Chola and Tambralinga also occupied. The purpose of Chola was
to dominate the trans-peninsula trade route of San-fo-chi. At that
time, the headquarters of San-fo-chi was temporarily collapsed. The
biggest problem for the Angkor Dynasty was that Suryavarman I
could not get military support from Tambralinga.
    Since the invasion by Chola, the military headquarters of
Tambralinga was probably moved to Lopburi. Lopburi became
practically independent kingdom but with smaller military power.
Chola did not interfere with Lopburi, which was out of trade route
to China.
    Since the beginning of the 9th century (Jayavarman II) to the
end of Suryavarman I's reign, for 250 years, Mahayana Buddhism
had been rapidly spread among Cambodian people and Cambodia
became a great Buddhist country. This was obviously the influence
of Srivijaya.

4-6-2   After Suryavarman I
    Suryavarman I died in 1050 and his posthumous name is
Nirvanapada. He was an ardent Mahayana Buddhist. His
successor Udayadityavarman II (1050-1066) is Suryavarman I's
army commander but not direct relative. Suryavarman I probably
abandoned the Phimeanakas as a central temple and to have started
construction of a giant pyramid-shaped temple 'Baphuon' in the
premises of Angkor Thom (completed by Udayadityavarman II). the
Baphuon is the last large Siva temple. He apparently discontinued
the exclusive privilege guaranteed by Jayavarman II to the family of
Sivakaivalya of furnishing purohitas (Chief Priests) of the Devaraja
(Briggs, p167).
    Udayadityavarman II was crowned in 1050. He had no blood
relation with Suryavarman I, but relative of Viralakshmi, chief queen

162   THE HISTORY OF SRIVIJAYA, ANGKOR and CHAMPA

of him, who was descendant from the line of Yasovarman's wife, the mother of Harshavarman I and of Isanavarman II (C. Jacques, p136)

The SKT (Sdok Kak Thom) Inscription, dated 1053 was established in remote areas from Angkor, so it was unharmed by the Jayavarman VIII. Udayadityavarman II should be called a wise king. About the author of SKT Inscription, Briggs assumes that Jayendrapandita (Aninditapura, nephew of Suryavarman I) continued as guru for Udayadityavarman II, for some time and was the builder of the Inscription of Sdok Kak Thom in 1053, after which the family of Sivakaivalya disappeared from history. Sankarapandita was purohita for Udayadityavarman II and established his Udayadityasvera in his new central temple for Baphuon (the Devaraja temple), after which he was to continue as purohita for his successor, Harshavarman III (Briggs, p167)

Udayadityavarman II was marked by various upheavals, but he conquered them by his commander Sangrama. In the later years of Udayadityavarman II a former general Kambau revolted in 1066. At that time, general Sangrama served the commander of Udayadityavarman II and crushed Kambau revolt.

Udayadityavarman II appears to have been a supporter of 'Siva', one of reaction against the Buddhism of Suryavarman I who seems never to have adopted the cult of Devaraja. All the important foundations and inscriptions of his reign were Sivaite. He established a magnificent temple and set there a golden linga, Udayadityesvara. (Briggs, p175)

Harshavarman III (1066-1080) succeeded the throne from his elder brother, Udayadityavarman II, born of the same mother. His capital was the second Yasodhrapura, which had its centre in Baphuon, built by his brother, and located at northwest of the Bayon. His reign was relatively peace, except war with Champa. According to the Ta Prohm Inscription, Harshavarman III was the descendants of the first Chenla King of Bhavavarman. Harshavarman III died in 1080. The posthumous name is Sadasivapada. By his death, the

Tambralinga line was finished in the Angkor Dynasty.

Harshavarman's younger brother, Nripatindravarman, attempted to ascend to the vacant throne, but was probably not even crowned. (C. Jacques, p145). However, Briggs says Jayavarman VI did not claim any connection with Harshavarman III, and for several years in strife against those who remained loyal to the legitimate line of Harshavarman III and his heir Nripatindravarman. Suryavarman II, successor of Dharanindravarman I, achieved the unity of Cambodia by conquering two kings, one of whom was his grand-uncle, Dharanindravarman I. The other seems to be the unnamed claimant of Harshavarman III's line. (Briggs, p179)

4-7 THE MAHINDHRAPURA DYNASTY

4-7-1 Hiranyavarman group, from the north of the Dangrek Range

The traditional ruler, influenced by Srivijaya had changed after the death of Harshavarman III.

From the northeastern area near Phimai, Jayavarman VI (1080-1106) appeared as the new ruler of the northeastern region in 1080, and later took the throne of the Angkor Dynasty, but he had nothing to do with the Srivijaya group. The exact date of his coronation is unknown. He once occupied Angkor and was crowned there, but came back to Mahindharapura and lived there. He adored Chaupesvara (Vishnu) and made a rich donation to the Vaisnavite temple of Kok Po (Sharan, p245). Jayavarman VI's posthumous name is Paramakaivalyapada.

Jayavarman VI's chief adviser was Vrah Guru Divakarapandita, who seems to have been the guiding star of the early destinies of the house of Mahindharapura. Udayadityavarman II had chosen him, as a very young man, to serve Devaraja at the dedication of Baphuon and Harshavarman III had made him the chief priest. Jayavarman VI had made him Vrah Guru and had been crowned by him. (C.

164   THE HISTORY OF SRIVIJAYA, ANGKOR and CHAMPA

Jacques, p179)

Hiranyavarman and Hiranyalaksmi had at least three sons and a daughter. The eldest son, Dharanindravarman at first chose a religious life (Buddhist). Jayavarman VI was the second. The youngest is known to history as the Yuvaraja (Crown Prince). The daughter became the grandmother of Suryavarman II. (Briggs, p178).

According to the My-Son inscription, between 1074 and 1080, Angkor had been attacked by Champa prince Pang, a younger brother of Champa king, Harivarman IV. The Sambhupura temples were destroyed and inhabitants were taken into slavery to My-Son, including the prince Sri Nandavarmadeva. Harivarman IV was a strong Cham king. However, this incident was not recorded in the Angkor inscription. In 1076, Cambodia and Champa were driven by the Song court in an attack against the Tonkin. But the Chinese army was defeated.

M. Vickery points out the so-called Mahindharapura kings, whose origin was north of the Dangrek Ranges, did not descend directly from the previous kings of Angkor, and that is why no earlier members of their kingdoms were mentioned before the end of the 11th century.

There are, however, inscriptions showing that high-ranking officials of the previous court continued in their functions under the new king, suggesting a peaceful transition, or at least a split in the previous court, with some favoring the new king. (M. Vickery, Bayon, p7).

Anyway, after the invasion of Chola, the Srivijaya group had lost power to control the Angkor Dynasty. Without military assistance from Thambralinga, Lopburi had not enough power to 'support' the Angkor rulers.

On the other hand, the Isaan group (Phimai group) had accumulated economic power and started to dominate Angkor.

4-7-2　Suryavarman II

Probably Jayavarman VI (1080-1106) was consecrated in 1080 by purohita Divakarapantita at Yasodharapura (C. Jacques, p147). Divakarapantita had been in service of Udayadityavarman II and Harshavarman III and made the coronation ceremony for Suryavarman II in 1113.

Jayavarman VI auto-claimed king and established his authority on the northern province, while Harshavarman III still reigned at Angkor. At the death of Harshavarman III in 1080, his successor Nripatindravarman continued to reside at Angkor who attempted to ascend to the vacant throne, but he had no power and was probably not even crowned. (C. Jacques, p145).

During this period, Jayavarman VI had to fight Nripatindravarman, but he succeeded to reconcile the favor of Harshavarman III's chaplain, Divakarapandita, and to consecrate his authority by Divakarapandita.

In 1107, after Jayavarman VI died he had no child, Divakarapandita transmitted the crown to his eldest brother Dharanindravarman I (1107-1113). At that time, he was in Buddhist monastery. However, in 1113 he was overthrown by Suryavarman II (1113-1149?).

The Mahindhrapura Dynasty originated in Phimai region, so Jayavarman VI probably constructed this important temple. However, in the temple wall, a re-used stone engraved with a Buddhist inscription of the 8th century was found, together with a curious stele which has a homage to Siva on one side, and another side to Buddha. Both date from the reign of Suryavarman I. (C. Jacques, p149).

While the lintels of the interior are Buddhist in inspiration, the main pediments and exterior lintels are clearly Hinduist (C. Jacques, p149).

On the Phimai Temple South Gate (main gate) the image of Trailokyavijaya was placed. This is Vimaya God, and became the origin of the word 'Phimai'.

166   THE HISTORY OF SRIVIJAYA, ANGKOR and CHAMPA

Jayavarman VI was a son of Hiranyavarman, a local ruler of Phimai area, northeast of Thailand. He called himself of Kambujadesa and claims that Mahindharapura had related to the 'royal family', but no evidence. There is no inscription about the circumstances of his accession. (C. Jacques, 1997, p147)

Dharanindravarman I (1107-1113) was an elder brother of Jayavarman VI, but succeeded him. Prior to the throne Dharanindravarman I was a great priest, and had served as a minister in the Angkor court. Before he achieved remarkable job, he was killed by their big sister's grandson Suryavarman II.

Suryavarman II (1113-1149?) is not relative of Suryavarman I, and he is free from the Srivijaya group. After the invasion of Chola, San-fo-chi (Srivijaya) had lost the controlling power toward Angkor.

M. Vickery says that Suryavarman II and Jayavarman VII came from Phimai. He also shown diplomatic attention to the Chola, in 1114 he reportedly presented a gemstone to the Chola king. He frequently dispatched a military expedition from East to West, but none ultimately ended successful. Especially in the eastern front Suryavarman II, in 1128 with Champa army support fought against Dai Viet (Vietnam=大越), but defeated. And in 1132, he tried again with Champa but failed again. Then in 1136, Jaya Indravarman III of Champa did not join Suryavarman II's war. Suryavarman II got angry and in 1144-5, invaded Champa, as the result the capital Vijaya (Binh Dinh) was occupied by Suryavarman II.

In 1145, Suryavarman II placed 'Prince Harideva', the younger brother of one of his chief queens (herself a Cham) on the Harivarman throne of the Cham king of Vijaya. This deed provoked fury of Jaya I, another Cham king, who killed Harideva in 1149 and proclaimed himself 'supreme king of the Cham kings' apparently defying Suryavarman II.

When Suryavarman II died is not clear, but supposed between 1149 and 1150, probably killed in the battle against Champa. He

4. Angkor Dynasty 167

could not receive army support from Tambralinga and Lopburi, because he had no relation with Srivijaya. He had challenged San-fo-chi (Srivijaya) by sending tribute to Song in 1116.

Militarily, he had to use the mercenaries of the Thai and Mon people. Thai people originally lived in Yunnan province, at that time they were emigrating to the northern and northeastern Thailand as farmers and some of them worked as mercenaries for the Angkor army. Later Thai people became important villagers in Thailand. The Mon people lived in the Menam Chao Praya basin and the lower Burma. However, these mercenaries were not so strong, and Suryavarman II was often defeated.

Suryavarman II ascended to the throne in 1113, with the coronation ceremony by Divakarapandita, high priest attended the enthronement ceremony at Wat Phu.

In 1116, in case of the first Suryavarman II's tribute to Song. The king's name was not recorded in the event of the following mission in 1120, the king was assigned to the king of Champa (Nominal). However, the real king of Champa got independence and sent its own tributary mission to the South Song in 1127 and continued sending the envoys further in 1129, 1132, 1155 ,1167 and1168. Champa kept independence during these years.

Suryavarman II constructed 'Angkor Wat' which is the greatest achievement under his reign. He was an ardent follower of Vishnu. This temple, with the length 1030m, width 820m was enclosed by a laterite fence. The central tower's height is 45m, which symbolizes 'Mount Meru' (centre of the universe). This construction was done by Brahman Damodar Pandita, from India. Suryavarman II made this Vishnu Temple, Angkor Wat as his mausoleum (Zhou described this temple like the miracle of the ancient Chinese architect, 'Lu Pang's work'). His posthumous name is 'Paramavishnuloka', and after his death he entered the world of Vishnu.

He officially avoided Sivaism and Buddhism, but Suryavarman II is known to have granted aid for the propagation of Buddhist education (Sharan, p184).

Suryavarman II constructed irrigation reservoir at Beng Mealea and Kompong Svay, from the Angkor 40 km away. The Beng Mealea irrigation reservoir is located south of Phnom Kulen and Mealea means 'Lotus pond'. The Beng Mealea Temple is one of the largest temples of Angkor era with 11 towers.

Suryavarman II's successor was his cousin Dharanindravarman II (1150-1160). Formal accession to the throne is not certain, but he lived in Yasodharapura (Angkor). He married a daughter of Harshavarman III, princess Chudamani, by whom around 1125 he had a son, later Jayavarman VII.

In addition, during his reign, he sent the tributary mission with Lavo (Lopburi) to the South Song in 1155. Lopburi used to be the forward-base of San-fo-chi, but at this time Lopburi became independent. Lopburi probably kept within territory, the Chantaburi port. Angkor had been placed under the supervision of Tambralinga, and Lopburi was its forward base. However, C. Jacques considers contrarily that Angkor supervised Lopburi (C. Jacques p198). If Lopburi was a subordinate state of Angkor, Lopburi's name should not have been mentioned with Angkor which sent tributary mission to Song.

By the invasion of the Chola (in 1025), the military power of Tambralinga collapsed and Lopburi became free and independent from Tambralinga. Originally Lopburi used to be a city of the Mons and was prospering as a commercial and manufacturing (iron and salt) centre. So, with remaining army of the former Srivijaya group, the position of Lopburi was so far strong in the 12th, 13th century and afterward.

Many historians believe that Lopburi had been under control of the Angkor Dynasty, but the fact is on the contrary, Angkor was placed under control of Tambralinga and Lopburi. Around 1090, San-fo-chi recovered independence from Chola, but after 1178, the South

4. Angkor Dynasty

Photo 25: Angkor Wat (back)

Photo 26: Phimeanakas

170   THE HISTORY OF SRIVIJAYA, ANGKOR and CHAMPA

Song Court stopped 'the tributary system', so San-fo-chi dissolved as a matter of course. At Tambralinga, King Chandrabhanu declared independence in 1230, from the Srivijaya group. But he failed after two times invasions to Sri Lanka, and finally Thambralinga was absorbed by King Ram Khamhaeng of Sukhotai kingdom at the end of the 13th century. On the other hand, the Lopburi kingdom kept independence, and prospered economically. Later, Lopburi played a significant role to form the Ayutthaya Kingdom. After the foundation of the Ayutthaya Kingdom in the 14th century, Lopburi was a stronghold of Ayutthaya's rulers. It became the capital of the Ayutthaya Kingdom during the reign of King Narai the Great in the mid-17th century.

C. Jacques says that on the death of Suryavarman II, around 1150, the supreme crown passed to Yasovarman II, a king whose origin and accession to the throne are completely mysterious. For a long time, it was assumed that between Suryavarman II and Yasovarman II, there could have intervened the reign of the father of the future Jayavarman VII: Dharanindravarman II. There is no trace of such a reign. (C. Jacques, p197).

However, Briggs says that Suryavarman II was succeeded by Dharanindravarman II (1150-1160). Dharanindravarman II was a cousin of Suryavarman II. This genealogy shows that Dharanindravarman II was a son of Mahindraditya, brother of Suryavarman II's mother, Narendralakshmi, and one Rajapatindralakshmi. (Briggs, p204).
After his death, Yasovarman II succeeded him in 1160. Yasovarman II was a close relative of Dharanindravarman II, but no evidence. The Ta Prohm Inscription says Dharanindravarman II was an ardent Buddhist and the posthumous name is 'Paramanishkalapada'. (Briggs, p204).
In the Central Thailand, independence movement came out from

the Angkor Dynasty. In Nakhon Sawan, Sri Darmasoka appeared as the king. At Dong Mae Nang Muang, Nakhon Sawan, an inscription written in Pali and Khmer (1167 A.D.), was discovered. That also existed in the current Suphan Buri (region called Shin Li Fu 眞里富) self-government. (Piriya, p138). Yasovarman II is supposed to suppress the movement of independence of these rebels.

4-8 JAYAVARMAN VII

The Inscription of Say-Fong (in Laos) introduced Jayavarman VII as the son of Dharanindravarman II (ardent Buddhist). Through his father, he was a second cousin of Suryavarman II and through his mother, Jayarajachudamani who was daughter of Harshavarman III, he was a great grand-son of Suryavarman I. So, Jayavarman VII had remote relation with the Srivijaya group.

He was born at the latest in 1125 and was married to the princess Jayarajadevi who had a great deal of influence over him. The Inscription of Phimeanakas inscribed by his second queen Indradevi provides the rest of information about his early life before he was crowned (Inscriptions du Cambodge II: Grande stele du Phimeanakas).

The queen Indradevi was the elder sister of the late queen Jayarajadevi. According to the inscription, Jayavarman VII left Cambodia to conduct a military expedition in Champa, at Vijaya (Binh Dinh). During the campaign, he learnt the death of his father and the accession of Yasovarman II. During the usurpation of Triphuvanaditya, he returned in great haste to safeguard the Angkorian throne, but it was too late. Tribhuvanadityavarman, once a faithful minister of Yasovarman II, killed the king and ascended the throne in 1165. It is said that the Cham King Jaya Indravarman IV attacked Angkor in 1177 and killed the usurper king. However, M. Vickery says this story is impossible and raised serious doubts. Probably what M. Vickery says is correct. This incident in 1177, was

172   THE HISTORY OF SRIVIJAYA, ANGKOR and CHAMPA

the substantial 'coup d'état' by Jayavarman VII.

In 1177, Jayavarman VII might have hired the Cham King Jaya Indravarman IV to attack Tribhuvanadityavarman. Jayavarman VII seems to have worked behind him. The *Song Shi* describes about this battle, but a Cham king could not have enough power to attack Angkor and killed the king. Tribhuvanadityavarman said to have asked peaceful solution, but was refused. M. Vickery doubts this battle in 1177 itself, because in Champa there is no inscription of this war.

M. Vickery points out the inscriptions of Champa side. Cham King Jaya Indravarman IV won in 1163-65, 67, 68 and 1170, when he donated to the shrine. However, in 1177, there is no record about the war. Therefore, there was no big war, nor victory of Champa in the year 1177. Probably M. Vickery's view may be correct. In the following inscriptions (C92B and C92C) of My-Son dated in 1181, 1182 and 1190, 92, 93, 94, there is no mention of the victory of Jaya Indravarman IV. Jayavarman VII ascended the formal throne of Angkor in 1181, and then in 1190 Cham King Jaya Indravarman IV was assigned the king of Champa. Cham King Suryavarmadeva i.e. Vidyanandana Prince in 1182 had served at the Jayavarman VII's court as a general of the Angkor army.

The story of the '*Song Shi*' is probably written based on the explanation of the Angkor mission of Jayavarman VII in 1200.

The reason why Jayavarman VII had stayed at Vijaya is unclear. His wife Jayarajadevi told him to wait for the opportunity to get the throne (C. Jacques, p203). After the usurpation of Tribhuvanadityavarman, Jayavarman VII quietly went back to Vijaya. At Vijaya he was looking for a favorable occasion to intervene. In 1166-1167 at Vijaya Jaya Indravarman IV killed the former Champa king and took the throne. He was a very ambitious young king and caused a lot of trouble with Arab merchants and the Song court.

Jayavarman VII seems to use the armies of the Cham, and later he is said to have fought against the Cham King at Preah Khan (holy

4. Angkor Dynasty 173

Photo 27: Phimai & Jayavarman VII

sword). In the last battle at Preah Khan, he defeated Cham King Jaya Indravarman IV. However, M. Vickery suggests this (Preah Khan) battle might be fictious. He claims the existence of inscriptions that wrote Jaya Indravarman IV died at home. Certainly, Jayavarman VII had no reason to fight against Jaya Indravarman IV and formally acceded to the throne 4 years later in 1181.

The point of M. Vickery's theory seems to be correct, especially on the 1177 incident, the Cham King Jaya Indravarman IV could not have been strong enough to defeat the army of Angkor. I can't find evidence that he was alone to attack Angkor. Jayavarman VII seems to have overthrown the usurper Tribhuvanadityavarman, teamed up with Cham generals. Jayavarman VII seems to plot a coup d'état against Tribhuvanadityavarman. Probably he borrowed the army of the Champa King Jaya Indravarman IV. However, 4 years later, in 1181 Jayavarman VII probably asked Champa forces to retreat from Angkor, and ascended to the throne. After Jayavarman VII ascended

174   THE HISTORY OF SRIVIJAYA, ANGKOR and CHAMPA

the throne, the relation between Angkor and Champa was peaceful. Jayavarman VII acted as the Buddhist King earnestly, Mahayana Buddhism was also more prevailed than before. Jayavarman VII was very cautious to take the throne.

Jayavarman VII had pushed 'Buddhism first' policy. Many inscriptions of both Khmer and Cham sites reveal that he had spent the rest of his life to fulfill that mission (Buddhism first). In the campaign, he enlisted many Yuvarajas (crown princes) who were brought up in Angkor and tasks were assigned to them to stabilize many parts of the empire. Vijaya (Binh Dinh) was the most key place for him. He constructed the royal road to Vijaya. Vijaya was the important port for international trade with China at that time.

After 1181, Jayavarman VII had employed another Cham Prince (Sri Vidyanandana later Suryavarmadeva) as the Angkor commander to defeat the rebellion of Battambang, and he successfully played his role. The Cham Prince In, married Jayavarman II's younger sister. In 1190, when Indravarman IV rebelled against Jayavarman VII, at that time Cham Prince Sri Vidyanandana (Suryavarmadeva) was sent and captured Jaya Indravarman IV, who was transported to Angkor.

The My-Son pillar inscription says: "In 1112 saka (1190), King Sri Jaya Indrvarman Ong Vatuv (IV) made war against the King of Kambujadesa. The latter sent the Prince (Vidyanandana) as the head of the troops of the Kambuja to take Vijaya and defeated the king (Indravarman IV). He captured Indravarman IV and brought him to Kambujadesa by the Kambuja troops. He proclaimed Suryavarmadeva Prince In, brother-in-law of the king of Kambujadesa (Jayavarman VII), as the king of the city of Vijaya."

Indravarman IV expressed allegiance to Jayavarman VII and he was allowed. Vidayanandana Prince and then King Vijaya was transferred and appointed once Rajaputra (= Phan Rang). However, a revolt in 1191 drove Vidayanandana Prince out and seated in

4. Angkor Dynasty 175

his place called Rashupati, who ruled under the name of Jaya Indravarmadeva (Jaya Indravarman V).

In 1192 Jayavarman VII sent Jaya Indravarman IV (Ong Vatuv) to help the prince (Vidyananda) to reconquer Champa. They met at Rajapura, took Vijaya, defeated and killed Jaya Indravarman V (Radhupati) and ruled over Vijaya. Again, Vidayanandana was assigned the King Vijaya formally.

After this victory, Jaya Indravarman IV fled from the Angkor Court and went to Amaravati (Thu Bon area) where he revolted and invaded Vijaya; but Vidayanandana defeated him and put him to death.

After the occupation of Champa, Jayavarman VII appointed his brother-in-law (Vidyanadana Prince) as the King of Vijaya, but he (later Suryavarmadeva) betrayed his former patron, Jayavarman VII. In 1193, Jayavarman VII got angry and sent an army into Champa, which Suryavarmadeva defeated. The next year, he sent a larger army, which also met the same fate. That year (1194), Suryavarmadeva renewed tribute to Dai Viet. In 1198, he was formally consecrated and sent an embassy to the Chinese Court asking for investiture, which he received in 1199. (Briggs, p216).

The *Song Shi* writes, Angkor revenged after 1995, about the Champa's attack in 1177.

「(淳熙) 四年 (1177年), 占城以舟師襲眞臘, 傅其國都。慶元以來,眞臘大舉伐占城以復讎, 殺戮殆盡, 俘其主以歸, 國遂亡, 其地悉歸眞臘。」

"Champa's navy attacked Angkor in 1177, and King Tribhuvanadityavarman was killed. After Kei-Yuan time (慶元、1195-), Chenla (Angkor) attacked Champa with large army for revenge, killed many people and the king was captured. Champa area was totally occupied by Angkor". As above mentioned this

176   THE HISTORY OF SRIVIJAYA, ANGKOR and CHAMPA

story is very doubtful from the beginning. In 1177 Jayavarman VII practically killed Tribhuvanadityavarman. He must be very happy about this incident. He had no reason to revenge Champa on this incident.

Probably this story was also reported to the South Song Dynasty, by the envoy of Angkor in 1200. However, many facts were cut off and distorted in this story, but partly correct.

Jayavarman VII had been betrayed by his most reliable Champa king (Suryavarmadeva), and finally in 1199, he invaded Champa with big army of Cambodia and defeated Suryavarmadeva. He fled to Dai Viet and probably he was killed there.

Jayavarman VII progressively promoted the network of 'royal roads' (paved with stone base and then straight road) around the territory, and even extended to the conquered area deep in Champa. He constructed accommodations (121 places) for travelers and for residents 102 Arogyasala (= Hospital Chapel) were constructed. The construction had been started gradually since Yasovarman I period. (C. Jacques p270).

Later Phimai had re-emerged as the centre of politics. The main road connecting Angkor with Phimai became called typical 'Royal Road'. This 'Royal Road' network had been extended to many places.

Jayavarman VII brought a Burmese priest Hrishikesa as hotar. He was called later Jaya Mahapradhana and performed the coronation of Jayavarman VIII. Jayavarman VIII (1243-1295) was an ardent Sivaist and fulfilled anti-Buddhist movement violently. Jayavarman VII was betrayed here again.

Jayavarman VII was later called the 'Mahiharapura' King and introduced a new type of Mahayana Buddhism. Later Srindravarman, son-in-law of Jayavarman VIII, put his faith in Theravada Buddhism, and since 1308 Khmer was switched to Theravada Buddhism. The

4. Angkor Dynasty

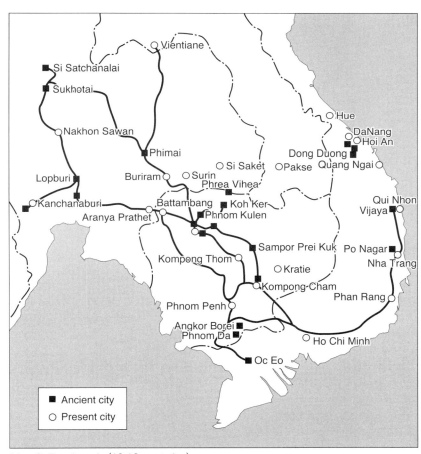

Map 8: Royal roads (12-13 centuries)

Photo 28: Ta Prohm Temple

kings of this group were born in the north of the Dangrek Ranges (now Northeast Thailand) and Phimai area. They had not a direct lineal connection with the kings of earlier Angkor. However, royal followers are often carried over from the earlier kings.

Jayavarman VII in his reign made effort for the benefit of people as much as possible and unified the kingdom. However, he met rebellion in Malyan, South of Battambang. He used above Champa (Tumprauk-Vijaya born) Prince Sri Vidyanandana and dispatched as the commander to repress the rebellion. He relied upon more the Champa generals than the generals of Khmer.

Jayavarman VII became a mild authoritarian, but few allies in the court. He gave privileges to many local monarchs, and gave the government rights. They were not necessarily faithful to Jayavarman VII, and many were Hindu followers who had secretly resisted the introduction of Mahayana Buddhism. Later Jayavarman VIII completely took anti Buddhism action.

Jayavarman VII as a Mahayana Buddhist constructed many temples where he set inscriptions and Buddha images. Jayavarman VII constructed the Bayon along with the Angkor Thom where he completed a residence there. Ta Prohm temples should be called the Royal Mausoleum (1186) which is a famous temple covered by the roots of Banyan trees.

Jayavarman VII made Buddha's mother universal Bodhisattva (Prajnaparamita = Perfection of Wisdom = Wisdom completed 觀自在) in the likeness of the mother of Jayavarman VII, which is enshrined in the form of the statue. The temple also contained many shrines, including an image of his Kru (guru). The resident monks of the temple were Buddhist, Sivaite and Vaisnavite. In addition, the Banteay Kdei Temple was constructed. The Preah Khan Temple was also completed in 1191, which is a Buddhism temple, but with factors of Siva and Vishnu. At the Preah Khan Temple, Jayatataka (Baray) was constructed. In the temple, Jayavarman VII placed his father, Dharanindravarman II's statue of Lokesvara, named Jayavarmesvara.

The trinity of Avalokitesvara, Pranjaparimita and Buddha was central to his thinking and manifest in the projects he commissioned in his lifetime.

He used a former residence of King Tribhuvanadityavarman. Jayavarman VII is dedicated to the God for the former king. Also, Champesvara the form of Vishnu that honors God was installed. This is a name derived from the Champa. Everything might be integrating for the future prosperity of the Angkor Dynasty and Jayavarman VII and propagation of the Buddhist philosophy.

Jayavarman VII's best temple is the 'Bayon'. This is said to commemorate the victory over Champa, but originally built as a Mahayana Buddhist temple. The Bayon, with the faces looking out

Photo 29: The Bayon

in the four cardinal directions, represents himself, Jayavarman VII, as Buddha.

However, crazy Sivaite, Jayavarman VIII strongly hated Buddhism and especially Jayavarman VII, he intentionally tried to convert the Bayon to Hindu temples.

The image of Buddha enshrined by Jayavarman VII was smashed to pieces and thrown them into the central well of Bayon. The 3.6m statue was recovered and restored in 1935, by French scholars. He demolished many of Buddhism temples and Buddha statues, but also transformed the central shrine of Bayon. The images of Buddha, especially those on the pediments, were all transformed into linga. (C. Jacques, p281). Jayavarman VIII freely moving stones of the Bayon, built a new Tower as much as what Jayavarman VII had constructed including inscription and bas-relief. There is evidence that the Angkor Thom also was made modifications and transformed to the Siva statue.

Photo 30-1, 30-2: destroyed and repaired Buddha Image (presented by Mr. Khieu Chan, APSARA)

Jayavarman VIII ordered the demolition of the sixteen chapels on the first level of Bayon, and their stones had been used to build the new angels of the second crucified enclosure.

In addition, In the reign of Jayavarman VIII, the texts of these steles were almost completely erased. The images of Buddha, especially those on the pediments, were all transformed into linga. (C. Jacques, p281).

He was believed to have destroyed also the Inscription on the

182   THE HISTORY OF SRIVIJAYA, ANGKOR and CHAMPA

Phimeanakas, which was recovered from underground later. Jayavarman VIII destroyed mainly what Jayavarman VII had ordered to construct. It is said that the older Buddha images were not so much harmed. But, from Angkor Wat in the Northeast 6 km, there is the Banteay Kdei from which large and small 274 Buddha buried statues were found by the Sophia University's restoration team. Jayavarman VIII is believed to have ordered this destruction of Buddha images.

Fortunately, the SKT Inscription was made far away from Angkor, so even Jayavarman VIII could not have touched it. Jayavarman VIII was the ruler of the outdated concept of anti-Buddhism and an ardent Sivaist. Naturally common people distrusted him.

In addition, Jayavarman VII constructed the Banteay Chhmar temple at near the Thailand border in northwestern Cambodia, which is called the 'Cat fortress = Citadel of the Cat'. The Banteay Chhmar temple was reportedly built for his son, Crown Prince, Srindrakumara Rajaputra who died before him. But in fact, it was for his grandmother Rajapatindralakshmi. Banteay Chhmar is mysterious place, where was the site of ancient kingdom of Chambak Borei (Briggs, p206)

Adjacent to the Banteay Chhmar, an irrigation reservoir (1.6km × 0.8km) had been constructed. In the middle of the pond and the mebon (island), there is a Buddhist temple. This pond has around the 1.9km × 1.7km of the surrounding moat. This land was barren ground of sand, was in his grandmother's land.

There are historians, like Cœdès, who think Jayavarman VII had made a huge construction and exhausted wealth of the government, as the result later Angkor Dynasty led a path of decline. However, the construction work was mainly done in the off-season, and the government had not depended on debt finance, so his criticism for Jayavarman II is not proper. His investment of roads, hospitals and traveler lodge were mainly for the convenience of common people.

Photo 31: Banteay Chhmar (Mr.Pirapon Pisnupong, Fine Arts Department, Thailand)

Jayavarman VII had distributed 23 statues of 'Jayabuddha Mahanatha' to the major cities. As the major cities, Lavodayapura = Lopburi, Svarnapura = Suphan Buri, Sambukpattana (Central Thailand cannot be specified), Jayarapapuri (= Ratchaburi), Jayasimjapura (= Muang Singh, Kanchanaburi), Jayavajrapuri (= Phetchaburi) are recorded. These cities were important for the Angkor Dynasty, but most of them are the Mons cities. Currently 17 statues still exist. The image of the Kanchanaburi Muang Singh is exhibited in the Bangkok National Museum.

Jayavarman VII's posthumous name is 'Mahaparamasaugata'. There are many inscriptions related with Jayavarman VII in Cambodia, Laos and Champa. The inscriptions of Champa often speak of him as a great conqueror. (Briggs, p236).

Jayavarman VII was a 'Bodhisattva King'. He had a sincere earnest belief of his destiny as a Bodhisattva whose path in life was to save his people from suffering. The people were objects of

Photo 32: Jayabuddha Mahanatha statue in Muang Singh, Bangkok National Museum

his compassion, an audience for his merit-making. Images of Jayavarman portray him in the ascetic seated meditation posture with a serene, enlightened expression.

Inscriptions say: "he suffered from the maladies of his subjects more than from his own; for it is the public griefs that make a king's grief." Another inscription reads: "filled with a deep sympathy for the good of the world, the king swore this oath; 'All beings who are plunged in the ocean of existence, may I draw out, by this good work. And may the kings of Cambodia who come after me, attached to goodness...attain with their wives, dignitaries and friends, the place of deliverance where there is no more illness." But his will was simply betrayed by Jayavarman VIII.

Jayavarman VII's successor is his son Indravarman II (1218? -1243), and he was sought to complete his father's unfinished construction (C. Jacques, P278). He was believed Sivaite. After his death, the Brahman Jaya Mahapradhana (Hrishikesa) went to the shrine of Siva at Bhimapura (Phimai) to offer prayers for the peace of the king's soul. It is not certain that Indravarman II was a son of Jayavarman VII or that he succeeded him directly. But it is known that he was reigning just before 1243 and Jayavarman VIII's chaplain seems to have served Indravarman II also. (Briggs, p238)

His successor is Jayavarman VIII. C.Jacques says, "It is a fact that Jayavarman VIII stands out, in contrast to his predecessors, not only as a Hinduist king but also as a fierce opponent of Buddhism, and this is what seems to this author (C. Jacques) to be the most significant feature of his reign."

4-9 DECLINE OF THE ANGKOR DYNASTY

After Jayavarman VII's death, Angkor retreated from Champa in 1220 due to the decline of the military power. Angkor fought against Dai Viet in 1216 and 1218, but defeated. In the northern Thailand and the Menam Chao Praya basin area, the Thai people were making independent small kingdoms and later they formed the Sukhotai Kingdom (1238-1438). In such circumstances, Angkor could not gather sufficient mercenaries of the Thai and Mon people, so the military power of Angkor declined drastically.

In 1222, Ansaraja was placed on the throne of Champa under the name of Jaya Parameshvara IV. Ansaraja was a commander of the Angkor army. After that Angkor could not have intervened Champa again.

C.Jacques says that Jayavarman VIII had a lengthy reign of around 50 years. It is highly likely that his accession was determined by political causes. There is strong indication that he belonged to a lineage which had been dispossessed by Jayavarman VII. His zeal in destroying any testimony to the previous reigns is remarkable (C. Jacques p283).

In 1283, Kublai Khan's forces tried to attack Cambodia from Champa. The attempt was unsuccessful, but Jayavarman VIII sent the tributary missions in 1285 and 1292 to the Yuan Dynasty. By the tribute to Yuan, Angkor spared military invasion. But Angkor never tried to fight the Sukhotai Kingdom of Thailand which had risen in the Chao Phraya basin. Jayavarman VIII was old and incompetent, rarely left the Palace.

186   THE HISTORY OF SRIVIJAYA, ANGKOR and CHAMPA

In Thailand, the Sukhothai Kingdom and then the Ayutthaya Dynasty, the Lanna Dynasty had emerged, and Khmer was gradually squeezed. In Thailand, Theravada Buddhism was introduced from Ceylon and Burma, became state religion, which united the people together and became a source of national power. On the other hand, the Angkor Dynasty led to a decline by the reign of Jayavarman VIII, whose regime was unfortunate for Angkor. As the Buddhist country, Cambodian people were united, but Buddhism was attacked by Jayavarman III without reason. Distressed Buddhist farmers began to neglect the repair of irrigation facilities and the water system was decayed, as the result which caused epidemics of diseases such as malaria and farmers were more impoverished. That was in a vicious cycle. Jayavarman VIII seemed to be indifferent of the farmers' suffering and he lacked the ability to resolve such disaster. His main concern was worship of Sivaism, and hatred toward Buddhism and Jayavarman II.

Jayavarman VIII was abdicated in 1295 under pressure from his son-in-law, Srindravarman.

Zhou Daguan (周達觀), the author of "*Memoirs on the Custom of Cambodia*" (眞臘風土記) came to Cambodia (1296-1297) as an attendant of the mission of the Yuan Dynasty. He wrote that the new prince (Srindravarman) is the son-in-law of Jayavarman VIII and his daughter stole the golden sward from him and took it to her husband (Srindravarman). Jayavarman's son plotted to raise troops, but Srindravarman discovered the plot, cut off his heels, and locked him in a dark prison.'

In the description of the Zhou Daguan, Buddhist ministers were active and came out everywhere. His observation of people's lives and practices is quite important. Probably they were Brahmen and worked at the palace as the king 's staff.

From the 14th century to the middle of the 16th century the inscriptions and other resources are rare and even the king's name is also unclear.

4. Angkor Dynasty

In 1431, the Angkor district was occupied by the force of Ayutthaya, so the Angkor Dynasty's palace was shifted to the South. In 1431 Rajadhipati captured Angkor. This is written in the Ayutthaya period. O. W. Wolter claims 1369, but without basis in theory and M. Vickery opposes him.

Jayavarman VII is accused that he destroyed the government wealth and the people were battered by a huge construction project. However, these damages could be recovered relatively in short times, at most in a few subsequent decades. Later Jayavarman VIII was indulged in superstition and Sivaism and opposed Buddhism.

Buddhism faith of the people was very deeply damaged, which was the base for the unity of the Angkor kingdom. Jayavarman VIII and his court officials were ignorant of the management of economy. They were indifferent of collapse of the irrigation pond. Maintenance and management of this magnificent water supply system depended upon the cooperation of talented civil servants and farmers. After the middle of the 15th century Cambodia was placed under the rule of the Ayutthaya Dynasty. It later became the Ayutthaya territory. However, the Ayutthaya Dynasty had been busy to fight against Burma and had not governed Cambodia properly, so non-government situation lasted for long time. Further in the 19th century Cambodia was colonized by France. And recently the people were seriously damaged by the Pol Pot regime.

188   THE HISTORY OF SRIVIJAYA, ANGKOR and CHAMPA

Table 2: Angkor Kings

1	Jayavarman II	802-834	In 790 or earlier he had title of King?
2	Jayavarman III	834-877	The son of Jayavarman II. Killed before 877? Vishunaite.
3	Indravarman I	877-889	The suspicion of usurpation. Completion of irrigation ponds in Roluos.
4	Yasovarman	889-910	son of Indravarman I, Yasodharapura
5	Harshavarman I	910-922	The son of Yasovarman I
6	Isanavarman II	922-928	Yasovarman's elder sister's son.
7	Jayavarman IV	928-941	Yasovarman Sister's husband, Moved to Koh Ker
8	Harshavarman II	941-944	Son of Jayavarman IV
9	Rajendravarman II	944-968	Yasovarman's elder sister's son
10	Jayavarman V	968-1000	The son of Rajendravarman II, Ascended the throne at the age of 10
11	Udayadityavarman I	1000-1002	Jayavarman V's commander
12	Jayaviravarman	1002-1007 ?	Nephew of Rajendravarman II
13	Suryavarman I	1002 ? -1050	Tambralinga King's son, Buddhist
14	Udayadityavarman II	1050-1066	Suryavarman I's military commander

4. Angkor Dynasty

15	Harshavarman III	1066-1080 p	Last king of Srivijaya group
16	Jayavarman VI	1080-1106	Phimai, provincial royalty
17	Dharanindravarman I	1107-1113	Jayavarman VI's brother, Buddhist
18	Suryavarman II	1113-1149?	Jayavarman VI's sister's grandson, in 1116, resume tribute to Song Construction of Angkor Wat, Vishnu
19	Dharanindravarman II	1150-1160	Jayavarman VII's father, Buddhist
20	Yasovarman II	1160-1165	Dharanindravarman II's relative?
21	Tribhuvanadityavarman	1165-1177	Usurper murdered Yasovarman II
22	Jayavarman VII	1181-1218	Buddhist King, Construction of Bayon
23	Indravarman II	1218-1243	Son of Jayavarman VII, Sivaist
24	Jayavarman VIII	1243-1295	Sivaist, Destroyer of Buddhism
25	Srindravarman	1295-1307	Jayavarman VIII's son-in-law, Theravada Buddhism
26	Srindra Jayavarman	1307-1327	
27	Jayavarman IX	1327-1353?	

CHAPTER
5
HISTORY OF CHAMPA
GENERAL ASPECT OF THE HISTORY OF CHAMPA

The original Lin-yi had very small population and small rice field, so they strongly intended to expand its territory to the north, and international trade with China.

Michael Vickery says, "Champa was neither a unitary polity nor even a federation, but rather consisted of several separate entities, the interrelationships among which varied from time to time (total separation, alliance, peace, hostility, trade). (M. Vickery, Vietnam, p385-6)

Michael Vickery elaborates further:

"These different Champa centres were never unified into a single state of kingdom. The far south, ancient Panduranga, including Phan Rang, perhaps Phan Thiet, and sometimes Nha Trang, was always independent of the Thu Bon valley polities. The Vijaya-Quy Nhon region was often independent of both Panduranga and the Thu Bon, its separate character seen even in its architecture and sculpture. Each of these centres called itself 'Champa' in the forms Champa nagara, Champapura, Champadesa: 'Champa country city, region.' When the Vietnamese chronicles refer habitually to Chiem Thanh or the Chinese histories to Zhan-cheng (占城＝Cham city), it is not always possible to know which Champa they meant."

192   THE HISTORY OF SRIVIJAYA, ANGKOR and CHAMPA

5-1 THE INSCRIPTIONS OF CHAMPA

THE OLDEST INSCRIPTION; VO CANH INSCRIPTION

The inscriptions of Champa are in two languages, Cham and Sanskrit. The oldest inscription is considered 'Vo Canh', from a site near Nha Trang. It has been dated between the 2nd and 4th centuries.

Coedes's opinion is that it belonged to Funan, that apparent chief named Sri Mara was the Funan ruler known to the Chinese as 'Fan (Shi) Man., (范師蔓＝or 范蔓)'. This inscription may not be ascribed to either Funan or Champa, and certainly not to Lin-yi. This inscription is isolated and may not be integrated with the rest of the corpus. Basically, in the Funan times, the rulers had left few inscriptions. Funan used to be a commercial state so their leaders had not left any personal monument'.

Around the 4th century, some small states existed in the southern region, and the cultural level of them was possible to leave the epitaph of the Sanskrit.

5-1-1   Distribution of Inscriptions by M. Vickery

M. Vickery's summing up of the distribution of inscriptions is as following:

"The first coherent group of inscriptions is linked with the early development of the Thu Bon valley, site of My-Son, at time when there are only isolated texts elsewhere.

From the 5th to the late 8th centuries, there are 20 inscriptions, all in Sanskrit and all but two located in or near My-Son.

Then from the mid-8th to mid-9th centuries ─between 774 and 854─ there are a coherent group of eight inscriptions in the South. Most of these are in Phan Rang but some are in Nha Trang; five of them are entirely or partly in Cham.

Following that, from 875 until 965, there are 25 inscriptions

Photo 33: My-Son sanctuary

ascribed to the Indrapura / Dong Duong dynasty, a little south of the Thu Bon area, and near My-Son. The Buddhist city, Dong Duong prospered after the 9th century.

These inscriptions delineate a coherent area from Quang Nam to Quang Binh and include the only epigraphy in the published corpus found north of Hue. Four inscriptions of this group are in the South, and 16 are entirely or partly in Cham. One more Cham-language inscription, possibly related, is from My-Son dated 991.

Thereafter inscriptions are rather equally distributed between North and South until the early thirteenth century, of which there are 32 in the South and only 6 in My-Son, the last dated 1263. After 991, of the 75 known inscriptions until the last in 1456, only 5 are Sanskrit (all of them before 1263), and the rest in Cham. (M. Vickery, Champa Revised, 2004, p367)

5-2 Three Stages of Champa History Lin-yi, Huan Wang, Champa

However, the Chinese historical texts write the word of 'Champa' as if it were a single polity and only the name of the country separates into three steps. However, each doesn't tell the state which unifies the Indochinese Peninsula.

According to the Chinese text,' Lin-yi （林邑）' had sent the first mission in the 2nd century and the last mission was in 750. The reason is not explained. Next 'Huan Wang （環王）' had sent the tribute missions to the Tang Dynasty only three times. Huan Wang was not so active. The final player was 'Champa （Chang Zheng 占城, 877 - 1471）'.

But, the name of 'Champa' began to be used in the epitaph of the Fan Shambhuvarman （范梵志王） at the beginning of the 7th century. Original name of 'Champa', is from the Indian city's name of the Indus riverside.

Xuan Zhan （玄奘） in the Tang times wrote as 'the Maha Champa （摩訶瞻婆） '. Yi Jing （義淨） too, used a word, ' Champa （占波） ' in the *'Nan-hui Chi-kuei Nei-fa Chuan* （南海寄歸內法傳）', in the late 7th century.

About the location of capital, it is often difficult to identify the exact place. Of course, the original meaning of 'Lin-yi' had been lost earlier, but the Chinese officials used this word until 758.

The cultural pre-history of Champa is known as the 'Sa Huynh' culture, dated between 600 BC, and early CE. The location of Sa Huynh makes a perfect geographical fit, along the Thu Bon Valley near My-Son and Hoi An, with the area of Cham centres known from local epigraphy, and the period is late enough to say that Cham speakers must have been there when Sa Huynh culture flourished （Vickery, Toyo, p 62）. However culturally Sa Huynh culture

5. History of Champa 195

and Lin-yi culture are not necessarily lined directory, after the archaeological survey.

The role of the Cham speaking people in the Thu Bon valley is not confirmed. The Mon-Khmer people were major residents at the original Lin-yi area and Cham people (Austronesian) is considered to live south part of Indochina and sea-side area along the Indochina peninsula. The Cham people gradually migrated from south to north, and they handled the international trade of Lin-yi.

Until 7th century, the religion of rulers was Hindu, but Buddhism came in Lin-yi also before the 7th century. Many Buddhism Canons were robbed by the Sui army in 605, when they attacked Lin-yi. The Bodhisattava Lokesvara is known in Champa but Siva was dominant religion among the rulers at that time. The religion of Srivijaya had been Mahayana Buddhism, so which might have penetrated into Champa gradually.

In the 8th century, in Champa there appeared Bodhisattava images. In the Bakul inscription (near Panduranga, dated 829), which records the donations of two temples to God Jina (Buddha) and Sankara (Siva) by Samanta (local ruler). (Majumdar, p65-66).

Buddhism became the official religion later probably around the 2nd half of the 9th century under the reign of Indravarman II. His posthumous name is Paramabuddhaloka. Probably, since this period, Mahayana Buddhism began to spread widely among the common people. Dong Duong is called 'Buddhist City'.

5-2-1　Lin-yi　(林邑)

Champa history began with a polity named 'Lin-yi (林邑)'. Lin-yi was first noted in the Chinese histories as having revolted against the authorities in Jiaozhou (交州) in the 2nd century A.D. Originally 'Lin-yi' means the village of Xiang-Lin Xian (象林縣), which located at the inland area.

The name 'Lin-yi' disappeared from the Chinese histories after 758. Lin-yi was depicted as an aggressive entity constantly pressing

196   THE HISTORY OF SRIVIJAYA, ANGKOR and CHAMPA

northward against Chinese provinces what is now known Vietnam

The *Latter Han Shu* (後漢書) says in 137 AD at Rinan (日南) district, Xiang-Lin Xian (象林縣) a Chinese official of the region, named 'Qu Lin (區隣)' had revolted against the governor of Xiang-Lin with thousands of mobs, and they burned down temples and killed the governor and his subordinates. The *Jin Shu* (晋書) (the history of Jin dynasty, 265-420), says Qu Lian (區連) after killing the governor, declared independence and called himself as 'king'.

At first Lin-yi established at the mountain side of the region where had a rich gold mine, but later Lin-yi shifted its capital to the seaside 'Xitu (西圖)' for the convenience of maritime trade. Xitu had been populated around 2,000.

Lin-yi had sent the first tribute mission to the 'Wu dynasty (呉)' during 226-231, Funan's first envoy was in 225.

M. Vickery writes that in the Lin-yi times during the 5th century to 774, around 20 inscriptions were found of which 19 inscriptions were at Quang Nam province, of which 12 inscriptions were at My-Son, all written in Sanskrit. So, in the Lin-yi times the political centre had existed around the Thu Bon valley, near Da Nang and Hoi An.

From 758, the name of Lin-yi disappeared from the Chronicle of the Tang Dynasty and a new epigraphy appears in the south, and there are no Chinese records of rulers, but they called 'Huan Wang (環王)'.

5-2-2　Huan Wang (環王)

Huan Wang's name, believed' came from Panduranga (Today's Phan Rang). However, Huan Wang's inscriptions are discovered, dated in 875 - 965 and they are mainly related with the Indrapura / Dong Duong dynasty far north from Phan Rang. Perhaps, Chinese officials misunderstood that Huan Wang was a new single state after

Lin-yi, but several missions went to China from different ports.

Also, some of them belong to the Thu Bon area (the centre of the old Lin-yi) and in Hue. Four are in the south.

The Cham words are used for the whole or the part in 16 inscriptions.

5-2-3　Champa -Zhancheng（占城）

The inscriptions of Zhancheng（占城）era, since 991 to 1456, 75 inscriptions were found and they spread from the North to the South almost evenly. South has 32 and 18 inscriptions (the last is 1263) are based at My-Son (North). Only five were written in Sanskrit, the rests were in Cham language. In the Zhancheng age, state powers had been divided into several regions. (M. Vickery, *'Champa Revised'*, p363-420').

The flow of the history of Champa can be understood roughly by observing the distribution of inscriptions. From the change of Sanskrit inscription into the Cham language is also notable.

5-3 EARLY RELATION WITH CHINA. WAR AND TRIBUTARY MISSIONS

As for Lin-yi, it settled at Tra Kieu in the Quang Nam province and it became the capital of Lin-yi. The Thu Bon River basin has the Sa Huynh culture which has ruins of Iron Age, a lot of Dongson bronze drums are discovered from within the region and, many funerary urns are unearthed there and bronze mirrors in the Han times are discovered. However, the relation between the Sa Huynh culture and Lin-yi is not clear.

The ancient Sa Huynh culture is regarded as continuing until the middle in the 1st century.

The material of beads, such as carnelian, agate, glass beading

198   THE HISTORY OF SRIVIJAYA, ANGKOR and CHAMPA

ball seems to have been brought from India. They are discovered together with iron tools in the region. The same material of beads was discovered also in the Malay Peninsula and Thailand.

Supposing that Indians had come in and out frequently and the activity of Indian merchants was similar as in case of Funan, their original purpose was maritime trade but some of them settled in this region.

However, the leading people of Lin-yi seem to have been a local people (including the Chinese). At first, the kings of Lin-yi were Chinese, but gradually changed to the Indian and Cham people.

In case of Funan, the ruling class had been dominated by the Indian origin people.

Also, here is the area called 'Amaravati', which is famous of the Buddhism images, came from south India.

However, Lin-yi seems to have been expanding their territory to Quy Nhon and Binh Dinh in the southern part on the Indochinese Peninsula. Binh Dinh was called 'Vijaya' later.

Da Nang and Hoi An region, as the centre of the trade states had the relations with the smaller states in the southern part for a long time. Then the Cham people came up to this region as seafarers and traders.

A lot of funerary urns (Sa Huynh style) were discovered from the An Bang ruins, the Hau Xa ruins in Hoi An city and iron knives and beads were also discovered.

These remains are estimated to be around the 3rd century BC.

The gem stones and beads were uncovered from the ruins. They were imported from India.

Rinan (日南) region had trade relation with the outside in early times and contacted the central empire of China.

The people of Rinan and its neighbors often sent the tributary

Photo 34: Sa Huynh Museum funerary urns

missions to China, and the 'barbarians of Rinan 'paid tribute white pheasants (雉) and rabbits to the Latter Han Dynasty, in 37 AD. (*Ce-fu Yuan-Gui* (冊府元亀).

Also, in 84, 122, 131, 159, 173, and 183 several states from near Rinan area sent tribute to China, it contributes from ' Jiuzhen (九眞) and suburbs (徼外)' . In 183, Rinan and suburbs sent tribute to China and thereafter their tributes were frequent.

The foreign merchants also came from Rinan region and India, in 166, the envoy of the Roman Emperor (Antoninus) too came with tribute in 159 and in 161.

The Roman envoy said he came from abroad and brought tribute of several pieces of ivories, rhino-horns and turtle-shells, but which were products of the Southeast Asia and whether he really came from Rome was doubtful.

200   THE HISTORY OF SRIVIJAYA, ANGKOR and CHAMPA

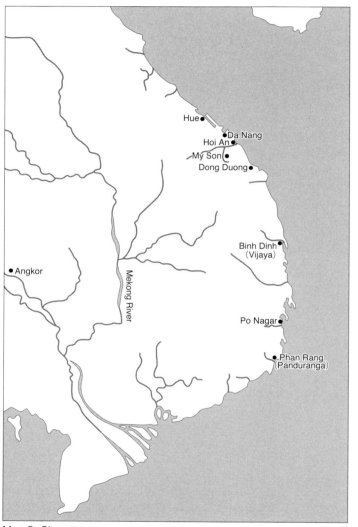

Map 9: Champa

5. History of Champa

The contents of the tributary articles are usually unclear, but it is sure that the most of them were local products and trained elephants. However foreign-made goods were included among them which were brought by Indian merchants and imported from the west countries.

In Lin-yi, Fan Xion (范熊) is the first king (270-80) who had the title of 'Fan' (范). In Funan, Fan (Shi) Man (范蔓) is the first king (225-230) who had 'Fan' title. There might be something common between Funan and Lin-yi. The *Sui Shu* (the history of the Sui) says that the titles of the state officers in Chenla (Cambodia) are the same as Lin-yi. So, possibly there was some political and economic relation between Funan and Lin-yi in the 3rd century.

R.C. Majumdar says; "He allied himself with the king of Funan for this purpose (extending its territory to the north) and continually ravaged the Chinese possessions in Tonkin". (Majumdar, p22)

After Fan Xion's death, his son Fan Yi (范逸 280-336) succeeded him. The tribute mission was sent to Emperor Sun Quan (孫權 = reign 229-252) of the Wu (呉) Dynasty. The tributary mission was sent in the year Wu-di (武帝)of the Western Jin (西晋) during 268 to 284. Funan also had sent missions in 265, 268, 285, 286 and 287. Sun Quan of Wu was assigned king of Wu in 200 and in 229 he was assigned 'Emperor (皇帝)' and died in 252 at the age of 71 years old.

The man who came up from the servant, Fan Weng (范文) plotted the murder of the princes of King Fan Yi who died in 336.

Fan Weng (范文 336-49) was said to be a sold Chinese servant, came from Yangzhou and escaped to Lin-yi. After that he promoted to the king's staff and approached King Fan Yi (范逸). He often went to China following Chinese merchants and got many kinds of technological knowhow.

202 THE HISTORY OF SRIVIJAYA, ANGKOR and CHAMPA

He was very tricky and killed two princes beforehand and when the king died he usurped the throne and threatened all concubines and mistress saying he would kill them who would not obey him without giving food.

He placed the nearby small states under his control and the number of resident reached 30,000-40,000.

He attacked Rinan, in 344 getting into his territory and he killed 5,000-6,000 people including the governor of the region. He proceeded his army to the Ngang Pass (Quang Binh) and where he claimed to be his territory, but was rejected by the Chinese governor Zhu Fan (朱藩).

Fan Weng stayed there for three years, but finally his army was defeated by China and he was wounded and died in 349.

His son, Fan Fo (范佛; 349-380) succeeded him, and he was also defeated. While he sent tribute missions in 372 and 373-375, he still continued invasion. He had invaded Rinan, Jiuzhen (九眞, Tain Hoa) and Jiute (九德) but in vain, and finally he surrendered. After his death, Fan Hu Da (范胡達, 380-413) took the throne, who was probably King Fan Fo's son, but uncertain. He was killed by the governor of Jiaozhou (交州), Du Hui Duo (杜慧度).

The capital of Lin-yi at that time, was located at Tra Kieu near the sanctuary of My-Son with the good ports such as Da Nang and Hoi An. From Tra Kieu to My-Son is about 20km.

Srisanabhadresvara, to deify Siva is built in My-Son and the builder was considered Bhadravarman. He is supposed to be King 'Fan Hu Da (范胡達, 380-413) ', son of Fan Fo (范佛). All the inscriptions erected by King Bhadravarman existed in the Thu Bon valley. His activity seems limited around the Thu Bon valley. Bhadravarman installed a Siva-linga in a temple and called it, after his name, Siva-

Bhadresvara, which is an epitaph of the first Sanskrit. Furthermore, Bhadravaman has a title of 'varman' which is attached to the 'Kshatria' class.

Apparently, he is a different type of king, who first introduced Sivaism. Some historians say that Bhadravarman is said to come from Funan, or at least an Indian origin.

His name 'Hu (胡)' means 'Western foreigner' in Chinese script, so there is possibility he comes from other country, for instance India or Funan. His wife is an Indian origin, a Hinduist, and she tried to go to the Ganges after King Fan Hu's death with her second son.

Dr. Rokuro Kuwata supposes that Indianization of Lin-yi started since this king (Kuwata, 1932, p349).

At the My-Son sanctuary, the mausoleums of many kings from Bhadravaraman to the king of 14th century were built.

The wooden built temples in My-Son were burned down, by the fire in the 7th century but they were reconstructed by King Fan Zhi (梵志) (577-629).

It is carved in the epitaph as the Sambhu-Bhadresvara. Sambhuvarman is Fan Zhi (梵志) himself.

The *Liang Shu* (梁書) says that after King Hu Da (胡達), his son Di Zhen (敵眞) succeeded him. M. Vickery agrees this description of the *Liang Shu* and adds that Fan Yang Mai (范陽邁) I took throne 421, and his son Yan May II succeeded his father in 425-46.

M. Vickery says:

"The name-title Di Zhen (敵眞) is entirely outside the Lin-yi tradition as recorded by the Chinese, and their report that Di Zhen abdicated and went on a pilgrimage to Ganges in India following his mother. He is called the first king of the 'Gangaraja Dynasty', in My-Son the inscription (C96). Dich (Di) Zhen

204   THE HISTORY OF SRIVIJAYA, ANGKOR and CHAMPA

was from the Thu Bon valley, probably Xitu（西圖）, and this is
the earliest clear correspondence between a king known from
Chinese sources and a ruler listed in epigraphy from the Thu
Bon valley".

5-3-1   Tributes of Lin-yi before the Tang Times

Wu Dynasty（呉）once during 226-231.

West Jin Dynasty（西晋）in 268 and 284, each.

East Jin Dynasty（東晋：317-420）
Fan Weng（范文）sent envoys 2 times, in 340 brought trained
elephants and in 372.
Fan Fo（范佛）sent missions during 373-375 and in 377 two times.
Fan Hu Da（范胡達）sent mission in 382.
Lin-yi sent mission during 405-418（in 414 and 417）.

Liu, South Song（劉氏南宋：420-479）
After the civil war, Fan Yang Mei（范陽邁）ascended the throne in
420. His origin is unknown, but he is said to be a son of Fan Hu Da,
probably by a mother of inferior rank. King Fan Yang Mai（陽邁）I
（421-425?）sent mission in 421. At the same time he invaded Rinan
and Jiuzhen（九眞）in 424. Fan Yang Mai II invaded in Jiuzhen again
in 431 with 100 boats. The Song Dynasty counter attacked with
3,000 soldiers but could not defeat Lin-yi and retreated. Lin-yi asked
Funan for support, but Funan refused.

Lin-yi continued tributes, but Emperor Wen Di（文帝）finally got
angry and in 446 dispatched General Long Xian（龍驤將軍）and
ordered Tan-he-zhi（檀和之）Governor of Jiaozhou（交州）to conquer
Lin-yi.

5. History of Champa

However, Yang Mai (陽邁) II demanded 10,000 Jin (斤) gold and 100,000 Jin silver but the South Song Court rejected his demand and Song sent strong army to crush Lin-yi and occupied Lin-yi's capital in 446. Yang Mai II fled away and disappeared from the history.

The South Song army got huge amount of gold. Lin-yi's damage was tremendous.

Lin-yi assigned new King Fan Shen Cheng (神成454-80?) who was gentle and obedient to the Song (Liu). His ambassador Fan Long Ba (范龍跋) was assigned to General Yang Wu (揚武將軍) by the Song (Liu) Court.

Yang Mai I sent tribute in 421 and Yang May II sent tributes often in 430, 433, 435, 438, 439 and 441, but the South Song Court had not appreciated the tributes, because they were poor and nominal. After the defeat, new King Shen Cheng (神成) sent envoy in 455, 458 and 472.

(The tributary missions during the South Ji and the Sui Dynasty from Lin-yi.)

South (Nan) Ji times (南齊 : 479-502)

After King Fan Shen Cheng, Lin-yi was in political confusion, and after all a foreigner Fan Dang Gen Chun (范當根純) took the throne in 484. He said himself , a prince of Funan, but actually he was an Indian slave of Brahman Nagasena (那伽仙). As the ambassador of Funan, Nagasena disclosed Fan Dang Gen Chun's origin to the Nan Ji Court.

Fan Dang Gen Chun sent tribute in 491. However a former royal family killed him, and Fan Zhu Nong (范諸農 491-498) ascended the throne, who was supposed a son of Yang Mai II. In 498, King Fan Zhu Nong went himself to tribute to the Nan Ji Court, but on the

206   THE HISTORY OF SRIVIJAYA, ANGKOR and CHAMPA

way, he was drowned. His son Fan Wen Huan（文欵）succeeded him. He was assigned to the General of An-Nan（安南將軍）and King of Lin-yi.

The *South Jin Shu*（南齊書）describes that Lin-yi was located at its distance of 3,000li（1,200Km）, south of Jiaozhou（交州）, and Lin-yi was south of Jiuzhen（九眞）. Since the 'Shin（秦）times', it was called 'Lin-yi' province.

（About successions of kings, Chinese texts made confusion）

About the linage of Lin-yi kings, between the *Liang Shu* and the *South Ji Shu*, there are some difference. I need not go into detail here about both documents. I write down the conclusion here.

Fan Hu Da 胡達 ⇒Di-Zhen 敵眞（the first King of Gangaraja）⇒Wen-Di 文敵 ⇒Yang-Mai I 陽邁 1st ⇒Yang Mai II 陽邁 2nd ⇒Shen Cheng 范神成 ⋯ Dang Gen Chun 當根純（Indian, from Funan）⋯ Zhu Nong 諸農 ⇒Wen Huan 文欵 ⇒Wen-Zan（文贊）⇒Tien-Kai = Devavarman 天凱 ⇒Vijayavarman 弼毳跋摩 ⇒Ku Sri Vijayavarman 高式勝鎧 ⇒Ku Sri Rudravarman I 高式律陀羅跋摩 ⇒Sambhuvarman 范梵志 ⇒Tou Li, Kandarvarman 頭黎 ⇒Zhen Long, Prakasadharma 鎭龍, who was killed by his subordinate Mahamantradhikrta（摩訶慢多伽獨）.

Fan Hu Da（胡達）was killed in 413 by Jiaozhou Governor Tu-kei-du 交州刺史杜慧度. His son Di Zhen（敵眞）succeeded him. He is later called King Gangaraja. But his younger brother Di Kai（敵鎧）fled to India with his mother, fearing killed by his elder brother（King Di Zhen）. King Di Zhen also wanted to follow his mother, abandoning the throne to his nephew Manorathavarman, but his minister Zang Ling（藏麟）opposed King Di Zhen's intention. His nephew got angry and killed the minister. But the nephew was also killed by the son of the minister.

Finally one of brothers of Di Kai , Wen Di（文敵）succeeded the

5. History of Champa

throne. What happened to King Wen Di is not known, and Yang Mai I (陽邁) took the throne in 421. He was aggressive and invaded Rinan, but defeated and his son Yang Mai II succeeded him. He was also defeated and disappeared from the history.

Nan Ji times (南齊: 479-502)

Lin-yi sent only two tributes to the Nan Ji in 491and 498.

The *Nan Ji Shu* (南齊書) recorded that after 472 (The Liu, South Song), in the Nan Ji time, in 491 Fan Dang-Gen-Chun (當根純 Proclaimed himself a prince of Funan and took over the throne of Lin-yi 483-491) and in 498 King Fan Wen Zan (范文贊) sent missions to Nan Ji. Nan Ji accepted Fan Dang-Gen-Chun, because as a king of Lin-yi, his performance was not so bad. But a descendant of the royal family of Lin-yi (probably a grandson of Yang Mai II), Fan Zhu Nong (諸農) killed him and took the throne in 492. The Nan Ji Court assigned him to 'An Nan (安南) General and the King of Lin-yi'.

But unfortunately, King Fan Chu Nong drowned on his way, leading the tribute mission to Nan Ji in 498. His son Fan Wen Huan (范文欵) succeeded him and was given the same title as his father.

Liang times (梁: 502-557)

During the Liang times, Lin-yi sent 9 missions, Funan sent 10 and Ban-Ban sent 9 to China. Actually, Ban-Ban was a subordinate state of Funan.

R. C. Majumdar says:
"Some important information about Rudravarman is obtained from inscription (No.7). Rudravarman I belonged

208 THE HISTORY OF SRIVIJAYA, ANGKOR and CHAMPA

to the Brahma-Kshatriya family, during his reign, the famous temple of Mahadeva, called Bhadresvarasvami after its builder the King Bhadravarman, was burnt by fire. Rudravarman I is identified with Ku Sri Rudravarman (高式律陀羅跋摩) mentioned in the Chinese annals who sought for his investiture from the Chinese Emperor in 529, and renewed the tribute again in 534."

About this time the Chinese province of Jiaozhou (交州) had revolted and thrown off the imperial yoke under the leadership of Ly Bon (李賁).

Rudravarman I proceeded his army to the north, but was defeated by Ly Bon in 541.

Rudravarman I was succeeded by his son Prasastadharma who took the name Sambhuvarman (范梵志王) at the time of his coronation. He is the author of the inscription No.7. He re-established the temple of Bhadravarman which was burnt at the time of his father, and re-named the image as Sambhu-Bhadresvara, thus adding his name to the original founder. He also gave the endowments to the temple of Bhadravarman. The two embassies sent to China in 568 and 572, probably belonged to his time. (R. C. Majumdar p 36, 37).

Lin-yi had sent tribute in 502, 510, 512, 514, 526, 527, 529, 534 and 542.

The Sui time (隋: 581-618)

Lin-yi sent tribute envoy to Sui in 595. Afterward, during the Sui Dynasty, Lin-yi was heavily invaded by General Liu Fang (劉方) of Sui, without reason.

The war continued during 604-605, and the Sui army occupied Tra Kieu, the capital of Lin-yi.

5. History of Champa   209

King Sambhuvarman, son of Rudravarman fought against the Sui army, with elephants, but General Liu Fang (劉方) dug holes against advancing elephants and he got victory. Liu Fang occupied Tra Kieu and got the 18 pieces of gold plates memories of Lin-yi's kings and destroyed then to make gold ingot. King Sambhuvarman fled to Quy Nhon and change the name of Lin-yi to Huan Wang (環王) for a short term. The Sui army returned to China after victory and Sambhuvarman recovered the occupied territory. Sambhuvarman sent an ambassador to the Sui Court to ask for 'pardon'.

He had reconstructed the sanctuary of My-Son, and in the inscription, he used the name of 'King of Champa' for the first time.

5-3-2   Relation with Tang
To the Tang Dynasty, Lin-yi had sent many envoys. In the seventh century Lin-yi sent 18 missions including 2 times of Huan Wang (環王). In the 8th century until 749, Lin-yi sent 18 missions. After 758, the name of Lin-yi disappeared from the Chinese chronicles. The reason is not explained. However, the attack of Sailendra (Srivijaya group) had strong relation. The inscriptions of Champa recorded the attack of 'Java' navy in 774. But actually Sailedra probably attacked Lin-yi (north) and destroyed its merchant ship around 760. The purpose of Sailendra's attack was to destroy Lin-yi's capability to send trade envoy to China and monopolize the tributary mission from the Southeast Asia.

Shumbuvarman (范梵志) who fought against the Sui invasion, survived until 629, and his son Kandrapadharm (頭黎) succeeded him. Sambhuvarman was very clever king and he kept good relations with Chenla (Cambodia).

On the other hand Huan Wang (環王) sent missions 2 times, during 618-626 and 629-649. At that time Huan Wang seems to have located

210   THE HISTORY OF SRIVIJAYA, ANGKOR and CHAMPA

at South (probably Panduranga and Nha Trang). The inscriptions of
Huan Wang were mostly discovered around Nha Trang, north of
Panduranga.

The contents of Lin-yi's tributes were in many cases not clear.
However, elephants were clearly recorded in the Chinese texts as
following. In 628, Lin-yi presented tamed rhinoceros. In 631, King
Kandarpadharma (頭黎 Fan Tou Li) sent a crystal ball of chicken egg
size which can make fire using sun-shine and parrot with five color
feather. In 640, Lin-yi presented rhinoceros and jewelry. In 654, King
Zhu Ge De (諸葛地) Prakasadharma-Vikrantavarman presented
trained elephants. In 686 and 691, Lin-yi presented trained elephants
and 695, war elephants, and 699 and 707 trained elephants. In 709
Lin-yi presented a white elephant. In 713, King Vikrantavarman
presented 5 trained elephants. In 731, Lin-yi presented 4 elephants
and 735, presented trained elephants and a white elephant. In 748
Lin-yi presented ivories and colorful felt sheets. In 749 Lin-yi
presented special delicious food, black agila wood (沉香) incense
and 10 bright white felt sheets. In other missions, they brought
various kind of tributes which were not specified. They were in
square boxes containing many kind of local products (incenses).
The last mission from Lin-yi was in 749, sent by Rudravarman II.

During the Tang times, Lin-yi could not have imported west
goods so easily, due to Srivijaya's interference. So, Lin-yi must have
presented mainly elephants and other local products. Later after
the 10th century, Arab merchants came to Champa and made trade
agreement with Champa, which presented frankincense (乳香) in
965 to the Song Court.

M. Vickery says that the predominance of My-Son and Tra Kieu
among the Champa centres from the time of the first epigraphic and
architectural remains came to an apparent sudden end in mid eighth

5. History of Champa

century when new epigraphy and architecture began in Nha Trang and Phan Rang (Panduranga) and there was no more of either in My-Son for a century. The reason is not clarified, but perhaps, Lin-yi was attacked by the Srivijaya (Sailendra) navy around 760 and their base of the international trade was destroyed by Srivijaya.

M. Vickery adds more that the shift in relative importance of the two areas (Nha Trang and Phan Rang) was no doubt related to a change in the international trade routes linking the Cham ports to China, Nusantara and India.

But this is not the decisive reason of the change of trade route. However, the change of the trade route is not positive reason. As above mentioned, Lin-yi ports were attacked by the 'Sailendra navy' and Lin-yi had probably lost their fleet to trade. The same thing had happened at Nha Trang 10 years later.

On the other hand, Huan Wang which located in the south-central part of Champa (Nha Trang and Panduranga), sent tribute two times, during 618-626 and 629-649. The royalty of Lin-yi was moving the capital city to Panduranga (Phan Rang) temporarily. Or a new political power emerged at Panduranga area. This Huan Wang is an independent state different from 'Lin-yi'.

However, Lin-yi had dominated the Amaravati region and My-Son was its sanctuary. The capitals were separated into the north (Tra Kieu and Dong Duong) and the south (Nha Trang and Panduranga) independently.

In 877, in the Tang Court, it officially unified a name, to Champa (占城) from Huan Wang. However, actually the name of Champa (占城), had been used in Tang since the 7th century. As above mentioned in the 7th century Xuan Zhan (玄裝) wrote as 'the Maha Champa (摩訶瞻婆)'. and Yi Jing (義淨) too, used a word, 'Champa (占波)'.

212   THE HISTORY OF SRIVIJAYA, ANGKOR and CHAMPA

At the court of Lin-yi, after Shambuvarman, his son Kandarpadharma （頭黎 Fan Tou Li) succeeded him. However his successor Prabhasadharma （鎮龍 Zhen Long) and all of his family were killed by his subordinate, Mahamantradhikrta （摩訶慢多伽獨） in 645.

The male descendants of the Fan （范） family were extinguished with the king. However, the usurper was also killed. Then the people raised a Brahman, a son-in-law of king Fan Tou Li the throne. He was replaced by the daughter of King Fan Tou Li. However, she was unable to restore order, so they summoned from Cambodia, Zhu Ge De （諸葛地）, son of the paternal aunt of Fan Tou Li, who is also grandson of Isanavarman, Chenla King.

Zhu Ge De married a daughter of Fan Tou Li and was proclaimed the king of Lin-yi and called Prakasadharma （迦舍波摩 653-687?）. He is also called as Prakasadharma-Vikrantavarman and that he believed in Vishnu god as well as Siva. （Briggs, p52)

At this time, the relation of both countries （Chenla and Lin-yi) was friendly. Isanavarman （611-635?） sent the envoy to Tang in 628 with Lin-yi but Chenla could not have used the marine-route so many times. The political good relation between Chenla and Lin-yi had not lasted long after the death of Isanavarman.

Prakasadharma-Vikrantavarman sent tribute to Tang in 653 and 669. However, the political influence of Chenla over Lin-yi seems not so strong and faded away.

R.C. Majumdar says that the latest known date of Prakasadharma is 687 and the earliest date of Vikarantavarman II is 713. Naravahanavarma's reign, therefore falls between these dates. We hardly know about his reign. Vikrantavarman II established an image of Laksmi in the year 731. （Majumdar, p46). Rudravarman sent the last envoy as a king of Lin-yi in 749.

5. History of Champa   213

After him all the inscriptions of the new dynasty exist at the Kauthara region (Nha Trang) in the south. However, rulers of Kauthara seem to have suzerainty over the entire former Lin-yi kingdom (Majumdar, p49). The founder of this dynasty is named Prithivindravarman. The inscription (No.24) says that he enjoyed the lands by having conquered all his enemies by his own power. But the Java (Srivijaya group) navy might have destroyed Lin-yi's major trading ships before his throne.

5-3-3 Srivijaya's invasion
The Chinese history also contains reference to a raid as early as 767. Prithivindravarman probably survived until 774. His successor is Satyavarman, nephew of Prithivindravarman. He left the inscription (No.22), and by the Glai Lamow inscription (No.24) we know about his younger brother Indravarman I, and of his sister's son King Vikrantavarman III (No.29) (R.C. Majumdar, p50).

Majumdar continues that in 774, the Javanese, "vicious cannibals coming from other countries (Malay Peninsula) by means of ships -burnt this temple and carried away the image together with all the properties of the temple. King Satyavarma pursued these marauders in his own ships and inflicted a crushing defeat upon them. But the object of the pursuit was not fully realized and Satyavarman was very much dejected to learn that the Sivamukha, together with its property which was in the empty ships, was thrown into water, and that Sivalinga was destroyed (No.22). The 'victorious king', unable to recover the old images, installed a new Sivamukhalinga, together with images of other deities, in 784, and gave rich endowments to the God. For this reason, he came to be regarded as the second Vicitrasagara or an incarnation of that king."

These are the description of the inscriptions of Cham side. However, what is the reality? As the result, the 'Java' navy (Srivijaya group)

Photo 35: Po Nagar

had attacked Po Nagar area and destroyed their merchant ships first and robbed Cham property and burned temples and they retreated as scheduled. Siva linga was abandoned into the seawater, because the Srivijaya people were Mahayana Buddhists and they did not pay respect to the symbol of Sivaism. Above all, Srivijaya restarted sending mission in 768, and had established sea-faring superiority on the South China Sea before that.

King Satyavarman's reign was not so long after 784, and he was succeeded by his younger brother Indravarman I. He is the author of the Yang Tikuh and Glai Lamow Inscription (Nos.23 and 24) in which his glory is sung in most extravagant terms (Majumdar, p51).

The Srivijaya group had never cared about Champa after the destruction of shipping facilities at Nha Trang and Panduranga. However, before this incident, the Srivijaya group might have attacked the Thu Bon area, so Lin-yi could not send envoy to Tang after 749.

5-4 DONG DUONG DYNASTY

After the dynasty near Panduranga and Nha Trang, in the 9th century a new dynasty appeared near Dong Duong which is called the Buddhism Dynasty. Dong Duong city is near My-Son, nearly 20km apart.

However, the 'Dong Duong' kingdom had sent only one mission to Tang, so this kingdom had little records in the Chinese text.

An inscription dated 875 is left by Indravarman II, which writes that from the son (or family) of Paramesvara was born Uroja, the legendary king of Champa. Indravarman II is known that he had introduced Mahayana Buddhism to Champa. The epitaph of Indravarman II dated in 875 was discovered from Dong Duong (called Buddhism city). Indravarman II was a great king, who was called the king of kings (Maharaja).
'The Goddess of Mercy' belief is one by the popularization and the name of 'Lokesvara' can be seen in the name of 'Laksmindra Lokesvara Svabhayada' there.
The last verse is echoed again in a prose passage Sri Jaya Indravarman Maharajadiraja became the King of Champa, by virtue of peculiar merits accruing from austerities of many previous births.

Indravarman II must have enjoyed a long and peaceful reign between 854, the date of Vikrantavarman III, and 898 the earliest date of his successor.
So far as we know he sent only a single envoy to China in 877 as he had nothing to fear from that quarter of its internal conditions. Indravarman II seems to have been succeeded by Jaya Simhavarman

Photo 36: Buddhism relics of Dong Duong, Da Nang Museum

Photo 37: Image of Tara, Da Nang Museum

5. History of Champa   217

(895-904). The relationship between the two kings is not definitely known. The Dong Duong inscription (No.36), however says the mother of Jaya Simhavarman had a younger sister Pov ku lyan Sri Rajakula, also known as Haradevi. Haradevi's husband was Sri Parama-Buddhaloka, and she installed Sri Indraparamosvara for the sake of religious merit of her own husband. This might be taken to imply that the coronation-name of her husband was Indravarman, as the name of the gods is often formed by the addition of the name of the king. It may be held therefore that Haradevi was the queen of Indravarman II.

An inscription says that from Indravarman II was born the fortunate and intelligent Dharmaraja, Sri Rudravarman. The son of the latter was far-famed King Sri Bhadravarma. The son of Sri Bhadravarma (III), known as Sri Indravarman (III), had become the king of Champa through the grace of Mahesvara (Siva God). Thus, the sovereignty of the king was transmitted in this entirety from those kings. It was not given by the grandfather or the father. By the special merit of the authorities, and by the virtue of his pure intelligence, he gained (the kingdom), not from his grandfather or father. (No.31, A18-22)

According to this view, Shimhavarman would be the son of the elder sister of Indravarman's queen, and Indravarman would have the epithet of Parama-Buddaloka.

The founder of this family, Sarthavaha, was a nephew of Rudravarman III, the first king of the dynasty, and a brother of the principal queen of Indravarman II. (Majumdar, p64)

Bhadravarman III must have a short reign (905-911). His known dates are 909 or 911. His reign, therefore, falls between this date and 903 the last date of Jaya Simhavarman. At one king intervened

218   THE HISTORY OF SRIVIJAYA, ANGKOR and CHAMPA

between the two, he did not probably reign for more than a period of five years, 905 to 910. During Jaya Simhavarman's reign, Pilih Rajadvarah was sent to Yavadvipa as an ambassador. His mission was very successful. In this case, Yavadvipa was Srivijaya (San-fo-chi). So, Srivijaya had a friendly relation with Champa at the beginning of the 10th century.

Bhadravarman III was succeeded by his son Indravarman III (911-959). His literary accomplishments are described in the Po Nagar inscription (No.45). (Majumdar p65). Despite of obvious exaggerations, the king must be taken to have been a remarkable scholar in his date.

In the inscription of Nhan Bieu of Indravarman III, dated 911 (No.43), there is description that King Sri Jaya Simhavarman sent a diplomatic mission to Yavadvipa (Malay Peninsula, Srivijaya) headed by Pov Krun Pilih Rajadvarah. After this mission the relation between San-fo-chi (Srivijaya) and Champa became familiar. San-fo-chi got the friendly intermediary port in Champa. Pilih Rajadvarah is close relative of the king and continues to occupy a high position.

The development of the relation of both kingdoms was not recorded in any document, but San-fo-chi must have helped Champa strongly. Later Champa had established the 'Vijaya Kingdom' at the end of the 10th century.

A stele dated 918 by Cham King Indravarman III states an order to build a gold statue of the goddess Bhagavati. According to the Po Nagar inscription (No.47), the gold image installed by Indravarman III was carried away by Angkor King Rajendravarman II in 946, and Jaya Indravarman III replaced the lost statue with a new stone one in 965.

This event tells us, the Dong Duong Dynasty had dominated Nha Trang in the 10th century, even though its capital was located at

5. History of Champa

Dong Duong.

After collapse of the Tang Dynasty in 907, Champa King, Sri Indravarman III（釋利因德漫）sent tributary envoy, led by Abu Hasan （甫訶散）to Latter Zhou（後周）in 958.

From Latter Zhou （951-960）, General Zao Kuangyin （趙匡胤, Emperor Taizu, 太祖 960-976）took the throne and founded the 'Song Dynasty' in 960. He was succeeded by his younger brother Zao Kuangyi（趙匡義, Emperor Taizong, 太宗 976-997）.

R.C. Majumdar says that Indravarman III enjoyed a long term reign of more than sixty years during 911 and 972. But there is a different opinion that Indravarman III died in 959, and Jaya Indravarman I （釋利因陀盤）succeeded the throne（959-972）. He sent ambassador Abu Hasan to the Song Dynasty in 960. The Song Dynasty started in 960;（North Song 960-1126, South Song 1127-1279）

In any case, the *Song Shi*（宋史）recognizes that Zhan-cheng（占城）was situated near Da Nang and Hoi An, and put Panduranga under control in the south. Champa had been separated several by area from north to south.

For a century, after the death of Indravarman III, the history of Champa is obscure. because there is no inscription, so we must depend upon the Chinese chronicle and the Annam text. From the north, Annam started invasion to Champa and Champa had to remove its capital to the southern area.

Majumdar says:"Indravarman III seems to have been succeeded by a king whose name is differently spelt in Chinese histories and may be taken to Paramesvavarman（972-982）. He sent embassies to China in 972, 973, 974, 976, 977 and 979. But he was soon involved in a quarrel with the Annamites which brought upon himself and

220   THE HISTORY OF SRIVIJAYA, ANGKOR and CHAMPA

kingdom." Probably Dong Duong might be occupied and Annamite king (general) Liu Ji-Zong (劉繼宗, killed in 988) usurped the throne.

5-4-1   Champa's missions to Song

The *Song Shi* recorded Champa's missions as follows:

In 960, Champa sent an embassy.

In 961, Sri Indravarman (釋利因陀盤 = Sri Jaya Indravarman I) sent ambassador Abu Hasan (甫訶散) with the official letter and many gifts (including, rhinoceros horns, ivories, incense, peacocks and big Arabic glass bottles). The Emperor of Song awarded them plenty.

In 962, Champa brought tribute of 22 pieces ivory and 1,000Jin (斤) of frankincense (乳香). Arabic frankincense is the most favored by Chinese.

In 966, Sri Indravarman (釋利因陀盤) sent ambassador, accompanying queen and prince.

In 967, 968, 970 Champa sent envoys to Song.

In 971, King Sri Jaya Indravarman I (悉利多盤),Viceroy Ali-Nou (李耨), queen and prince visited the Song Court.

In 972, King Paramesvara Indravarman I (波美税褐印茶) sent ambassador Abu Hasan (甫訶散).

In 973, King Sri Jaya Indravarman I (悉利盤陀印茶) sent ambassador .

In 974, King Paramesvara Indravarman I (波利税褐茶) sent tribute (peacock umbrella 2 and 40 Jin of West Indian iron bar).

In 976, Champa sent envoys (without king's name).

In 977, King Paramesvara Indravarman I (波利税陽布印茶).

In 978, 979, 982, 983, Champa sent envoys (without king's name)

In 985, Sri Indravarman IV (施利陀般呉日歡) sent ambassador, Brahman Jin-ge-ma (金歌麻).He appealed to the Emperor that Jiaozhou (交州) invades Champa. In 986, King Liu Ji-Zong (劉繼宗) sent ambassador with various presents (rhino-horns, ivories,

5. History of Champa

Photo 38: Khmer Tower, Vijaya

incense). But he was killed in 988 possibly by Cham people. Soon after his death, Champa probably changed its capital to Vijaya (Quy Nhon).

King Liu Ji-Zong is an Annam general, so he might have usurped the throne of the Dong Duong dynasty, around 982.

R.C. Majumdar explains these situations as follows:
"The downfall of the Tang Dynasty in 907 was followed by a period of anarchy. The Annam took full advantage of this situation and freed themselves from the iron yoke of the Chinese. The first independent royal Annam dynasty was founded by Ngo Quyen in 939. By 965 twelve important chiefs had partitioned their country. In 968 Dinh Bo Linh defeated the twelve chiefs and proclaimed himself emperor. He ruled for 12 years but was murdered in 979.

222   THE HISTORY OF SRIVIJAYA, ANGKOR and CHAMPA

Ngo Nhut Khanh, one of the twelve chiefs defeated by the emperor, had taken refuge in the Court of Champa. As soon as news of the emperor's death reached him he planned to seize the throne and asked for the aid of Paramesvavarman. The latter readily consented and led a naval expedition to Tonkin in person. The Cham fleet made good progress and reached within a few miles of the capital, but storm destroyed his navy."

Le Hoan (黎桓; life 941-1005) was elected by Annam chiefs as their emperor in 980. He opposed a Chinese expedition sent by the Emperor Kuang -yi (光義). He sent an ambassador to Paramesvavarman, but the latter imprisoned him. Le Hoan was furious and led an expedition against Champa. Paramesvavarman was defeated and killed in 982, and Le Hoan marched towards capital.

A new king was set up, but he could not compete Le Hon and retreated to the South in 982. The new king was recorded as Indrvarman IV (982-983).

Le Hoan, the first emperor of the Early Le Dynasty, succeeding the Dinh Dynasty as the ruler of Annam.

5-5 Vijaya Kingdom

The new Vijaya kingdom had sent the first mission to China in 990. Apparently Champa change its capital from Dong Duong to Vijaya (Quy Nhon) after King Liu Ji-Zong (劉繼宗) was killed in 988.

In 990, King Vijaya Sri Harivarman II (楊陀拜), sent mission led by the first ambassador Ali Sin (李臻), 2nd ambassador was Abu Hasan (甫訶散) with tributes (rhino-horns, ivories, wax, various incense, cardamom, perfume etc.).

5. History of Champa

Champa （占城、Zancheng） was at first located at Indrapura and moved to Dong Duong （Buddha city）, south of Hoi An, but being occupied by Le Hoan （黎桓） of Annam. The Annam general Liu Ji-Zong （劉繼宗） rebelled against Le Hoan and usurped the throne of Champa. Le Hoan advanced his army to punish Liu Ji-Zong, but failed. However, Liu Ji-Zong was killed in 988 probably by the Cham hero appeared at Vijaya. During this confusion Champa removed their capital to Quy Nhon （Vijaya） area and in 989 Champa fixed Vijaya as it capital.

The first king is Sri Harivarman II （楊陀排, 988-998） who sent the first envoy from Vijaya in 990. His ambassador explained to the Song Court that King Sri Harivarman II set up the new throne at Vijaya （Binh Dinh）. The origin of 'Vijaya' is unknown, but it might have some relation with Srivijaya （San-fo-chi）, since the beginning of the 10th century.

Shortly after his accession, Harivarman II found his territory again ravaged by Le Hoan. He sent an embassy to the Song Court with rich tribute and complained about the conduct of Le Hoan. And the Emperor commanded Le Hoan to stay within his territory. Champa did not help Annam rebel against Le Hoan, so he appreciated friendship of Champa king and released many Cham prisoners in 992. During the same year the Song Emperor sent a rich present to Harivarman II, who was glad and sent in return an envoy with plenty of tribute.

Until being destroyed by Annam in the second half of the 15th century, Vijaya had survived., sometimes under the control of Angkor. However, kings of 'Vijaya' kept contact with Indrapura area and left some inscriptions there. Vijaya had been strong as the trade centre of Champa.

224   THE HISTORY OF SRIVIJAYA, ANGKOR and CHAMPA

In December 990, a new King Harivarman II (楊陀排) sent tribute mission, who self- claimed new king of Vijaya state. But where was the Vijaya state? The Vijaya (Binh Dinh) theory is popular, but M. Vickery doubts about it. (M. Vickery, p386)

M. Vickery says: 'Vijaya' has been misunderstood as both a name and a location, leading to erroneous interpretations in the historical narrative. The name Vijaya in all modern literature on Champa is conventionally understood as the old Champa centre in Binh Dinh near the modern city of Quy Nhon. 'William Southworth' has most strongly and correctly insisted that 'Champa' was neither a unitary polity nor even a federation, but rather consisted of several separate entities, the interrelationship among which varied from time to time (total separation, alliance, peace, hostility and trade).
However we cannot ignore the description of the *Song Si* (宋史).

　　「淳化元年,新王楊陀排自稱新坐佛逝國， 楊陀排遣使李臻貢馴犀方物,表訴爲交州國中人所攻,民財皆爲寶所略。」

The new king, Sri Harivarman II (楊陀排, 988-998) sent the first envoy in 990. His ambassador explained to the Song Court that King Sri Harivarman II set up the new throne at Vijaya.

Apparently 'Vijaya' was set up earlier than in 990, even though the location is not mentioned at that time. The problem is why new state was set up at Vijaya. It is natural to think that Champa in Indrapura district (Thu Bon area) was removed to the south to avoid direct attack of Annam troops.

The word 'Fo-shi = 佛逝' means 'Vijaya'. Srivijaya is 'Shi-li-fo-shi = 室利佛逝', so there may be some relation between the names of the two polities. However, we cannot solve this problem now. M. Vickery apparently ignores this text.

Vijaya was certainly connected with Binh Dinh area. I suppose Champa had two capitals. One was at the north such as Dong Duong, and another was at Binh Dinh and usually the king had stayed Binh Dinh for the security reason. In Binh Dinh region, there are several brick towers of Khmer style. I cannot solve the relation between Champa and Angkor and Srivijaya, but certainly some relation existed.

In January 990, San-fo-chi sent envoy to Song, and the same year the ambassador went back to San-fo-chi, but he stopped at Champa, because he heard that 'Jawa (Medang, King Dharmawangsa)' was attacking San-fo-chi. In 991, the ambassador could not go back to his country, so he reported the invasion to the Song Court. In 992, Jawa sent mission to Song with huge tribute, but the Song Court prohibited Jawa to send mission for 200 years until 1192.

Around 990, the relation between Champa and San-fo-chi was friendly. The good relation had continued from the beginning of the 10th century. Probably the ambassador of San-fo-chi stopped over at Binh Dinh port in his return to San-fo-chi in 990.

M. Vickery wants to say it was 'Dong Duong (Buddha city). Later in the middle of the 12th century, Jayavarman VII said to have stayed at Vijaya, he might have no reason to stay at Dong Duong where was too far from Angkor. Jayavarman VII constructed 'royal road' to Binh Dinh at the end of his reign.

It is recorded that King Rajendravarman II and his son Jayavarman V of Angkor had sent forces to Champa.

There was Harivarman IV, who left his inscription at My-Son, dated 1081. He has re-established the edifices and city of Champa, during the troublesome days of the war…and seeing Srisanabhadresvara despoiled of all his possessions at the end of war, he came to worship the god with a pious heart.

226 THE HISTORY OF SRIVIJAYA, ANGKOR and CHAMPA

Siva cult had been practiced in the My-Son Sanctuary between the 8th and the 12 / 13th centuries.

Vijaya is conventionally understood as the old Champa centre in the Binh Dinh district near the modern city of Quy Nhon.

5-5-1 Vijaya's tribute to Song

In March 997, Champa King Harivarman II（Yan Pu Ku Vijaya Sri 楊甫恭毘施離）sent an ambassador to Song. The ambassador explained that his king was Yan Pu Ku Vijaya Harivarman（盈卜皮紫訶哩援焉）.

In February 999, Harivarman II （楊普俱毘茶逸施離 Yan Pu Ku Vijaya Sri), sent an envoy to the Song Court again, with tributes (rhino-horn, ivory, turtle-shell and incense).

In September 1004, King Harivarman II（楊甫毘茶逸施離）、sent an envoy.

In 1005, Champa sent tribute to Song.

In 1007, King Harivarman II （楊普俱毘茶室離） sent an envoy together with Da Shi (Arab countries, 大食) to Song. Arab merchants started to use Champa as trade partners. Thereafter, Champa can tribute large volume of 'frankincense' to the Song Court. Formerly frankincense（乳香）had been almost monopolized by San-fo-chi（三佛齊）from Southeast Asia. San-fo-chi purchased frankincense from Arab countries, which was the most important tributary item to the Song Court.

In 1008, Da Shi and Champa sent tributes together to Song.

In April 1009, Champa sent an envoy. (The *Song Hui yao* 宋會要)

In April 1010, King Sri Harivarmadeva （施離霞離鼻麻底 Harivarman II) sent an envoy. Dr. Naojiro Sugimoto interprets that 施離 = Sri, 霞離 = Hari、鼻麻底＝Varmadeva, so this king is Sri Harivarman II.

In 1011, Champa King Harivarman II （楊普毘茶室離 Yan Pu Ku Sri Harivarman) presented to the Song Court lions with two native persons who take care of them. The Emperor pitied lions and let them come back with sufficient food. Other presents are ivory, rhino-horn, turtle-shell, incense, clove, cardamom, etc.

5. History of Champa 227

In February and May 1015, Champa sent an envoys with many presents including frankincense.

In 1018, Champa King Sri Harivarman II (尸嘿排摩) sent an envoy with tributes (ivories 72, rhino-horns 86, turtle-shells 1000Jin (斤), frankincense 50 Jin, clove 80 Jin, cardamom 65 Jin etc.

In May 1029, Champa sent an ambassador. (The *Song Hui Yao*, 宋會要)

In October 1030, Champa King Yan Pu Sri Vikrantavarman (陽補孤施離皮蘭德加拔麻疊) sent an ambassador with tribute of incense, turtle-shell, frankincense, ivory, rhino-horn.

In November 1042, Champa King Yan Pu Sri Jaya Simhavarman II (刑卜施離值星霞弗) sent an envoy, and presented 3 trained elephants, ivory, rhino-horn, incense etc.

In January 1044, Le Tai Song (李太宗) of Vietnam invaded Champa and battles took place at Hue and Da Nang. Champa was defeated in every battle, and Vietnam army occupied Dong Duong after 7 months' battle. Champa king (probably Yan Pu Sri Jaya Shimhavarman II) was killed and 5,000 Chams were captured together with palace women.

However, M. Vickery opposes this history,
"The period from the war of 1044 to the war of 1069, which Maspero---on the basis of one Vietnamese source but not the official chronicles---called another attack on Vijaya, is perhaps the most fictionalized segment of his story. (M. Vickery, Vietnam, p 390)

In January 1050, Champa King (俱舍波微收羅婆麻提楊卜＝Ku Sri Paramesvarmadeva Yang Pu) sent an envoy to Song with 201 ivories and 79 rhino-horns and presented official letter.

In April 1053, Champa King sent an envoy to Song, with presents (168 ivories, 20 rhino-horns, 60 Jin turtle-shell and many volume and many kinds of incense).

In November 1054, Champa sent tribute of elephants and

228   THE HISTORY OF SRIVIJAYA, ANGKOR and CHAMPA

rhinoceroses.

In March 1056, Champa sent tribute. In the same year, Sri Yuvaraja Mahasenapati said to have attacked Sambhupura, one of big cities in Angkor. This story is recorded in the inscription of My-Son, but Angkor side said nothing about this invasion. Sambhupura was the old capital of the former 'Land Chenla' and in 1050s, there was little importance for the Angkor dynasty. At that time, Angkor king was Udayadityavarman II (1050-1066), former commander of Suryavarman I.

R. C. Majumdar explains in detail about Champa King Sri Paramesvaravarmadeva and his nephew Yuvaraja Mahasenapati and Devaraja Mahasenapati.

They conquered the rebellion of Panduranga in 1050. An inscriprion says: "All the troops of Panduranga came to fight. Yuvaraja (crown prince) pursued and crushed them all and they took shelter in mountains and caverns. On behalf of king Paramesvaravarmadeva Dharmarja, Yuvaraja, who had a powerful army, ordered his troops to pursue them in all directions. And these troops got hold of all the people of Panduranga with oxen, buffaloes, slaves and elephants. The kings installed lings to commemorate their victory".

Next, the king turned his attention towards his western enemy, the commander Yuvaraja proceeded to the Angkor dynasty and crushed the Angkor army and took the town of Sambhupura. The commander Yuvaraja destroyed many temples there and distributed the Khmer captives among the temples of Srisanabhadresnara. However, Angkor left no record of this invasion. So, this story is quite dubious. Probably 100 years later, Angkor occupied Vijaya, by Jayavarman VII (or Suryavarman II in 1145)

At this time Champa probably dominated Thu Bon area, but

5. History of Champa

Southern area (Phan Rang and Nha Trang) was out of control. Panduranga had enjoyed a semi-independent status, when it was not the chief seat of power in Champa, and was a constant source of irritation to the Cham kingdom ruling at the north. A strong king, Jaya Paramesvaravarman, came to the throne of Champa about 1050 or a little earlier and, with his son (or nephew) Yuvaraja Mahasenapati, thoroughly subdued Panduranga, according to the several inscriptions of Po Klang Garai, Phan Rang dated 1050.

The Song Court who did not register the war of 1044 and 1069 (between Dai Viet and Champa), seems to have been in contact with Rudravarman of Phan Rang, for they recorded a tribute mission from 'Champa' in 1069, and it is not certain that all the envoys recorded as coming to China from 'Champa' were from the same region. For the Chinse officials, they could not have identified the separate relations with the Thu Bon- Quang Nam-Quang Ngai rulers and with Panduranga rulers.

Epigraphy toward the end of the eleventh century shows two groups of royalties, one in the Thu Bon area leaving inscription in My-Son and another in the South with the inscriptions in Nha Trang and Phan Rang.

R. C. Majumdar gives us the detailed explanations in his book (Champa) as follows.

"Jaya Paramesvaravarman cultivated good relations with the Emperors of China and Annam. To the Song Court he sent ambassadors in 1050, 1053 and 1056. On the last journey, his ambassador was shipwrecked and lost all his cargo, whereupon the Chinese Emperor sent him 1000 ounces of silver."

Champa's ambassadors also visited the Court of Annam Emperor in 1047, 1050, 1055, 1060 and sometimes between 1057 and 1059.

Jaya Paramesvaravarman was probably succeeded by Bhadra-

230   THE HISTORY OF SRIVIJAYA, ANGKOR and CHAMPA

varman IV."

He probably sent tribute to China in 1061. He was succeeded by
Rudravarman III. He was born in the family of Jaya Paramesvara,
but the relation is unknown. From the beginning, he prepared
attacking Annam. He sent an ambassador to China in 1062 for
securing assistance against Annam but the Chinese Emperor did
not want to attack Annam. So, Rudravarman III sent tributes to
the Annam Emperor 1063, 1065 and 1068. But all the while he
continued preparations and opened hostility towards the end of
1068. The Annamite Emperor, Ly Thanh Ton (李聖宗、1054-72) took
up the challenge and moved his troops on February 1069.

The inscriptions of Champa refer to troubles in the past,
approximately the 1060s-70s, but not to war with Vietnam (Annam).

However, R.C. Majumdar gave us the detailed explanations in his
book (Champa) as follows.

Majumdar says as follows:
"After long fierce battle, Champa was defeated, on the 17th
July, the Annamite army occupied the capital. Rudravarman
with his family was caught near the Angkor border. About
50,000 prisoners were taken to Tonkin, and Rudravarman was
freed after he gave 3 districts to Annam, Dia Ly, Ma Linh and
Bo Chanh in 1069."
" This meant the cession of the whole of Quang Binh and the
northern part of Quang Tri and brought the frontier of Champa
to the mouth of the river Viet. However, Champa was to fight to
regain these territories in the future many times. On his return
to Champa, Rudravarman III found Champa was in the state of
anarchy and several persons had claimed themselves as kings in
different parts of the kingdom." (Majumdar, p. 82).

However, the *Song Hui Yao* (宋會要) tells nothing about the wars in 1044 and 1069. M. Vickery does not believe this story as above mentioned.

M. Vickery says as follows:
"Ma Linh and Bo Chinh far north of Indrapura-Dong Du (r) ong, had already been reported as lost at the end of the tenth century, and their possession again by the Cham until the war of 1069 belies the interpretation of a Cham retreat from Indrapura to Vijaya at the end of the 990s. Here we see the confusion in the sources concerning Viet-Champa relation."

However, there might be no reason for Champa rulers to tell a simple lie to pretend the removal of capital to Vijaya.

The Song Court who did not register the war of 1044 and 1069, seems to have been in contact with Rudravarman III of Phan Rang, for they recorded a tribute mission from Champa in 1069, and it is not certain that all the envoys recorded as coming to China from 'Champa' were from the same region. It would have been unusual for China to have separate relations with the Thu Bon- Quang Nam-Quang Ngai rulers and with Pandurang rulers which at different times they considered a distinct separate polity.

Epigraphy toward the end of the eleventh century shows two groups of royalties, one in the Thu Bon area leaving inscription in My-Son and another in the South with the inscriptions in Nha Trang and Phan Rang. (M. Vickery, Short History of Champa, p52).

Champa sent tributes to Annam in 1071, 1072 and 1074, and to China in 1072.

Among many competitors after Rudravarman III, in 1074 Harivarman IV took the throne of Champa. He was the son of Pramesvara Dharmaraja of the Coconut Clan. His mother belonged to the Betelnut Clan, so he represented the two chief rival families of the kingdom.

232   THE HISTORY OF SRIVIJAYA, ANGKOR and CHAMPA

After defeat of Rudravarman III, Harivarman IV established his authority over the greater part of Champa. But the civil war continued throughout his reign and he had to fight with rival chiefs for the throne of Champa. To make matters worse, the Annam king sent a new expedition in 1075, and the king of Angkor began plundering raids.

Harivarman IV, Cham prince who reigned 1074-81, boasts of a victory at Somesvara over Khmer troops commanded by a prince, Nandanavarman, who was captured by him. Nandanavarman had a royal title, but left no trace in Khmer epigraphy. (C. Jacques, p145)

The Annam forces were also defeated, so Harivarman IV assured the safety of the newly established power. King Harivarman IV celebrated his coronation. He had to repair the damages by Annam invasions and civil wars. The inscription writes: "The Majesty Vijaya Sri Harivarmadeva, Yan Devatamuti ascended the throne. He completely defeated the enemies, proceeded to the Nagara Champs and restored the temple of Srisanabhadresvara. (No. 61).

Two inscriptions of My-Son (Nos. 61, 62) describe in detail the work of restoration by the king and his brother Yuvaraja Mahasenapati. (Majumdar, p. 86)

With the exception of Panduranga, the whole of Champa was united under his authority. In 1081, at the age of 41 Harivarmn IV abdicated in favor of his eldest son, Pulyan Sri Rajadevara, and devoted himself to spiritual exercises and worship of Siva. However, he died soon in 1081. His 14 wives followed him to death in right Indian fashion.

Pulyan Sri Rajadevara ascended the throne under the name of Yan-pu-ku Sri Jaya Indravarmadeva II. He was a boy of 9 years old then and was obviously unfit to hold the reign of government

5. History of Champa

in those troublesome days. He had hardly reigned for a month, and the throne was offered to Pu-lyan Sri Yuvaraja Mahasenapati, prince Pan, younger brother of Sri Harivarman IV. The event is thus described in the My-Son Inscription of Jaya Indravarman II himself.

The Yuvaraja ascended the throne under the title Paramabodhisattva in 1081 A.D. He recovered Panduranga and achieved the unity of Champa. At Panduranga a usurper (name is unknown) had set up an independent kingdom after the Annamite invasion of 1069. And maintained his position for 16 years. However, Paramabodhisattava resigned in 1086, and his nephew regained the throne, and revived the name of Sri Jaya Indravarman II at the age of 14 years old.

Jaya Indravarman II (1086-1114) paid his tribute to Annam regularly, but he deplored the loss of the three districts ceded by Rudravarman III.

The two peoples (Champa and Annam) were so much estranged over this question, that when their ambassadors, having arrived at the Chinese court on the same day, they kept themselves aloof from each other. At a dinner time in which they were invited they sat at two ends of the table. At last in 1092. Indravarman II stopped the payment of tribute to Annam (Chiao Zhi = 交趾) and approached the Chinese emperor with a proposal to make common cause against Annam. The Chinese emperor, however, refused to fight with Annam. Nevertheless, Jaya Indravarman II continued to withhold the tribute till a formal complaint was made by the Annamese Court in 1094. Jaya Indravarman Ⅱ was seized with terror, and hastened to comply with the demand of tribute. The tributes was sent in 1095, 1097, 1098, 1099 and 1102.

Jaya Indravarman II tried to attack Annam to recover the ceded districts in 1103, but he was easily defeated by Annam. He immediately sent tribute to Annam. Henceforth the two countries

234   THE HISTORY OF SRIVIJAYA, ANGKOR and CHAMPA

live in peace and tributes were regularly sent from Champa to Annam.

Jaya Indravarman II was succeeded to his nephew Harivarman V in 1114. (No.68). Harivarman V died in 1139, but left no children and succeeded by Jaya Indravarman III. (1139-1145).

Jaya Indravarman III was born in 1106, and he became Devaraja in 1129 and Yuvaraja in 1133. Finally, he ascended the throne in 1139 (No.69). He was involved in a quarrel with the Angkor king, Suryavarman II, who ascended the throne in 1112 and began to harass Champa. Suryavarman II sent a tribute mission to Song in 1116, thereafter he started invasion to Annam 1128, with 20,000 army and induced the king of Champa to join the Angkor force. But the both armies were separately defeated by the Annamite army. Next Suryavarman II dispatched a navy of 700 vessels to harass the coast of Than Hoa. A similar attempt was again made in 1132 when Jaya Indravarman III invaded Nghe An in concert with the army of Angkor, but was easily defeated. He then settled matters with Annam by paying off the tribute in 1136.

At the same time, he withdrew from the offensive alliance with Angkor. Suryavarman II got angry and in 1144-5, he invaded Champa and made himself the 'master of Vijaya'. Jaya Indravarman III was killed in this battle. During 1145-49, Angkor had dominated Vijaya.

After this incident, a descendant of king Paramabodhisattva proclaimed himself king and took refuge in Panduranga. His name was Rudravarman Parama Brahmaloka. He was a son of eminent king Rudraloka, who was the successor of Harivarman V. However, he died in 1147.

On the death of the king, the people of Panduranga invited his son

5. History of Champa

Ratnabhumivijaya to be the king of Champa, and he ascended the throne in 1147, under the name of Sri Jaya Harivarman I (鄒時蘭巴).

Sri Jaya Harivarman I ascended the throne in the difficult time. The greater part of Champa was under the attack of Angkor and Annamite. In 1147, Jaya Harivarman I defeated the Angkor army at the field of Kayev.

The Angkor army commanded by general Sangkara was aided by Cham soldiers of Vijaya. Jaya Harivarman I met at Chaklyan (probably the southern village of Phan Vijaya) to fight in the plain of Virapura and defeated the Angkor army. The next year in 1148, Jaya Harivarman I met the Angkor troops at the field of Kayev and also defeated them.

Suryavarman II consecrated his brother-in-law, Harideva, as King of Champa and commanded generals to lead the Angkor troops and to protect Prince Harideva until he became king of Vijaya. Jaya Harivarman I marched northward, seized Vijaya and totally destroyed the Khmer and Cham forces at Mahisa. Harideva was killed at that time. Then Jaya Harivarman I was consecrated at Vijaya in 1149.

But the relative of Jaya Harivarman I betrayed him. The brother of his wife called Vanaraja now joined his enemies. But Jaya Harivarman I defeated them all.
At last he integrated Champa from Panduranga to Vijaya, and later My-Son area.
However, civilian war took place, first at Amaravati (1151) and then Panduranga (1155). Jaya Harivarman I defeated both. He restored all the damaged temples and set up Sivalingas.

Like Jaya Indravarman II (Buddhist King, Dong Duong, 875),

236   THE HISTORY OF SRIVIJAYA, ANGKOR and CHAMPA

king Jaya Harivarman I also believed that he was an incarnation of Uroja (legendary hero). He sent tribute to China in 1152 and in 1154. To the Ammanite court he also sent tribute in 1155 and 1160. He died in 1162, and he was succeeded by his son Jaya Harivarman II, He is referred to as a king by his son's inscriptions (No.94 and 95). Within a year of the death of king Jaya Harivarman II, the throne of Champa was occupied by Pu Ciy Anak Sri Jaya Indravarman IV, an inhabitant of Gramapura Vijaya. He sent tributes to Annamite court in 1164 and 1165.

Jaya Indravarman IV was formally consecrated to the throne about in 1165. He sent an envoy to the Song Court. The tributes from Champa was plundered from Arab merchants. The Emperor, who had been informed the source of tribute, refused to accept them. The offered tributes from Champa was extremely huge as follows:

By 6 vessels, white frankincense 20,435 Jin (斤), common grade frankincense 80,295 Jin, ivory 7,795 Jin, various kind of incense. Frankincense was the most important and variable item for the Song Court.

Jaya Indravarman IV paid big present to the Emperor of Annamite and secured the neutrality of Annam. On the other hand, he began to attack the Angkor 1170, At that time the king of Angkor was Tribhuvanadityavarman. Jaya Indrvarman asked China for purchasing horses, but China was not affirmative.

(Tribute missions: 1061-1176)

In 1061 Champa sent an envoy with tribute of trained elephants.
In May 1062, Champa ambassador Ton-pa-ni (頓琶尼) presented tribute in box.
In June 1062, The Song Court gave the Champa king, Yan Pu Sri

5. History of Champa

Rudravarman III（施里律茶盤麻常楊溥）one white horse.

In June 1068, The Champa king Yang Pu Sri Rudravarmadeva （卜尸利律陀般摩提婆）sent ambassador Abu Mohamed（蒲麻勿）to the Song Court with tribute and asked for permission to purchase mules (not horses) in the market. The Emperor gave him one white horse with silver saddle, and instruction to Kanton officials to help him purchasing mules.

In 1069 Dai Vet is said to attack Binh Dinh (Vijaya), but M. Vickery is suspicious. (M. Vickery, p393). Vijaya is too far from Dai Vet.

In April 1072,the ambassador Ali Po-liu（李蒲薩）was sent to Song, with tribute of grass-ware, camphor, frankincense, pepper and so on.

In 1076, 1086, 1127 Champa sent missions but very fewer times compared with San-fo-chi. There was political turmoil in Champa.

In 1084, Paramabodhisattava（波羅摩菩提薩）set up his political base at the Thu Bon area, after the victory of war between Nha Trang and Panduranga.

In 1088, Jaya Indravarman II regained the throne of Champa.

Around in 1113、Harivarman V（楊卜麻疊）ascend the throne (Yuko Dohi, 2017, p398).

In 1117, Champa sent tribute, with golden flower to Dai Vet (Annam).

In 1129, Champa king Harivarman V（楊卜麻疊）sent an ambassador to Song.

In 1132, the Champa king sent an envoy with present of rhinoceroses, elephants, turtle-shells and incense.

Since 1139 Jaya Indravarman III, retained the throne of Champa (1139-1145).

In October 1155, Jaya Harivarman I（鄒時蘭巴）sent mission with tribute rhino-horn 20, ivory 168, turtle-shell 60 Jin and various incenses.

In November 1155, Angkor and Lopburi sent a joint mission to the

238   THE HISTORY OF SRIVIJAYA, ANGKOR and CHAMPA

Song Court. (The *Song Shi*)

In December 1116, Angkor king Suryavarman II, sent tribute mission to the Song Court after 300 years' absence.

In 1119, Angkor sent mission (14 officials) to Song, and the next year they were awarded Chinese officials costume and the King was assigned to the king of Champa (nominal).

5-5-2 Confusion of Champa and Jayavarman VII

In 1166 or 1167 Jaya Indravarman IV (鄒亞娜) killed Jaya Harivarman II and took the throne.

In 1167 Jaya Indravarman IV (鄒亞娜) robbed the cargo of Da Shi and sent an envoy with huge present to the Song Court. But the Song Court rejected to accept it and no reward was given. But finally, the Song Court bought up all of the 'frankincense'. (p236)

Jaya Indravarman IV was not authorized by Song as the king of Champa, but treated as the heir-apparent of the king.

He is Jaya Indravarman on Vatun, came from Gramapuravijaya and a typical usurper, who sent tribute to Annam too. And he fought against Angkor.

China recorded in 1170, Jaya Indravarman IV attacked Angkor but unsuccessful.

In 1174 Jaya Indravarman IV again sent tribute to Song. In 1176, he sent the last official mission to Song and rewarded silk and silver. But his title was still 'heir-apparent of King. He was not authorized as king of Champa. (文忠集、卷111)

In 1177, here is a story that Jaya Indravarman IV attacked Angkor and killed King Tribhuvanadityavarman and returned with enormous booty. But M. Vickery denies this story, because no inscription about this war   recorded in Champa. However, King Tribhuvanadityavarman was certainly killed by someone. Jayavarman VII took the Angkor throne 4 years later in 1811.

5. History of Champa

This attack in 1177, is recorded in the Chinese text, but probably the Chinese official was told this dubious story by the ambassador of Jayavarman VII in 1200. The incident in 1177, was basically 'coup d'état' by Jayavarman VII, by using the military assistance of Champa, led by Indravarman IV, so the inscription of Champa might have been quiet about this incident.

In 1182, Champa prince Vidyanandana of Tumpraukvijaya (later Cham king Suryavarmadeva) went to Angkor and was taken into the service of Jayavarman VII. In that capacity, he led troops to put down a rebellion in Malyang, near Battambang and defeated the enemy. He was then assigned Yuvaraja (crown prince) by Jayavarman VII.

He entrusted this campaign to a young Cham refugee prince named Sri Vidyanandana, native of Tumprank-Vijaya. The king of Champa was at that time was Jaya Indravarman IV. The story of this prince is told in the My-Son pillar inscription:

In 1190, king Sri Jaya Indravarman IV made war against the king of Kambujadesa (Jayavarman VII). Prince Vidyanandana as the head of the Angkor troops to take Vijaya and defeat the king. He captured the Indravarnan IV and had brought him to Kambujadesa (Angkor). He proclaimed Suryavarmadeva Prince In, brother-in-law of the king of Kambujadesa (Jayavarman VII), as the king of Vijaya.

In 1190, Sri Jaya Indravarman IV was captured by Jayavarman VII and in 1911 he was released, but killed by his subordinate. (Dohi, p460) But there is a different story as below.

The Cham inscription, Po Nagar says that Jayavarman VII took the capital and carried off all the lingas, because he is Buddhist.

240   THE HISTORY OF SRIVIJAYA, ANGKOR and CHAMPA

However in 1191, a revolt drove Prince In (Vidyanandana) out of Champa and seated in his place a Cham prince Rashupati, who ruled under the name of Jaya Indravarmadeva Jaya Indravarman V. In 1192, Jayavarman VII sent Jaya Indravarman IV (Ong Vatuv) to help prince Vidyanandana reconquer Champa. They met at Rajapura, took Vijaya and killed Jaya Indravarman V, and ruled over Vijaya.

Then Jaya Indravarman IV fled from Cambodia and went to Amaravati where he raised a revolt and invaded Vijaya; but the prince Vidyanandana defeated and killed him. Henceforth the prince ruled without opposition (Briggs, p216).

Champa was united again under a Cham king Suryavarmadeva (prince Vidyanandana). However, he rebelled against Jayavarman VII later. In 1193, Jayavarman VII sent an army to Champa, but defeated. The next year Angkor sent a larger army, but defeated again. In 1194 Suryavarmadeva sent tribute to Dai Vet. In 1198, he was formally consecrated and sent an embassy to the Song Court asking for investiture, which he received in 1199.

However, Jayavarman VII, finally attacked Champa, Suryavarmadeva fled to Dai Viet. But he was involved in trouble at the Co-la port with the local governor of Dai Viet and heard nothing from the incident.

慶元(1195-)以來, 眞臘大舉伐占城以復讎, 殺戮殆盡, 俘其主以歸, 國遂亡, 其地悉歸眞臘。(The *Song Shi*)

The *Song Shi* says that after 1195, Angkor invaded with big army to revenge, and killed many people and captured the king. Champa was destroyed and occupied completely by Angkor.

Jayavarman   VII   died   in   1218,   post-humous   name   of

5. History of Champa

Mahaparamasaugata (reigned 1181-1218). Angkor pulled out from Champa in 1220. Angkor realized they had no power to put Champa under control. After 1222, Champa regained independence by Jaya Parameshvaravarman II. He used to be a general of Angkor, too.

Jayavarman VII had employed Champa princes, but they betrayed him finally. As the result, Jayavarman VII controlled Champa by himself. However, Angkor had lost military power and gave up Champa after his death. Angkor could not have gathered enough soldiers from Cambodia, so he used the Thai and the Mons as mercenary. However, they were getting stronger and establishing their own countries, so he could not amass them as mercenaries. As the result, he had to employ Cham princes as his generals and used Cham soldiers. But they finally betrayed Jayavarman VII. In the Angkor court, Jayavarman VII was also betrayed by his successors.

ABOUT THE AUTHOR

Takashi Suzuki

1938,	5 Aug. Born in Manchuria, Nationality Japanese
1962,	BS Economics, University of Tokyo
1962,	Sumitomo Metal industries, Economic Research Dept, Planning Dept
1975,	Singapore Office, Representative Manager
1979,	Manager, Business Research Section
1987,	General Manger, Overseas Investment Dept
1989,	President, Thai Steel Pipe Industries
1991,	Deputy Superintendent, Kashima Steel Works, Sumitomo Metals
1994,	Director, Japan Research Institute, Head of Asian Research Group
1997,	Professor, Kobe University, Faculty of Economics
2001,	Professor, Toyo University, Faculty of Economics
2003,	Doctorate of Economics, Kobe University
2004,	Retired Toyo university

(Others)
1995-8, Lecturer, Faculty of Agriculture, University of Tokyo
1996-8, Guest Professor, Ritsumeikan University, Faculty of Economics

(Writings: Japanese)
"The Economy of Southeast Asia", Ochanomizu Press Co., 1996.
"The History and Economy of Southeast Asia" Nihon Keizai Hyouronsha, 2002.
"The Mystery of Srivijaya" Asahi Krie Co., 2008.
"The History of Srivijaya-The ancient trade between the East and West, under the tributary system of China" Mekong Publishing Co., Ltd., 2010.
"The History of Funan, Chenla and Champa" Mekong Publishing Co., Ltd., 2016.
(Writings: English)
"The History of Srivijaya" Mekong Publishing Co., Ltd., 2012.

Appendix List of tributary countries

The Major Southeast Asia & Western Tributary Countries to China (From Wu to the end of South Song Period)

Wu （呉）222-280

225		Funan
226-31	Linyi	Funan
243		Funan

Western-Jin（西晋）265-316

265		Funan	
268	Linyi	Funan	
284	Linyi		Rome （大秦）
285		Funan	
286		Funan	
287		Funan	

Eastern-Jin（東晋）317-420

340	Linyi		
357		Funan	
372	Linyi		
373-75	Linyi		

377	Linyi		
382	Linyi		
389		Funan	
405-418			Ceylon
414	Linyi		
417	Linyi		

First South Song（Liu 劉氏南宋）420-479

421	Linyi			
424-53		Panpan		
428				Ceylon/ India
429				Ceylon
430	Linyi		Khalatan	Ceylon
433	Linyi		Khalatan	
434		Funan	Khalatan	
435	Linyi	Funan	Khalatan JavaPata	Ceylon
436			Khalatan	
437			Khalatan	
438	Linyi	Funan		
439	Linyi			
441	Linyi		Kandari	

Appendix

442			Pohang	
449			Pohang/Pata	
451			Pohang/Pata	
452			Khalatan	
455	Linyi	Panpan	Kandari Pohang	
456			Pohang	
457-64		Panpan		
458	Linyi			
459			Pohang	
464			Pohang	
466			Pohang	India
472	Linyi			
473			Poli（婆利）	

South-Ji（南齊）479-502

479		Funan	Khala（迦羅）
484		Funan	
491	Linyi		
498	Linyi		

246   THE HISTORY OF SRIVIJAYA, ANGKOR and CHAMPA

Liang（梁）502-557

502	Linyi		Kandari	M.India
503		Funan		India
504				N.India
510	Linyi			
511		Funan		
512	Linyi	Funan		
514	Linyi	Funan		
515			Langkasuka	
517		Funan	Poli	
518			Kandari	
519		Funan		
520		Funan	Kandari	
522			Poli	
523			Langkasuka	
526	Linyi			
527	Linyi	Panpan		Ceylon
529		Panpan		
530	Linyi	Funan		
531			Langkasuka Tan-tan	
532		Panpan		

533		Panpan		Persia
534	Linyi	Panpan		
535		Funan	Tan-tan	Persia
539		Funan		
542	Linyi	Panpan		
543		Funan		
551		Panpan		

Chin（陳）557-589

559			Funan		
563				Kandari	
568	Linyi			Langkasuka	
571			Panpan	Tan-tan*2	India
572	Linyi		Funan		
581				Tan-tan	
583		Dvaravati			
584			Panpan		
585				Tan-tan	
588			Funan		

248   THE HISTORY OF SRIVIJAYA, ANGKOR and CHAMPA

Sui（隋）581-618

595	Linyi				
608		Koloshefen		Chi-tu	
609				Chi-tu	
610				Chi-tu	
616		Chen-la	Panpan	Tan-tan Poli	Persia

Tang（唐）618-907

618-25	Huan Wang		Funan		
623	Linyi	Chen-la			
625	Linyi	Chen-la			
627-49	Huan Wang	Dvaravati	Funan	Duo-po-deng	
628	Linyi	Chen-la			
630	Linyi			Poli	
631	Linyi			Poli	
633			Panpan		
635		Chen-la	Panpan		
638		Dvaravati			
639					Persia
640	Linyi	Dvaravati		Old Khaling	
641			Panpan	India	

Appendix

642	Linyi			Poluo （婆羅）	
643		Dvaravati			
644				Malayu	
646				India	
647				Old Khaling Duo-po-deng	Persia*2
648			Panpan	Old Khaling	Persia
649		Dvaravati			
651		Chen-la			Arab
653	Linyi				
654	Linyi				
657	Linyi				
661					Persia
662		Koloshefen			
666				Old Khaling Tan-tan	
667					Persia
669	Linyi			Poluo	
670	Linyi			Khala/Tan-tan Ceylon	
670-73			Shilifoshi		
671					Persia
672				S-India	
673					Persia

250 THE HISTORY OF SRIVIJAYA, ANGKOR and CHAMPA

681					Arab
682		Chen-la		S-India	Persia/Arab
686	Linyi				
691	Linyi				
692				India*5	
695	Linyi*2				
698		Chen-la			
699	Linyi				
701			Shilifoshi		
702	Linyi				Arab
703	Linyi*2				
706	Linyi				Persia
707	Linyi	L.Chen-la			
708					Persia
709	Linyi			Konlon	
710		Chen-la		S-India*2	Persia/Arab
711	Linyi			Ceylon	Arab
712	Linyi				
713	Linyi			S-India	
714				W-India	
715	Linyi			India	

Appendix 251

716			Shilifoshi		Arab
717		Chen-la		M-India	
719				S-India	Persia*2 Arab
720				S-India*2 M-India	
722					Persia
724			Shilifoshi		Arab
725				M-India	Arab*2
727			Shilifoshi		
729				N-India	Arab
730					Persia*2
731	Linyi			M-India	
732					Persia
733					Arab
734	Linyi				
735	Linyi*2				
737				E-India	Persia
740					Arab
741			Shilifoshi		
743					B-Arab
744	Linyi				
745					Persia/Arab

252 THE HISTORY OF SRIVIJAYA, ANGKOR and CHAMPA

746				Ceylon	Persia
747					Persia/Arab
748	Linyi				
749	Linyi				
750		L-Chen-la		Ceylon	Persia
751					Persia
752					B-Arab
753		L-Chen-la			B-Arab*3
754					B-Arab
755		L-Chen-la			B-Arab
756					Arab
758					B-Arab
759					Persia
760					W-Arab
762				Ceylon	Persia*2 B-Arab*2
767		L-Chen-la			
768			Sailendra		
769			Sailendra		B-Arab
771		L-Chen-la			Persia
772					Arab
774					B-Arab

Appendix 253

780		Chen-la			
791					B-Arab
793	Huan Wang				
798		L-Chen-la			
802		Pyu			
806		Pyu			
813		W-Chen-la	Sailendra		
814		W-Chen-la			
815			Sailendra		
818			Sailendra		
820				Sañjaya	
827-33			Sailendra		
831				Sañjaya	
839				Sañjaya	
852			Jambi		
860-874			Sailendra		
871			Jambi		
904			Sanfochi		

254 THE HISTORY OF SRIVIJAYA, ANGKOR and CHAMPA

North Song（北宋）960-1126

960	Champa	Sanfochi			
961	Champa	Sanfochi*2			
962	Champa	Sanfochi*3			
966	Champa				
967	Champa				
968	Champa				Arab
970	Champa	Sanfochi			
971	Champa	Sanfochi			Arab
972	Champa	Sanfochi			
973	Champa				Arab
974	Champa	Sanfochi			Arab
975		Sanfochi			Arab
976	Champa		Brunei		Arab*2
977	Champa		Brunei		
978	Champa				
979	Champa				
980		Sanfochi			
982	Champa				
983	Champa	Sanfochi			
984					Arab

Appendix

985	Champa	Sanfochi			
986	Champa				
988		Sanfochi			
989		Sanfochi			
990	Champa*2	Sanfochi			
992	Champa		Sañjaya*2		
994					Arab*2
995	Champa				Arab
997	Champa				Arab
999	Champa				Arab
1001			Danmeiliu		
1003		Sanfochi			Arab
1004	Champa				
1005	Champa				
1006					Arab
1007	Champa				Arab
1008	Champa	Sanfochi			Arab
1009	Champa				
1010	Champa				
1011	Champa				Arab
1014	Champa				

1015	Champa			Chola	
1016	Champa			Chola	
1017		Sanfochi			
1018	Champa	Sanfochi			
1019		Sanfochi			Arab
1020				Chola	
1023					Arab
1028		Sanfochi-CL			
1029	Champa				
1030	Champa				
1033				Chola	
1042	Champa				
1050	Champa				
1053	Champa				
1054	Champa				Arab
1056	Champa				Arab
1060					Arab
1061	Champa				
1062	Champa				
1068	Champa				
1070					Arab

Appendix   257

1072	Champa				Arab
1073					Arab
1076	Champa				
1077		Sanfochi-CL		Chola	
1079		Sanfochi-CL Sanfochi-JB			
1082		Sanfochi-CL Sanfochi-JB	Brunei		
1084		Sanfochi			Arab
1085					Arab
1086	Champa				
1088		Sanfochi-CL Sanfochi			
1089					Arab
1090		Sanfochi-CL			
1094		Sanfochi			
1095		Sanfochi			
1099					Arab
1106	Pagan				
1109			Java (Kediri)		
1116	Angkor				
1120	Angkor				

258 THE HISTORY OF SRIVIJAYA, ANGKOR and CHAMPA

South Song（南宋）1127-1279

1127	Champa			
1128			Sanfochi	
1129	Champa			
1132	Champa			
1136		Pagan		Arab
1155	Champa	Chen-la/ Lopburi		
1156			Sanfochi*3	
1167	Champa			
1168	Champa			
1178			Sanfochi	
1196		Tambralinga		
1200		Chen-la		

Main source: *Ce-Fu Yuan-Gui*（冊府元亀）, *Song-Hui-Yao*（宋會要）
Official Chronicles of Chinese Dynasties

Appendix

Tributary countries in Chinese character（漢字）

Arab		大食	651-1136
Black(B)-Arab	Islam	黑衣大食	743-791
White(W)-Arab	Non Islam	白衣大食	760
Brunei		勃泥	976, 977
Ceylon		獅子/師子	405-762
Champa		占城	958-1168
Chen-la		眞臘	616-1200
Land(L)Chen-la	Wentan（文單）	陸眞臘	707-798
Water(W)Chen-la		水眞臘	813, 814
Chi-tu		赤土	608-610
Chola	Tamil	注輦	1015-1090
Danmeiliu		丹眉流	1001
Duo-po-deng	West Java	墮婆登	647
Dvaravati	Mons	墮和羅鉢底 投和/頭和	583-649

260   THE HISTORY OF SRIVIJAYA, ANGKOR and CHAMPA

Funan		扶南	225−649
Jambi		詹卑/占卑	852, 871
India		天竺	428−715
Middle(M)-India		中天竺	502−731
North(N)-India		北天竺	504
West(W)- India		西天竺	714
South(S)-India	Tamil	南天竺	672−720
East(E)-India	Bengal	東天竺	737
Java	Sañjaya Kediri	闍婆 闍婆	820−992 1109
Khalatan(Holotan)	Kelantan?	訶羅旦(單)	430−452
Kandai(Kantuoli)	Kedah	干陁利	441−563
Huan Wang	Champa	環王	618−793
Khala	迦羅 訶羅	Kedah 訶陵?	479 670
Kha-ling(Ho-ling)	Old(Sailendra)	訶陵	640−670

Appendix 261

Kha-ling (Ho-ling)	New (Sailendra)	訶陵	768−860+
Koloshefen	Ratchaburi?	哥羅舍分	608,662
Konlon		崑崙	709
Langkasuka	Nakhon S T	狼牙須	515−568
Linyi	Champa	林邑	226−749
Lopburi		羅斛	1155
Malayu	Near Jambi	末羅瑜	644
Pagan	Burma	蒲甘	1106,1136
Pan-pan	Chaiya	盤盤	(424−453)−648
Pata	Pattani?	婆達	435−451
Persia		波斯	533−771
Pohang	Pahang?	婆皇	442−466
Poli	Borneo	婆利(黎)	473−631
Poluo	Borneo	波羅	642−669

262 THE HISTORY OF SRIVIJAYA, ANGKOR and CHAMPA

Pyu	Burma	驃	802, 806
Rome		大秦	284
Sailendra	Srivijaya	訶陵	768-(860-879)
Sanfochi	Srivijaya	三佛齊	904-1178
Sanfochi-CL(Chola)		三佛齊注輦	1028-1090
Sanfochi-JB(Jambi)		三佛齊詹卑	1079,1082
Sañjaya		闍婆	820-992
Shilifoshi	Srivijaya(Chaiya)	室利佛逝	670-741
Tambralinga	Nakhon S T	單馬令	1196
Tantan	Kelantan	丹丹・單單	531-666

BIBLIOGRAPHY

【English Text】

Briggs, Lawrence Palmer, *The Ancient Khmer Empire* : Transactions Of The American Philosophical Society, V42, Part 1, February, 1951

Cowing, Hawai University George Coedès, *The Indianized States of Southeast Asia*: Translated by Sue Brown. 1968.

Honda, Megumu, *The Han-Chey Inscriprtion of Bhavavarman* : Japanese Association of Indian and Japanese Buddhist Histories, jibs 15(1), 441-438 1966.

Jaques, Claude, *ANGKOR, Cities and Temples*, River Books, 1997.

Piriya Krairiksh, *The Roots of Thai Art*, Bangkok, River Books. 2012.

Majmdar, R.C., *Champā : history & culture of an Indian colonial kingdom in the Far East, 2nd-16th century A.D.* Delhi : Gian Pub. House , 1985.

──*Svarnadvipa*, New Delhi, Cosmo Publications, 2004.

Sharan, Mahesh Kumar, *Studies in Sanskrit inscriptions of ancient Cambodia, on the basis of first three volumes of Dr. R. C. Majumdar's edition*, foreword by C. Sivaramamurti, New Delhi : Abhinav Publications, 1978.

Vickery, Michael, Society, *Economics and Politics in Pre-Angkor Cambodia: The 7th-8th Centuries*. Tokyo, The Centre for East Asian Cultural Studies for Unesco, The Toyo Bunko, 1998.

──*Coedès' Histories of Cambodia*, Silpakorn University International Journal (Bangkok, Thailand), Volume 1, Number 1, January-June 2000, pp. 61-108.

──*Funan Reviewed: Deconstructing the Ancients, Bulletin de l'École Française d'Extrême-Orient*, 90-91, 2003-2004, pp. 101-143

──*Champa Revised*, 2005, long version available as ARI WPS No. 37

──Bayon: New Perspectives Reconsidered, Udaya,VII, 2006, pp. 101-176

──Champa Revised, short version to be published March 2005, in a conference book by Asia Research Institute, +ARI working paper No. 37, University of Singapore.

──What and Where was Chenla?, Recherches nouvelles sur le Cambodge. Publiées sous la direction de F. Bizot. École française d'Extrême-Orient, Paris, 1994, pp. 197-212.

──The Cham of VIETNAM History, Society and Art , "Champa Revised" pp363-420, Singapore, NUS 2011

──The Reign of Sūryavarman I and Royal Factionalism at Angkor, Journal of South-

264 THE HISTORY OF SRIVIJAYA, ANGKOR and CHAMPA

east Asian Studies, Vol. 16, No. 2, September 1985, 226-244.

Wales, H.G. Quaritch, Towards Angkor in the footsteps of Indian invaders, London, George G. Harrap & CO. LTD. First published 1937.

Wheatley, Paul, The Golden Khersonese, University of Malaya Press, 1961.

【Japanese Text】

Doki, Yuko（土肥祐子）, 宋代南海貿易史の研究. 汲古書院、2017.

Kuwata, Rokuro（桑田六郎）, 南海東西交通史論考, 汲古書院, 1933. 2.

Miyabayashi, Akihiko（宮林昭彦）, Kato, Eiji（加藤栄司）,『現代語訳 南海寄帰内法伝―7世紀インド仏教僧伽の日常生活』,法蔵館, 2004.4.

Sugimoto, Naojiro（杉本　直治郎）, 東南アジア史研究 第1., 訂補再版, 巌南堂書店 , 1968.

INDEX

I. PERSONAL NAMES

Abu Hasan （甫訶散）　　219, 221

Agastya　　　134

Ali Po-lin （李蒲薩）　　222, 237

Ali Sin （李臻）　　222

Ali-Nou （李耨）　　220

An Nan （安南）　　206, 207

Antoninus　　199

Balaputra　　43, 50, 52, 56-59, 62, 70, 138, 158

Ban Ban （槃槃）　　2

Ban Kuang （盤況）　　2

Bhadravarman　　202, 203, 208

Bhadravarman III　　217, 218

BhavavarmanI　　35, 75, 85, 91, 111

BhavavarmanII　　87, 89-91, 111

Candana （旃檀）　　16

Chamdevi, princess　　155

Chandrabhanu　　51, 68, 170

Chang Jun （常駿）　　38, 45

Chao Ju-kua （趙汝适）　　39, 66

Culamanivarman　　64

Citrasena （Mahendravarman）　　71, 81, 85-87, 89, 91, 111

Chudamani, princess　　168

Coedès, G　　x-xii, xv-vi, 1, 10, 22, 29, 31, 35, 42, 43, 46, 54, 55, 78, 81, 83, 86, 91, 92, 95, 101-108, 125, 156, 182

Dapunta Hyang　　105, 114, 117

Dapunta Selndra　　36, 49, 55, 114, 117

Dharmasetsu　　52, 62, 114

Dharmadeva　　90

Dharmaraja　　155, 157, 217, 231

266 THE HISTORY OF SRIVIJAYA, ANGKOR and CHAMPA

Devaraja 116, 128-130, 139, 144, 145, 152, 153, 161, 163, 228, 234
Dharanindradevi 133, 137
Dharmaraja 155, 157, 217.231
Dharmasetu 52, 62, 113
Dharmawangsa（Medang） 225
Dharanindravarman I 163-166, 168
Dharanindradevi 133, 137
Dharanindravarman II 168, 170, 171, 179, 189
Divakarapandita 163, 165, 167
Dohi, Yuko（土肥祐子） 237, 239
Du Hui Duo（杜慧度） 202
Du You（杜祐） 27, 33
Fa Xian（法顕） x, xiv, 30
Fan Shou（范尋） 3, 16
Fan Chang（范長） 3
Fan Dang Gen Chun（范當根純） 205-207
Fan Di Zhen（范敵真） 203, 206
Fan Fo（范佛） 202, 204
Fan Hu Da（范胡達） 202-204, 206
Fan Jin-sheng（范金生） 3
Fan Man（范(師)蔓） 2, 3, 6, 7, 12, 14-16, 33, 40, 69, 70
Fan Shen Cheng（范神成） 205, 206
Fan Tien Kai（范天凱） 206
Fan Wen Di 206
Fan Wen Huan 206, 207
Fan Wen Zan（范文賛） 206, 207
Fan Weng（范文） 201, 202, 204
Fan Xion（范熊） 201
Fan Yang Mai I（范陽邁1世） 203, 204, 206, 207
Fan Yang Mai II（范陽邁2世） 204-207
Fan Yi（范逸） 201
Fan Zhan（范旃） 3
Fan Zheng Long（范鎮龍） →see Prakasadharma（鉢迦含波摩）
Fan Zhu Non（范諸農） 205-207
Ferrand, G. 120

Fujita Toyohachi   x, 27, 63, 64
Gnavarman（求那跋摩）   53
Haradevi   217
Harivarman V（楊卜麻畳）   234, 237
Harivarman II（楊陀拝毘茶室離）   222-224, 226, 227, 236, 238
Harshavarman I   144, 147, 148, 162, 188
Harshavarman II   145, 146, 153, 188
Harshavarman III   162, 163, 165, 168, 171, 189
Hiranhadama   116
Hiranyadama   130
Hiranyavarman   163, 164, 166
Hrishikesa   176, 184
Ibn Khordadbeh   x
Indradevi   133, 135, 136, 137, 139, 171
Indravarman I   125, 133, 136-140, 144-146, 188, 213, 214
Indravarman II（Buddhist King）   182, 184, 189, 195, 215, 217, 218, 233
Indravarman III（釈利因徳漫）   218, 219
Isanavarman II   144, 162, 188
Isanavarman（伊奢那）   77, 83, 86, 87-92, 98, 107, 111, 123, 152, 202, 212
Vijaya Harivarman   226
Jaya Harivarman I（娜時蘭巴） 235-237
Jaya Harivarman II   236, 238
Jaya Indravarman II   233-235, 237
Jaya Indravarman III   166, 218, 219, 234, 237
Jaya Indravarman IV（鄒亜娜） 172-175, 238-240
Jaya Indravarman V（Prince Rashputi）   174, 175, 240
Jaya Paramesvara   229, 230
Jaya Simhavarman   215, 217
Jayadevi, Queen   58, 90, 95, 98, 99, 111, 142
Jayanasa   104, 105, 114
Jayanta   51
Jayarajadevi   171, 172
Jayavarman I   78, 91-96, 98, 100, 101, 108, 111, 142
Jayavarman II   xiii, 32, 49, 55, 58, 62, 70, 77, 87, 90, 93-95, 98, 100, 107-
    110, 113, 115-117, 121-131, 133-140, 142, 147, 148, 156, 157, 161, 174, 182,

188

Jayavarman III   138, 140, 145, 186, 188
Jayavarman IV   144-146, 188
Jayavarman V   131, 145, 148, 150, 151, 153-155, 188, 225
Jayavarman VI   xiii, 159, 163-166, 189
Jayavarman VII   83, 98, 99, 131, 132, 142, 147, 152-155, 159, 166-185, 187,
    189, 225, 228, 238-241
Jayavarman VIII   131, 132, 159, 162, 176-189
Jayavarmesvara   179
Jayaviravarman   152, 153-157, 188
Jayendrapandita   162
Jia Dan（賈耽）   23, 24-28
Jayendradhipativarman   125
Jaya Parameshvaravarman II   241
Kambau   162
Kandarapadharma（頭黎）   206, 209.210, 212
Kang Tai（康泰）   1, 17
Karttikeya   136
Kaundinya I（混塡）   2, 100, 146, 156
Kaundinya II（僑陳如）   12, 16, 129
Kaundinya Jayavarman（僑陳如闍耶跋摩）   74, 128
Kavindrarimathan   147, 150
Kirtipandita   150
Kirttivarman   151
Ku Sri Harivarmadeva   226
Ku Sri Paramesvarmadeva（倶舍利波微收羅婆麻提）   221, 228
Ku Sri Rudravarman I（高式律陀羅跋摩）   206, 208
Ku Sri Vijayavarman（高式勝鎧）   206
Kuang-yi   219
Kuwata, Rokuro（桑田六郎）   x, 203
Land route   ix, xiiv, 3, 9, 12, 69, 73, 74, 78, 81, 82, 84, 87, 96, 98, 107, 123
Le Hoan（黎桓）   222, 223
Le Tai Song（李太宗）   227
Liu Ji-Zong（劉継宗）   220, 222, 223
Lie-ye（柳葉）   2, 100

Index   269

Liu Fang（劉方）   208, 209
Lu Dai（呂岱）   16
LyBon（李賁）   208
Ly Thanh Ton（李聖宗）   230
Ma Huang（馬歡）   xv
Mahamantradhikrta 206, 212
Mahapradhana, Jaya   176, 184
Mahipativarman   58, 110, 134
Majumdar, R.C.   51, 65-67, 195, 201, 207, 208, 212-214, 217-219, 221, 228-230, 232
Mangrai   42
Manorathavarman   206
Maspero   227
Maxwell T. S.   116, 133, 134
Mhipativarman   58, 111, 134
Bok-di（穆帝）   16
Nagasena（那伽仙）   12, 128, 205
Nandanavarman   232
Naravahanavarma   212
Narendravarman   134
Ngo Nhut Khanh   222
Ngo Quyen   221
Nitta, Eiji（新田栄治）   145
Nripaditya   95, 99
Nripatindravarman   101, 133, 137, 147, 163, 165
Obraja   155
Obyuvaraja   155
Ou Yang Xiu（欧陽修）   97
Panamkaran, Panangkaran   43, 49, 52, 55, 56, 60, 62, 70, 95, 113, 114
Paramesvara Indravarman I（波美税褐印茶）   220
Paramabodhisattava（波羅摩菩提薩） 233, 237
Paramesvaravarmadeva   228
Pelliot   78
Pikatan, Rakai   43, 50, 56, 57, 59, 62, 70
Pilih Rajadvarah   218

270   THE HISTORY OF SRIVIJAYA, ANGKOR and CHAMPA

Po Kho Su（蒲訶粟）   43
Pov ku lyan Sri Rajakula（Haradevi）   217, Queen of Indravarman II
Prakasadharma（鉢迦含波摩）   88, 206, 210
Pramesvara Dharmaraja   231
Pramesvaraindravarman I 220
Pramodawarddhani   43, 50
Prana, Kambujalakshmi   137
Prithivinarendra   128, 137
Prithivindravarman 133, 213
Pushakaraksha   101
Pu-yue-jia-ma（蒲越伽摩）   27
Qu-lian 区連（隣）196
Radhupati   175
Rajadhiraja   187, 51
Rajapativarman   135
Rajaputra   174, 182
Rajaraja   160
Rajendra Chola   65
Rajendravarman I   111
Rajendravarman II 129, 136, 145-148, 150, 153-155, 157, 159, 188, 218, 225
Rashupati   175, 240
Ratnabhumivijaya   235
Rudravarman I, Sri   135, 146
Rudravarman, Sri   217
Rudravarman II   210
Rudravarman III   217, 230-233, 237
Rudravarman（Funan）   15, 74-76
Rudravarman（Angkor）   117, 127, 133, 135, 137, 146
Rudravarman Parama Brahmaloka   234
Samaratunga   43, 50, 52, 54, 57, 59, 60, 62
Sambhuvarman（范梵志）   101, 203, 206, 208, 209
Sangkara   235
Sangrama   162
Sangrama Vijayottungavarman 65
Sankarapandita   162

Index

271

Saptadevakula	148, 153-155
Sarthavaha	217,
Satyavarman	xiii, 213, 214
Sharan	116, 129-131, 150, 153, 163, 168
Sivaddata	89, 90
Sivakaivalya	117, 127, 128, 130, 131, 137, 138, 161, 162
Sivavinduka	117
Soma	2, 91, 100, 146, 147, 157
Sresthavarnan	83
Vijaya Sri Harivarman II	222-224, 226, 227
Sri Harivarmadeva（施離霞離鼻麻底）	226, 232, HarivarmanII
Sri Harivarman II（新王楊陀排）	223, 224
Sri Harivarman II（尸嘿排摩）（同上？）	227
Sri Harvarman IV	231, 232, 233
SriIndravarman III	176, 186, 188
Sri Jaya Indravarman IV	236
Sri Indravarman IV（施利陀盤呉日歡）	220
Sri Jaya Harivarman I（鄒時蘭巴）	235-237
Sri Jaya Harivarman II（son of Harivarman I）	236, 238, killed by Indravarman IV
Sri Jaya Indravarman I（釈利因陀盤）	219, 220
Sri Maravijayottungavarman	64
Sri Nanda Varmadeva	64
Sri Parama-Buddhaloka	164
Sri Rudravarman III	237
Srindravarman（持黎陀跋摩）	施里律茶盤麻常楊溥, 237
Srindravarman（持黎陀跋摩）	176, 186, 188
Stanford Raffles, Sir	57
Sugimoto, Naojiro（杉本直次郎）	x, 2, 13, 226
Sukshmavindu	138
Sulaiman	58, 117
Suryavarmadeva（Jayavarman VII' s general）	172, 174-176, 238-240
Suryavarman I	xiii, 32, 62, 64, 128-130, 137, 148, 151-165, 188, 228
Suryavarman II	62, 98, 99, 114, 138, 142, 163-171, 189, 228, 234, 235, 238
Svamini Hyang Amrita	117

272   THE HISTORY OF SRIVIJAYA, ANGKOR and CHAMPA

Tai-Zong（太宗）　98
Takakusu Junjiro　x, xv, 104
Tan-he-Zhi（檀和之）　204
Tara（Sailendra）　52, 62
Tara（Champa）　216
Wyatt, David　103
Quaritch Wales　xiii, xv, 21, 26, 58, 81, 113, 114, 117, 126
Xuan Zhan（玄裝）　194, 211
Tou li, Kandarpadharma（范頭黎）　206, 210, 212
Tribhuvanadityavarman　171-173, 175, 176, 179, 189, 236, 238
Udayadityavarman I　152-156, 188
Udayadityavarman II　116, 159, 161-163, 165, 188, 228
Uroja　215, 236
Vijaya Sri Harivarman II　172, 174, 175, 178, 238-240
Vijayavarman（弼毳跋摩）　206
Vikrantavarman（Prakasadharma）（諸葛地）　88, 210, 212
Vikrantavarman II　212
Vikrantavarman III　213, 215
Vivavarman　81, 85
Vyadhapura　78, 93, 121-123, 134, 139
Wales, Quaritch　xiii, xv, 21, 26, 58, 81, 113, 114, 117, 126
Wen-di（文帝）　204
Wen-di（文敵）　206, 207
Wheatley, Paul　29, 37
Wu-di（武帝）　16, 34, 132, 201
Wolters, O.W.　103
Wyatt, David K.　103
Xuan Zhan（玄裝）　194, 211
Yan Devatamuti　232
Yan Pu Ku Sri Harivarman II（楊普俱毘茶室離）　226
Yan Pu Ku Vijaya Sri（楊普俱毘茶室離）　226
Yan Pu Ku Vijaya Sri（楊甫恭毘施離）（HarivarmanII）　226
Yan Pu Ku Vijaya Sri（楊甫(普)俱毘茶逸施離）（HarivarmanII）　226
Yan Pu Sri Jaya Shimhavrman II（楊普毘茶逸施離）　HarivarmanII, 226
Yan Pu Sri Rudravarmadeva（刑卜施離值星霞弗）　227

Yan Pu Sri Rudravarman III　　237
Yang-di（煬帝）　38, 45
Yan Pu Ku Sri Paramesvarmadeva（供舍波微收羅婆麻提楊卜）　227
Yan Pu Ku Sri Vikrantavarman（陽補孤施離皮蘭德加抜麻疊）　227
Yasovarman　116, 132-134, 136, 138, 140, 142, 144-148, 151, 153, 162, 176, 188
Yasovarman II　142, 170, 171, 189
Yi-Jing（義浄）　x, xii, xiii, xv, 15, 29, 45, 92, 105, 128, 194, 211
Yuvaraja　155, 164, 174, 228, 229, 232-234, 239
Yuvaraja Mahasenapati　228, 229, 232, 233
Zao Kuangyi（Taizong）（趙匡義）　219
ZaoKuangyin（TaiZu）（趙匡胤）　219
Zhen Long, Prakasadharma（鎮龍）　206, 212
Zhou Daguan（周達観）　159, 186
Chou Ch'u-fei（周去非）　53
Zhu Fan（朱藩）　202
Zhu Ge De（諸葛地）　88, 210, 212
Zhu Yin　1, 17
Zhu Nong（諸農）　205, 206

II. GENERAL ITEMS

Ak Yom　99, 141
Adhayapura　89, 90-92, 124
Amaravati　175, 198, 211, 235, 240
Andaman　69
Angkor Borei　13, 78, 80, 84
Aninditapura　91, 92, 96, 100, 101, 117, 121-123, 127, 130, 134, 136, 139, 147,
162
Annam（安南）　219-224, 229-238
Arab, Da Shi（大食）　x, 7, 12, 43, 46, 51, 57, 58, 63, 117, 118, 121, 132, 172,
210, 220, 226, 236
Aranyaprathet　123

274   THE HISTORY OF SRIVIJAYA, ANGKOR and CHAMPA

Arogyasala   176
Asramas   133
Austronesian   107.195
Avalokitesvara   179
Ayutthaya   4, 19, 170.187
BaPhnom   13, 78, 92, 122, 123, 128
Bakong   135-137, 139, 140
Baksei Changkrong Inscription   567, 144, 146, 147
Bakul Inscription   195
Baladitya   99-101
Baladityapura（婆羅提跋城）   92, 96, 98-101, 147
Ban Ban（盤盤）   xi, 2, 7, 9, 11-16, 27, 31, 33-38, 45, 46, 53, 70, 75-77, 82-85,
     89, 109, 128, 207
Ban Don Bay   49, 55, 75, 94, 145
Ban Dong Phlong Ruins   145
Ban Ta Khun   9
Bangka Island   36, 46, 53-55
Banteay Chhmar, Cat fortress   182
Banteay Prei Nokor   94, 99, 101, 122, 126
Baphuon   161-163
Battambang   83, 85, 93, 102, 122, 123, 126, 128, 157, 174, 178, 239
Beads   11, 17, 197, 198
Bengal   xi, xv, 2, 3, 7, 11, 17, 26, 45, 46
Bhagavati   148, 218
Bhavapura   88, 89, 101, 122, 130
Bhavaputra   88, 89, 101, 122, 130
black agila wood（沉香）   210
Borobudur   15, 56, 57, 60, 62, 125
Bronze   17, 18, 159, 161, 197
Buddha Footprint   4, 5, 14, 15, 18, 30, 31, 40-42, 53
carnelian   197
Caturvara   156
Ce-fu Yuan-Gui（冊府元亀）   27, 35, 198, 199
Chakravatin   116
Champasak   81, 82, 84, 85

Index   275

Chantaburi   85, 93, 94, 128, 168
Chaupesvara（Vishnu）　163
Chen Dynasty（陳王朝）　34, 40
Chi River   21, 32, 81
Chiem Thanh   191
Chi-tu（赤土）   xii, 34, 36-38, 42, 43, 45, 46, 70
Chola   xiii, 43, 64, 65, 67, 68, 70, 99, 160, 161, 164, 166, 168
Con Dao island   38
cotton   11, 17
Da Nang   196, 198, 202, 216, 219, 227
Dai Viet （大越）   166, 175, 176, 185, 229, 240
Dangrek   21, 81-83, 86, 89, 122, 124, 125, 139, 163, 164, 178
Devaraja   116, 128-130, 139, 144, 145, 152, 153, 161-163, 228, 234
Dharma-cakra   21
Dinh Dynnasty   222
Dong Duong（BuddhistCity）   193, 195, 196, 211, 213-223, 225, 227, 235
Dun-Sun（典遜）   6, 39, 40
Duo-Po-Deng（堕婆登）   54, 55
Durga   129
Dvaravati（堕和羅鉢底）   6, 21, 26, 37-41, 77, 99, 139, 155
Early Le Dynasty   222
East Baray   142, 147
Eastern Jin（東晋）   16, 204
East-West trade   xi, xv, 17, 29
elephant   16, 34, 65, 135, 136, 138, 159, 201, 204, 209, 210, 227, 228, 236, 237
Frankincense（乳香）   210, 220, 226, 236-238
Gangaraja   203, 206
General Commerce Trade System   xv, 25, 27-29, 36, 44-46, 66, 70
God Jina   195
Gold Tower   159
Guanyin Bodhisattava   131
Gulf of Thailand   4, 6, 19, 27, 36, 40, 50, 59, 62.64, 67, 89, 107, 128
Guru   162, 163, 179, 130, 136
Han Chey Inscription   35

276 THE HISTORY OF SRIVIJAYA, ANGKOR and CHAMPA

Harihara   87, 92
Hariharalaya（Roluos）   117, 118, 122, 123, 125, 127, 133, 138, 140, 142, 188
Hariphunchai   41, 42, 155
Hemasringagiri   151
Hoi An   194, 196, 198, 202, 219, 223
Hotar   130, 176
Hue   193, 197, 227
Hynayana   129
Indianization   11, 203
Indochinese Peninsula   194, 198
Indrapura   62, 99, 100, 101, 122, 130, 193, 196, 223, 224, 231
Indratataka   136, 140
Iron   9, 17, 18, 21, 33, 81, 82, 140, 168, 197, 198, 220, 221
Isanapura   83, 87, 88, 91, 93, 144
Ivory   199, 210, 220, 226, 227, 236, 237
Jambi   15, 25, 27, 36, 43, 46, 50, 54, 58, 59, 64, 66, 67, 70, 109, 138
Java（闍婆）   xiii, 25, 30, 50, 53-58, 107-110, 114-116, 121, 124, 126, 130, 132,
    208, 213
Jayabuddha Mahanatha   183, 184
Jerteh（日羅亭）   66
Jin-lin（金隣）   3
Jiu(old)TngShu（旧唐書）   11, 96, 97, 99
Jiuzhen（九真）   199, 202, 204, 206
Jiao(Chiao)zhou（交州）   195, 202, 206, 208, 224
KamaratenJagat   124, 129
Kambuja   116, 129, 132, 174
Kambujadesa   130, 166, 174, 239
Kampot   78, 89, 94, 133
Kanchanabui   3, 6, 18, 21, 73, 183
Kandari, Kindari   9, 10, 36, 39, 42, 43
Kanton（広東）   45, 237
Karimun Island   31
Kauthara（NhaTrang）   213
Kedah（羯茶, 箇羅, 斤陀利）   羯茶：xv, 9   箇羅：24, 25   斤陀利：9
Kedukan Bukit Inscription   xi, 23, 36, 104, 105

K(h)alatan（呵羅単）　　　10, 30, 42
Kha-ling（訶陵）　　24, 25, 33, 36, 46, 49, 54, 59, 70, 109, 113
Khao Luang, Mt　　39
Khao Phra Narai　　9
Khao Si Wichai　　9, 10, 45
Klong Sok River　　10, 45
KohKer, Lingapura　　144-146, 148, 150, 156, 188
Kok Po　　163
Ko-ku-lo（Ko Koh Khao Island）（哥谷羅）　　7, 23, 24, 26, 27, 84
Ko-lo-she-fen（迦羅舎分）（Ratchaburi）　　6, 18, 26, 27, 40, 41, 183
Kompong Cham　　35, 93, 94, 97-99, 101, 109, 116, 122-124, 126, 134
Kompong Thom　　83, 85, 91, 92, 94, 101, 122, 152
Kota Kapur Inscription　　53-55
Krabi　　14, 17, 30, 39
Kratie　　83, 96, 100, 101, 116, 122, 126, 156
Krishna　　19, 81, 154
Kshatria　　2, 13, 203
Ku-kang（旧港）　　xv
Kunrun（崑崙）　　34
Kurung　　130
Lamuri　　66
Land Chenla　　90, 96-101, 108, 122, 124, 126, 228
Land route　　xv, 3, 9, 12, 69, 73, 74, 78, 81, 82, 84, 87, 96, 98, 107, 123
Lang Barus（郎婆露斯）　　ix, x, xii, 105
Langkasuka（狼牙須）　　9, 36-39, 66
Lanna　　42, 186
Latter Han Shu（後漢書）　　196
Latter Zhou（後周）　　219
Le Dynasty　　168, 183
Liang Dynasty　　234, 207, 34
Liang Shu（梁書）　　2, 17, 16, 39, 74, 75, 78, 203, 206
Ligor（Inscription）　　xii, 48-52, 66, 95, 100, 108, 128
Lingwei Tai-ta（嶺外代答）　　53
Lokesvara　　179, 195, 215
Lolei　　136, 140

278 THE HISTORY OF SRIVIJAYA, ANGKOR and CHAMPA

Lopburi（Lavo） 19, 40, 62, 98, 99, 129, 153, 155, 156, 161, 164, 167, 168, 170, 183, 237
Lunarrace 75, 132, 211
Luo-yue（羅越） 23-27
Ma Linh 230, 231
Mae Sot 3, 4, 5
Maeklong River 6, 18
Mahayana Buddhism 13, 15, 32, 53, 56, 60, 64, 77, 95, 109, 110, 114, 115
Mahesvara 12, 128, 130, 217
Mahindhrapura Dynasty 163, 165
Malacca Straits xl, 7, 27, 30, 36, 46, 48, 50, 59, 65, 70, 109
Malyan 128, 178, 239
Martaban 3, 4, 39, 40
Maurya Dynasty 11
Mebon 142, 147, 159, 160, 182
Medang（Jawa） 225
Mediterranean 11
mercenary 241
Meru, Mountain 13, 92, 130, 140, 145, 151, 159, 167
Mon 13-19, 26, 39-42, 70, 73, 77, 78, 81, 129, 139, 155, 160, 167, 168, 183, 185, 195, 241
Monsoon xi, 7, 30
Muang Singh, Prasert 18, 183, 184
Muaro Jambi 15
Mun, River 19, 21, 32, 33, 81, 89, 101
Lower Myanmar, Burma 3, 11, 18, 21, 32, 33, 39, 41, 166, 167
My-Son 88, 164, 172, 174, 192-194, 197, 202, 203, 209-211, 215, 225, 226, 228, 229, 231-235
Nagapatam village 64
Na-fu-na（那弗那） 35, 78
Naked people（裸人国） xv, 45, 92
Nakhon Si Thammarat xii, xiii, 23, 38, 39, 44, 48, 51, 62, 66, 95, 108, 153
Nalanda xv
Nan Hui Chi Kuei Nei Fa Chan x, xv, 92, 194
Nan Ji Shu（南斉書） 12, 205, 207

Index 279

Nandi   133, 142, 143
Navanakar   78, 88
Ngang Pass   202
Nicobar Islands   ix, x, xv, 23, 24, 66, 105
North Song   63, 64, 132, 160, 219
Oc Eo   3, 4, 6, 7, 21, 69, 70, 73-75, 78, 84
Jiu（Old）Tang Shu（舊唐書）11, 96, 97, 99
Palem bang   ix, xi, xii, xv, 10, 23, 25-31, 36, 43, 46, 49, 54, 64-71, 104, 105,
    109, 114, 117, 156
Panduranga（Phan Rang）   28, 66, 89, 99, 132, 191, 195, 196, 200, 210, 211,
    214, 215, 219, 228, 229, 232-235, 237
Pasak Valley   19, 83, 84
Pa-Ta（抜沓）39
Pattani   38, 39, 66
Phatthalung   44, 45, 56, 62, 63
Pekalongan   36, 48, 53, 56, 117
Persia   x, xi, 7, 12, 17, 46, 73
Petchaburi   6, 40
Phimai   xiii, 32, 83, 86, 115, 159, 163-166, 173, 176-178, 184, 189
Phnom Bakheng   139, 142, 143, 146, 151
Phnom Da   13, 78, 80
Phnom Kulen   115, 123, 124, 127, 148, 150, 168
Phimeanakas   131, 148, 157, 159, 161, 169, 171, 184
Po Nagar   132, 148, 214, 218, 239
Prachuap Khiri Kan   6, 40
Prasat Khna   154
Prasert Thom   145
Preah Ko   133, 136-141
Preah Vihear   94, 133, 142, 144, 150, 152
Prei Veng   93, 121, 122, 133
Purandarapura   91, 94, 96, 99, 101
Purohita   128, 130, 131, 137, 138, 161, 162, 165
Quang Binh   193, 202, 230
Quang Nam   193, 196, 197, 229, 231
Quang Ngai   229, 231

280   THE HISTORY OF SRIVIJAYA, ANGKOR and CHAMPA

Quang Tri   230
Quy Nhon   191, 198, 209, 221-224, 226
Rahal Baray   144
Rajapura   175, 240
Ratchaburi   6, 18, 26, 27, 40, 183
Rhinoceros   75, 98, 199, 210, 220, 222.226-228, 237
Riau Islsmds   xi, xv, 25
Rinan（日南）   196, 198, 199, 202, 204, 207
Robang Romeas Inscription   154
Roluos   →see Hariharalaya
Royal road   159, 174, 176, 177, 225
Sa Huynh   194, 197-199
Salt   16, 18, 21, 82, 145, 168
Samanta   195
Sambhupura   101, 122, 125, 134, 137, 139, 154, 160, 164, 228
Sambor   83, 101, 122, 125, 126
Sambor Prei Kuk   83, 85
Sanguozhi（三國史）　16
Sanjaya   36, 37, 43, 46, 48, 50, 53-59, 62, 70, 109, 113, 138
Sankara（Siva）   162, 195
Sanskrit   x, xii, 9, 11, 29, 34, 45, 60, 66, 146, 192, 196, 197, 203
Sathing Phra   25, 44, 45, 50, 56, 58, 63
Satun   9
She-po（闍婆）   53, 127
Si Wichai, Khao   9, 10, 45
Siem Reap   93, 94, 126, 133, 134, 140, 144, 150
Silpakorn University 102
Sing Khon Pass   6
Sivalinga   130, 213, 235
SKT（Sdok Kak Thom）Inscription   62, 108, 116, 125, 132, 152, 162, 182
Sojomerto Inscription   53
Solarrace   75, 132, 146
Song Hui Yao（宋会要）   226, 227, 230
Song-Shi（宋史）   172, 175, 219, 220, 238, 240
Song-Shu（宋書）   30

Index   281

Songkhla（僧祇城） 7, 9, 36, 42, 45, 56, 63
South China Sea   17, 107
SouthJi Dynasty   12, 204, 206
South-Ji-Shu（南齊書） 128, 208
South Song,（南宋）   68, 70, 162, 167, 168, 176
South Song, Leu（劉、南宋）   9-11, 16, 30, 204, 205, 207
Sri Dharmaraja（Tambralinga） 155, 157
Sri Thep（SriDeva） 3, 4, 6, 18-21, 32, 73, 75-78, 81-83, 87
Srindrakumara   182
Sri-Vijayendra-raja 51
Srisanabhadresvara 202, 225, 228, 232
Stung Treng   83, 85
Sui（隋）   37, 38, 40, 45, 76, 97, 98, 195, 205, 208, 209
Sui Shu（隋書）   xii, 38, 39, 45, 49, 73, 88, 92, 201
Sukhothai Kingdom   170, 175
Sunda   xi, 29, 55
Sungai Batu   9, 17
Suphanburi   4
Surat Thani   ix, 9, 25, 26, 33, 70, 84
Surin   83, 86
Surya   19, 81, 82
Suw(v)arnadvipa   12, 50, 51
Ta Praya   83, 86, 155
Ta Prom   162, 170, 178, 179
Tai Ping Yu Lan（太平御覧）   1, 17
Tak   4, 5, 18
Takeo, Angkor   151, 154
Takeo, Angkor Borei   78, 84
Takola   55
Takua Pa   xi, 2, 6-9, 14, 15, 17, 23, 26, 27, 30, 35, 66, 67, 70, 74, 82, 84
Tamil   9, 43, 64, 66, 67, 70
Tamralipiti   xv, 2, 17, 45
Tanmeiryu（単眉流）   66
Tanbralinga（単馬令）   51, 50, 58, 59, 62, 66, 68, 153-157, 161, 163, 167-170,
   188

Tang Hui Yao（唐会要）　43
Tanjore　65
Tambralinga（単馬令）　50, 51, 58, 59, 62, 66, 68, 153-157, 161, 163, 167, 168, 170, 188
Tantra Vidya　130
tantrism　114
Taruma　54, 55
Tavoy　6, 21, 73
Tboung Khmum　124, 134
Temu（特牧城）　35
Tenasserim　2, 6, 17, 26, 39, 40, 73
Than Hoa　234
Thaton　3, 4, 17, 39, 73, 129
Theravada Buddhism　4, 176, 186, 189
Three Pagoda Pass　6, 18
Thu Bon 175, 191-197, 202, 204, 215, 224, 228, 229, 231, 237
Tong Dian（通典）　x, 27, 33
Tonkin　164, 201, 222, 230
TonleSap　83, 89, 92, 94, 96, 101, 122, 123, 125-127, 133
Tra Kieu　197, 202, 208-211
Trailokyavijaya　165
trans-peninsula　xi, 6, 7, 29, 46, 70, 161
Tri Tepusan Inscription　60
U Thong　4, 6, 18, 21, 32, 73, 78
Ubon Ratchatani　81, 83, 85, 86
vassal state　xii, 33, 37, 59, 69, 71, 73, 101, 144
Vo Canh　192
Vyadhapura　78, 93, 121-124, 139
Wat Kraison　9, 14
Wat Long　51
Wat Phu　32, 76, 81, 83-85, 92, 93, 122, 126, 167
Wat Wieng　51
Water Chenla　xii, 48, 49, 53, 55, 57, 58, 62, 70, 85, 90, 91, 94, 95, 98, 99, 108-110, 117, 121, 124-126
Wen-dan（文単）　96-98, 107, 124

Index 283

West Baray　　99, 142, 159
Western Jin（西晋）　16, 201
Wu Dynasty（呉王朝）　　1, 3, 17, 196, 204
Xiang-Lin Xian（象林県）　　195, 196
Xin Tang Shu（新唐書）　ix, x, xi, 23-26, 29, 32, 34, 36, 78, 88, 96, 97, 101, 105, 108
Xitu（西図）　196, 204
Yaba-dvipa（耶馬提）　x, 30,
Yasodharapura　132, 139, 142, 144, 145, 156, 157, 165, 168, 188
Yavadvipa　218
Ying Yai Sheng Lan（瀛涯勝覧）　xv, 69
Yun-nan（雲南）　116
Zhi（Chi 質）　24-26
Zhu Bo（諸婆）　17
Zhu-fan-zhi（諸蕃志）　39, 65, 66

Funan, Srivijaya, San-fo-chi		King's name	Remarks	Chenla & Angkor		King's name	王
1-2C	1-2Cen	混填 (Kaundinya)					
2-3C	2-3Cen	盤況(Ban Kuang)					
3C	3C	槃槃 (Ban Ban) 范(師)蔓 (Fan Man) 范金生 (Fan Jin Sheng) 范旃 (Fan Zhan) 范長 (Fan Chang)	Conquered 10 ports Son of Fan Man, killed Son of Fan Man, killed				
	265 Trb	范尋 (Fan Shou)					
4C	357 Trb	旃檀 (Candana)					
5C	5C1St / half	僑陳如 (Kaundinya 2)	Brahman				
	411		Fa-Xian Arrv Yabadvipa				
	434, 35, 38 Trb	持黎陀跋摩 (Srindravarman)					
	478-514	僑陳如闍耶跋摩 (Kaundinya Jayavarman)					
	484 Trb		Amb Nagasena				
	513, 11-12 Trib						
6Cen	514-540?	留陀跋摩 (Rudravarman)	Last king of Funan				
	514, 17, 19-20, 30, 35, 39, 43, 59, 72, 88 Trib		Chenla Defeat Funan	**Chenla**			
				550-600		Bhavavarman I	
7Cen	618-25	Funan tributed		600-611		Chitrasena Mahendra- varman	質多
	627-49	Funan tributed					
	638-645		Dvaravati Trb				
	670-673	Srivijaya Trib		611-635 628 Tribute		Isanavarman	伊奢
	671		Yi-Jing went to Sirivijaya	635-657		BhavavarmanII	
	683	Kedukan Bukit Insc (Palembang)	Srivijaya conquered (Dapunta Hyang)	657-681		Jayavarman I	

Champa

(籍)	Remarks		King's name	王名 (漢籍)	Remarks
		137, rebelion	Qu Lian	區連（隣）	Rebel against authority
		226-31 Tribute 268 Tribute 270-280 Tribute 280-336 Tribute	Fan Xio Fan Yi	范熊 范逸	
		284 Tribute			
		336-349 Tribute	Fan Weng	范文（元奴婢）	Chinese slave, usurper
		340 Tribute			
		349-380 Tribute 372 Tribute 373-5 Tribute 377 Tribute	Fan Fo	范佛	
		380-413 Reign 382 Tribute	Bhadravarman I	范胡達（須達）	Sivaite
		413?-421?	Fan Di Zhen Manorathavarman, nephew	范敵眞	(Gangaraja Dynasty)
			Fan Wen Di	范文敵	Younger brother of Di Zhen
		421-425 421, Tribute	Fan Yang Mai I	范陽邁1世	
		425-446 430, 33, 35, 38, 39, 41 Tribute	Fan Yang Mai II	范陽邁2世	Disappeared after war
		454? - 480?	Fan Shen Cheng	范神成	
		455, 58, 72 Trib 483?-491	Fan Dang Gen Chun	范當根純（元奴婢）	From Funan, not prince
		491 Tribute	Fan Zhu Nong	范諸農	498 drown on Tribute
		492-498 Tribute	Fan Wen Huan	范文款	
		498- Tribute	Fan Wen Zan, Same as above?	范文贊	
		502 Tribute			
		510, 12, 14 Tribute	Fan Tien Kai, Devavarman	范天凱	
		514-?	Vijayavarman	弼毳跋摩	
		526-?	Ku Sri Vijayavar-man	高式勝鎧	
	Son of Virvavarman	526-27, 29 Trib			
		530-?, 530 Trib	Ku Sri Rudravar-man I	高式律陀羅跋摩	
		534, 42, 68, 72 Tribute	Tou Li	范頭黎	No king's name
		595 Tribute to Sui			
那	2nd Son of Virvavarman	604 Sui invade 623 Tribute to Tang	Sambhuvarman	范梵志	Son of Rudravarman I
		625, 28, 30, 31 Tribute	Tou Li, Kandarpadharma	范頭黎	
	Expelled Funan Sent tribute with Linyi 2nd son of Isanavarman	643, Funan attack Linyi ?-645killed	Fan ZhengLong, Prabhasadharma	范鎮龍	Ask for help to Tang
		640, 42 Tribute 645-	Mahamantra-dhikrta	摩訶慢多伽獨	
	Maximised Chenla territory	645-	Brahman (Toi li's son-in-law)	婆羅門（頭黎婿）	

Funan, Srivijaya, San-fo-chi

Chenla & Angkor

		Events	Remarks		King's name
	686	Kota Kapur Insc	Srivijaya conquered Kha-ling (訶陵) (Dapunta Selendra) Sailendra Kingdom	713, Inscription Arnd 707	Queen Jayadevi
8Cen	701, 16, 24, 27 Tribute			**King of the Mekong Delta**	
				716-730?	Pushkaraksha?
	741	Last envoy of Srivijaya		730-760?	Sambhuvarman?
	Arnd745	Water Chela occupied Srivijaya (Chaiya)		760?-780?	Rajendravar-man I
			Sailendra navy		
	Arnd 760	Srivijaya recovered Sailendra attacked Chenla		780?-788?	Mahipativar-man
	768	Restrted tribute	New Kha-ling Panangkaran		
	775	Ligor Inscription	Sailendra Maharaja		
9Cen				**Angkor kings**	
	Arnd 800	Borobudur	Samaratunga	802-834	Jayavarman II
	Arnd 830	Balaputra defeated	Sailendra left Jawa	834-877?	Jayavarman III
	Arnd 855	Sanjaya kingdom Jawa	Prambanam Temple		
				877-889	Indravarman I
Mid 9Cen					
	813, 15, 18 860-74 Trib		Sailendra	889-910	Yasovarman
End 9Cen		San-fo-chi formed	Chaiya. Jambi, Kedah		
10Cen	904 Last tribute to Tang	San-fo-chi		910-922 922-928	Harshavarman I Isanavarman II
	960-962, 970-72, 74-75, 980, 83, 85, 88, 990	Start tribute to North Song		928-941	Jayavarman IV
				941-944	Harshavarman II
				944-968	Rajendravar-man II

Champa

Remarks		King's name	王名 (漢籍)	Remarks
		Queen (Tou Li's daughter)	女王 (頭黎娘)	
Daughter of Jayavarman I	653-687? 653, 54, 57, 70, 86 Triibute 691, 95, 99, 702, 03, 07, 09, 11, 12 Tribute	Prakasadharma Vikaratavarman （自称）	鉢迦含波摩 （諸葛地）	Grandson of Isanavarman
Division of Water & Land Chenla				No king's name No king's name
	713, 15 Tribute	Vikrantavarman II	建多達摩	
	731, 34-35, 44 Tribute			No king's name
	748, 49 Trib	Rudravarman II	盧陀	tributed 3 times
	貞元 (793) Trib	Tang apply new name after 756 Huan Wang	（環王）(Pandura-nga 王朝)	No king's name No king's name No king's name
	799 Inscription	Prithindravarma Satyavarman Indravarman I		
Landed Cambodia before 770 from Srivijaya	817 Inscription	Harivarman I		
		Vikrantavarman III		
Son of Jayavarman II				
Sivaite, Usurper?	（占城初期: 860-950）			
Move to Yasodarapura	854?-898?	Indravarman II		Propagate Buddhism
Phnom Bakheng	898?	Jaya Sinhavarman I		
Son of Yasovarman	910?	Bhadravarman II		
Son of Yasovarman	918-959	Indravarman III		
Brother-in-law of Yasovarman	958 Tribute to Latter Zhou	Sri Indravarman III	釋利因德漫	
Move to Koh Ker, Sivaite	960, Start tribute to North Song, 960, 61, 62	Sri Jaya Indravarman I	釋利因陀盤	
Son of Jayavarman IV				
Son of Yasovarman's elder sister	970, Tribute	Sri Jaya Indravarman I	悉利因陀盤	
	971, Tribute	Sri Jaya Indravarman I	悉利多盤	
Propagate Buddhism, East Baray. Phimeanakas	972, Tribute	Paramesvara-Indravarman I	波美税褐印茶	from Indrapura

Funan, Srivijaya, San-fo-chi		Events	Remarks	Chenla & Angkor	King's name	
				946	Rajendra-varman II	
				968~1000	Jayavarman V	
	991	Jawa invade San-fo-si				
11Cen	1006	Sri Culamanivar-man Donate, temple (Nagapatam)	King of Kedah	1000-1002	Udayadityavar-man I	
				1002-1007	Jayavivarman	
	1003, 08 Trb					
	1017, 18, 19 Trb			1007?-1050	Suryavarman I	
				1050-1066	Udayadityavar-man II	
	1025, Invade	Chola attack	San-fo-chi surrender	1053, Inscription		
	1028 Trb	Chola, Tribute		1066-1080	Harshavarman III	
	1068	Kedah freed	Chola gave up Kedah			
	1077	Chola Tribute	Use San-fo-chi name	Mahindra Dynasty		
	1079	Chola Tribute	Use San-fo-chi name	1080-1106	Jayavarman VI	
	1079	Jambi Tribute	Use San-fo-chi name			
	1082	Chola Tribute	Use San-fo-chi name			
	1082	Jambi Tribute	Use San-fo-chi name			
	1084, 85	San fo-chi Trib				
	1088	Chola Tribute	Use San-fo-chi name			
	1088	San fo-chi Trib				

Champa

Remarks		King's name	王名（漢籍）	Remarks
Attack Po Nagar	973 Tribute	Sri Jaya Indravarman I	悉利盤陀印茶	
	974 Tribute	Paramesva raindravarman I	波美稅褐印茶	
Son of Rajendravarman II Preah Vihear	976 Trib, 2times 977 Tribute	Paramesvara-Indravarman I	波美稅陽布褐印茶	No king's name from Indrapura
	978, 79 Tribute Abt. 982	Killed by Dai Viet		No king's name Dai Viet invade Indrapura
	982 Tribute			No king's name
	985 Tribute	Sri Indravarman IV	施利陀盤吳日歡	
	986 Tribute	Liu Ji-Zong	劉繼宗	988 killed
	990 Tribute	Vijaya Sri Harivarman II	新王楊陀排	King of new capital Vijaya
	991 Inscription	Ku Sri Harivarmadeva	Yan Po 碑文（異系列）	
	992 Tribute		楊陀排2世	Dai Viet return Cham captive
	995 Tribute		楊波占（楊波古?）	
	997 Tribute	Yan Pu Ku Vijaya Sri	楊甫恭毘施離	
	999 Tribute	Yan Pu Ku Vijaya Sri	楊甫（普）俱毘茶逸施離	
Commander, from Tambralinga	1004, 05 Tribute	Yan Pu Ku Vijaya Sri	楊普毘茶逸施離	
Elder brother of formaer king	1007, 08 Tribute	Yan Pu Ku Harivarman	楊普俱毘茶室離	Tribute with Da-shi
Prince of Tambralinga, Buddhist	1009 Tribute	(Yan Pu Ku Harivarman)	（楊普俱毘茶室離）	No king's name
West Baray, Phimai Commander of Suryavarman I	1010 Tribute	Sri Hari Varmadeva	施離霞離鼻麻底	
		Same as Harivarman II ?	（宋會要）毘茶室離	
SKT Inscripion 1053	1011 Tribute	Yan Pu Ku Sri Harivarman II	楊普俱毘茶室離	
Last king of Tambralinga line	1014, 15 Tribute			No king's name
	1018 Tribute	Sri Harivarman III?	尸嘿排摩傑	
	1021-1026 Dai Viet War			Dai Vet attack Vijaya
Phimai group, non-Srivijaya	1029, 30 Tribute	Yan Pu Ko Sri Vikantavarmeda	陽補孤施離皮蘭德加拔麻疊	
	1042 Tribute	Yan Pu Sri Jaya Shinhavarman II	刑卜施離值星霞弗	
	1044 Dai Viet Attack			Attack Vijaya, killed 30,000?
	1050 Tribute	Ku Sri Paramesva rmadeva Yan Pu	俱舍利波微收羅婆麻提楊卜	Reconstruct Po Nagar
	1053,54,56,57,61 Tribute			No king's name
	1062 Tribute	Sri Rudravarman III Harivarman III	施里律茶盤麻常楊溥	

Funan, Srivijaya, San-fo-chi		Events	Remarks	Chenla & Angkor	King's name	
	1090	Chola Tribute				
	1094	San fo-chi				
	1095	San fo-chi				
12Cen	1128	San fo-chi		1107-1113	Dhranindravar-manI	
	1156, 3times	San fo-chi				
				1113-1150?	Suryavarman II	
				1116, Tribute		
	1178 Final Tribute	San fo-chi	San-fo-chi disappear	1150-1160	Dhranindravar-man II	
			14century Palembang tributed to Ming telling lie, as San-fo-chi	1155, Tribute	With Lopburi	
				1160-1165	Yasovarman II	
				1165-1177	Tribhuvanadit-yavarman	
13Cen				1181-1218	Jayavarman VII	
				1200, Tribute		
				1218-1270	Indravarman II	
	1230, Tambralinga		King Candrabhanu			
	1292, Sukhothai		Rama hamheng merged Tambralinga	1270-1295	Jayavarman VIII	
14-15Cen				1295-1307	Srindravarman	
				1296-1297		
				1307-1327 1327-1353? 1431	Jayavarman IX	

Champa

Remarks		King's name	王名（漢籍）	Remarks
	1068 Tribute	Yan Pu Sri Rudravarmdeva	楊卜尸利律陀般摩提婆	Attack Dai Viet but defeated
	1072, 76 Tribute			No king's name
	1084 Inscription	Paramabodhisatva	波羅摩菩提薩	Thu Bon base
	1086 Tribute			No king's name
	1088 Inscription	Jaya Indravar-man II	重昨	
Brother of Jayavarman VI killed by Suryvarman II	1127 Tribute			No king's name
Grand son of JayavarmanVI' sister				
Angkor Wat, Vishunite	1129, 32 Tribute	HarivarmanV	楊卜麻疊	
	1139-55	Jaya Indravarman III		
Cousin of Suryavarman II, Buddhist tribute with Lopburi	1145-1149	Rudravarman IV Jaya HarivarmanI		War agaist SuryavarmanII
Relative of Dhra-nindravarmanII?	1155 Tribute	Jaya Harivarman II	娜時蘭巴	
	1167, 68 Tribute	Jaya Indravarman IV	鄒亞娜	
Minster of Yasovarman I, Usurper 1177, Indravarman IV killed king?	1177	Jaya Indravarman IV	Attack Angkor, killed usurper. Coup D'état of Jayavarman VII	JayavarmanVII's general
	1192, Killed	Jaya Indravarman V	Prince Rashputi	Control Vijaya but fail
Buddhist, Bayon, Ta Prom, Banteay Chhmar Royal Road network Used several Cham generals	1190-1203	Suryavarmadeva (Vijayananda)	Jayavarman VII's general Independent from Angkor	Vijaya
Son of Jayavarman VII, Sivaite	1203	Suryavarmadeva killed		Killed in Dai Viet
	1203-1220		Angkor re-control	
Sivaite, destroy Buddha images	1220-	Jy Paramesh-varavarman II	Independent from Angkor	
Son-in-law of JayavarmanVIII, Usurper Theravada Buddhist				
Zhou Daguan visied Angkor Sivaite				
Ayutthaya occupied Angkor				

鈴木　峻 (すずき　たかし)

1938年8月5日満州国・牡丹江市生まれ。

1962年東京大学経済学部卒業。住友金属工業、調査部次長、シンガポール事務所次長、海外事業部長。タイスチール・パイプ社長。鹿島製鉄所副所長。(株) 日本総研理事・アジア研究センター所長。

1997年神戸大学大学院経済学研究科兼国際協力研究科教授。2001年東洋大学経済学部教授。2004年定年退職。その間、東京大学農学部、茨城大学人文学部非常勤講師。立命館大学客員教授。

経済学博士 (神戸大学、学術)。

主な著書『東南アジアの経済』(御茶ノ水書房、1996年)、『東南アジアの経済と歴史』(日本経済評論社、2002年)、『シュリヴィジャヤの歴史』(2010年、めこん)、The History of Srivijaya (英文。2012年、めこん)、『扶南・真臘・チャンパの歴史』(2016年、めこん)

The History of Srivijaya, Angkor and Champa

初版第1刷発行　2019年4月5日

定価5000円+税

著者	鈴木峻
装丁	水戸部功
編集・組版	面川ユカ
発行者	桑原晨
発行	株式会社めこん

〒113-0033 東京都文京区本郷3-7-1
電話 03-3815-1688　FAX 03-3815-1810
URL: http://www.mekong-publishing.com

印刷	モリモト印刷株式会社
製本	株式会社新里製本所

ISBN978-4-8396-0316-8　C3022　¥5000E
3022-1903316-8347

JPCA 日本出版著作権協会
http://www.e-jpca.com/

本書は日本出版著作権協会 (JPCA) が委託管理する著作物です。本書の無断複写などは著作権法上での例外を除き禁じられています。複写 (コピー)・複製、その他著作物の利用については事前に日本出版著作権協会 (http://www.jpca.jp.net e-mail : data@jpca.jp.net) の許諾を得てください。